John F. Kennedy

Issues in the History of American Foreign Relations

Series Editor: Robert J. McMahon, Ohio State University

Forthcoming titles in the series, 2010:

How the Cold War Ended: Debating and Doing History
John Prados, National Security Archive

Previously published titles in this series:

The Triumph of Internationalism:
Franklin D. Roosevelt and a World in Crisis, 1933–1941 (2007)
David Schmitz, Whitman College

Intimate Ties, Bitter Struggles:
The United States and Latin America Since 1945 (2006)
Alan McPherson, Howard University

The Color of Empire:
Race and American Foreign Relations (2006)
Michael L. Krenn, Appalachian State University

Crisis and Crossfire:
The United States and the Middle East Since 1945 (2005)
Peter L. Hahn, Ohio State University

John F. Kennedy

World Leader

Stephen G. Rabe

Potomac Books, Inc.
Washington, D.C.

Library of Congress Cataloging-in-Publication Data
Rabe, Stephen G.
John F. Kennedy : world leader / Stephen G. Rabe. — 1st ed.
p. cm. — (Issues in the history of American foreign relations)
Includes bibliographical references and index.
ISBN 978-1-59797-147-8 (hardcover : alk. paper) — ISBN 978-1-59797-148-5 (pbk. : alk. paper)
1. Kennedy, John F. (John Fitzgerald), 1917–1963—Political and social views. 2. Kennedy, John F. (John Fitzgerald), 1917–1963—Influence. 3. United States—Foreign relations—1961–1963. 4. Political leadership—United States—Case studies. 5. United States—Foreign relations—1961–1963—Sources. 6. World politics—1955–1965—Sources. I. Title.
E842.1.R33 2010
973.922092—dc22

2009039255

Printed in the United States of America on acid-free paper that meets the American National Standards Institute Z39-48 Standard.

Potomac Books, Inc.
22841 Quicksilver Drive
Dulles, Virginia 20166

First Edition

10 9 8 7 6 5 4 3 2 1

To Elina Nikulainen, Sigrún Ólafsdóttir, Rïina Hildén Silvennoinen, and Iwona Swaiatczak-Wasilewska. Great students and wonderful citizens of the world.

Contents

List of Photographs ix
Series Editor's Note xi
Acknowledgments xiii
Chronology xv

CHAPTER 1. John F. Kennedy in History 1
CHAPTER 2. Background, Beliefs, People 13
CHAPTER 3. Soviet Union 27
CHAPTER 4. Cuba 51
CHAPTER 5. Latin America 75
CHAPTER 6. Vietnam 99
CHAPTER 7. Asia 125
CHAPTER 8. Middle East and Africa 153
CHAPTER 9. John F. Kennedy: The Future Versus the Past 179

APPENDIX OF DOCUMENTS
1. John F. Kennedy's Inaugural Address, January 20, 1961 191
2. President Kennedy and Chairman Khrushchev Debate the Fate of Berlin at the Vienna Summit, June 4, 1961 194
3. President Kennedy Urges Citizens to Prepare for Nuclear War, July 25, 1961 197
4. President Kennedy Exerts Command over U.S. Nuclear Forces, October 20, 1961 198
5. President-elect Kennedy Receives Advice from President Eisenhower on Cuba, January 19, 1961 199

6. Attorney General Robert Kennedy Is Briefed on CIA Contacts with Organized Crime in Plots against Fidel Castro, May 14, 1962 200
7. President Kennedy Explains His Decision Not to Launch an Air Strike against Cuba, October 22, 1962 202
8. Higher Authority (President Kennedy) Approves a Sabotage Program against Cuba, June 19, 1963 203
9. President Kennedy Debates the Issue of Communist Influence in Latin America with the President of Mexico, June 29, 1962 205
10. President Kennedy Expresses Reservations about Expanding the U.S. Role in South Vietnam, November 15, 1961 206
11. The Kennedy Administration Initiates the Process of Overthrowing President Ngo Dinh Diem of South Vietnam, August 24, 1963 207
12. President Kennedy Offers Conflicting Views on the U.S. Role in South Vietnam, September 2 and 9, 1963 209
13. President Kennedy Promises to Protect Taiwan's Seat on the Security Council at the United Nations, October 16, 1961 210
14. President Kennedy Seeks Soviet Cooperation to Prevent China from Developing Nuclear Weapons, July 15, 1963 211
15. President Kennedy's Commencement Address at American University, June 10, 1963 213
16. President Kennedy Ties Civil Rights Legislation to International Affairs, June 11, 1963 215
17. President Kennedy's Undelivered Remarks at the Trade Mart in Dallas, November 22, 1963 215

Notes 219
Recommended Readings 237
Index 241
About the Author 249

Photographs

John F. Kennedy, Thirty-fifth President of the United States 3
President Kennedy, Secretary of State Dean Rusk, and Secretary of Defense Robert McNamara, 1962 23
President Kennedy and Nikita Khrushchev in Vienna, 1961 42
President Kennedy addresses crowd in West Berlin, 1963 49
President Kennedy meets Soviet Foreign Minister Andrei Gromyko in the White House during the Cuban missile crisis, 1962 67
President Kennedy meets with his advisory committee during the Cuban missile crisis, 1962 69
President Kennedy at a land redistribution ceremony in Venezuela, 1961 90
President Kennedy, Gen. Maxwell Taylor, and Secretary of Defense Robert McNamara, 1963 117
Jacqueline Bouvier Kennedy and Prime Minister Jawaharlal Nehru in New Delhi, 1962 148
President Kennedy and President Kwame Nkrumah of Ghana, 1961 168
President Kennedy delivers commencement address at American University, 1963 183

Series Editor's Note

From the birth of the American Republic in the late eighteenth century to the emergence of the United States as a fledgling world power at the end of the nineteenth century, the place of the United States within the broader international system of nation-states posed fundamental challenges to American and foreign statesmen alike. What role would—and could—a non-European power play in a Eurocentric world order? The combination of America's stunning economic transformation and two devastating world wars helped shatter the old European order, catapulting the United States into a position of global preeminence by the middle decades of the twentieth century. Since the mid-1940s, it has become common to refer to the United States as a superpower. Since the collapse of the Soviet Union, America's only serious rival, and the concomitant end of the Cold War, it has become common to label the United States as the world's lone superpower, or "hyperpower," as a French diplomat labeled it in the late 1990s.

By any standard of measurement, the United States has long been, as it remains today, the dominant force in world affairs—economically, politically, militarily, and culturally.

The United States has placed, and continues to place, its own indelible stamp on the international system while shaping the aspirations, mores, tastes, living standards, and sometimes resentments and hatreds of hundreds of millions of ordinary people across the globe. Few subjects, consequently, loom larger in the history of the modern world than the often uneasy encounter between the United States and the nations and peoples beyond its shores.

This series, *Issues in the History of American Foreign Relations*, aims to provide students and general readers alike with a wide range of books, written by some of the outstanding scholarly experts of this generation, that elucidate key issues, themes, topics, and individuals in the nearly 250-year history of U.S. foreign relations. The series covers an array of diverse subjects spanning from the era of the founding fathers to the present. Each book offers a concise, accessible narrative, based upon the latest scholarship, followed by a careful selection of relevant primary documents. Primary sources enable readers to immerse themselves in the raw material of history, thereby facilitating the formation of informed, independent judgments about the subject at hand. To capitalize upon the unprecedented amount of non-American archival sources and materials currently available, most books feature foreign as well as American material in the documentary section. A broad, international perspective on the external behavior of the United States, one of the major trends of recent scholarship, is a prominent feature of the books in this series.

It is my fondest hope that this series will contribute to a greater engagement with and understanding of the complexities of this fascinating—and critical—subject.

ROBERT J. MCMAHON
OHIO STATE UNIVERSITY

Acknowledgments

FIRST, I WANT TO EXPRESS my gratitude to Dr. Hobson Wildenthal, the academic vice president and provost at the University of Texas at Dallas, and Dr. Dennis Kratz, the dean of the School of Arts and Humanities. Both men have consistently supported my teaching and research over many years. These two academic leaders have provided me with the generous Arts and Humanities Endowed Chair and have granted me released time for my writing. I also thank Robert McMahon, the series editor, for inviting me to write this study and for reading a draft of the manuscript. Hilary Claggett of Potomac Books has proved to be a fine and helpful editor. Keiko Makishima of the Audiovisual Archives at the John F. Kennedy Library in Boston helped me select photographs for the study. My friends, Dr. James N. Giglio, the Distinguished Professor of History at Missouri State University, and Dr. Thomas G. Paterson of the University of Connecticut, first persuaded me to think about analyzing the foreign policies of the Kennedy years. Finally, I thank the noted lawyer and my wife, Genice A. G. Rabe, for many things.

Chronology

1960

March 17	President Dwight D. Eisenhower authorizes the CIA to develop a program to overthrow Fidel Castro.
May 5	Premier Nikita Khrushchev announces that the Soviet Union has shot down a U.S. reconnaissance aircraft, a U-2, over Soviet territory on May 1.
May 16	Khrushchev walks out of a summit meeting with Eisenhower in Paris in protest over the U-2 incident.
August 19	The CIA begins to plot to assassinate Patrice Lumumba, premier of the Congo, after President Eisenhower expresses strong disapproval of Lumumba.
August 26	The United States breaks diplomatic relations with the Dominican Republic and its dictator, Rafael Leonidas Trujillo. U.S. officials subsequently supply arms to assist Dominicans who will assassinate Trujillo.
September 26	Senator John F. Kennedy and Vice President Richard M. Nixon engage in the first televised debate between presidential candidates.
November 4	The CIA begins to develop a Cuban exile force for launching an amphibious assault against Cuba.
November 8	Senator Kennedy narrowly defeats Nixon in the presidential election.
November 27	President-elect Kennedy receives a briefing on covert operations in Cuba.

December 6 — President-elect Kennedy meets with President Eisenhower to discuss the transition of power.

December 20 — Vietnamese Communists establish the National Liberation Front, political wing of the Communist movement in South Vietnam.

1961

January 3 — President Eisenhower breaks diplomatic relations with Cuba.

January 6 — Premier Khrushchev pledges that the Soviet Union will back "wars of national liberation."

January 17 — President Eisenhower gives a farewell address to the nation, warning of the influence of "the military-industrial complex."

January 17 — Congolese leader Patrice Lumumba is murdered by Congolese political opponents.

January 19 — President-elect Kennedy meets for the second time with President Eisenhower. Eisenhower emphasizes that the United States cannot allow Fidel Castro to govern Cuba. Kennedy also learns about U.S. difficulties in Southeast Asia.

January 20 — John F. Kennedy is inaugurated as thirty-fifth president of the United States. The president pledges "to bear any burden" in the defense of liberty.

January 30 — In an address to a joint session of Congress, President Kennedy calls for massive buildup of U.S. military forces.

February 6 — Secretary of Defense Robert McNamara admits to journalists, "There is no missile gap."

March 1 — President Kennedy establishes the Peace Corps by executive order.

March 7 — The first of sixteen U.S.-Chinese ambassadorial meetings during the Kennedy administration is held in Warsaw. The United States and the People's Republic of China do not reach substantial agreements at any of these meetings.

March 13 — President Kennedy proposes the Alliance for Progress for Latin America.

April 12 — Soviet cosmonaut Yuri Gagarin becomes the first human to orbit Earth.

April 17–19	Cuban exiles, backed by the CIA, invade Cuba at the Bay of Pigs. Fidel Castro's forces easily rout the invaders capturing over 1,000 exiles.
May 5	Astronaut Alan Shepard becomes the first U.S. citizen in space, making a suborbital flight.
May 5	At a National Security Council meeting President Kennedy rules that U.S. policy toward Cuba will continue "to aim at the downfall of Castro."
May 12	A conference in Geneva convenes to consider the status of Laos.
May 25	President Kennedy calls on the United States to land a man on the moon and return him safely to Earth by the end of the decade.
May 30	President Kennedy meets with Israeli Prime Minister David Ben-Gurion in New York City and presses Ben-Gurion on the purposes of the Dimona nuclear reactor.
May 31	Dominican dissidents assassinate Rafael Trujillo. The dissidents carry weapons supplied by the CIA.
June 3–4	President Kennedy and Premier Khrushchev meet in Vienna and debate the status of Berlin.
July 25	President Kennedy addresses the nation on Berlin. He asks Congress for additional military spending, authority to activate military reservists, and money for a civil defense fallout shelter program.
August 5	The United States begins meeting with Latin American nations at Punta del Este, Uruguay, to plan the Alliance for Progress.
August 12–13	East German forces close the border between East and West Berlin and begin to construct the Berlin Wall.
August 21	In Berlin Vice President Lyndon Johnson greets a U.S. battle group that has traveled overland through East Germany.
August 30	Premier Khrushchev announces the resumption of nuclear testing. The Soviets conduct fifty atmospheric tests in sixty days.
September 15	The United States resumes underground testing of nuclear weapons. Atmospheric testing will resume in March 1962.
October 16	President Kennedy confidentially assures Generalissimo Jiang

	Jieshi of Taiwan that the United States will use its veto power to bar China's admission to the United Nations.
October 17	Premier Khrushchev essentially retracts the Soviet ultimatum on Berlin.
October 21	Roswell Gilpatric, U.S. Department of Defense official, publicly affirms that the United States has an advantage in nuclear weapons over the Soviet Union.
October 26	U.S. and Communist forces confront one another at "Checkpoint Charlie," a border crossing in Berlin. President Kennedy subsequently works out a formula to defuse the tension.
November 3	Presidential advisers Maxwell Taylor and Walt Rostow recommend to President Kennedy a sizeable expansion of U.S. support for the government in Saigon.
November 7	President Kennedy has unsuccessful talks in Washington with Prime Minister Jawaharlal Nehru of India.
November 22	President Kennedy authorizes an expansion of the U.S. military effort in South Vietnam.
November 30	President Kennedy authorizes Operation Mongoose, a covert campaign of terrorism and sabotage against Cuba.
December 12	Indian troops commence attacks leading to annexation to India of the Portuguese colony of Goa.

1962

February 6	The Kennedy administration establishes the Military Assistance Command, Vietnam (MACV) in Saigon to oversee the expanded U.S. military effort.
February 7	The United States imposes a total embargo on trade with Cuba.
February 20	Astronaut John Glenn becomes the first U.S. citizen to orbit Earth.
July 23	The United States, the Soviet Union, and China sign accords at Geneva, providing for a neutral Laos.
August 5	South African police arrest Nelson Mandela after reportedly receiving information from the CIA on Mandela's location. Mandela will be imprisoned until 1990.

October 14	A U-2 reconnaissance plane photographs missile bases under construction in Cuba.
October 16	President Kennedy is informed of the discovery of missile bases in Cuba. He creates the Executive Committee of the National Security Council (ExComm) to consider the U.S. response.
October 18	President Kennedy meets with Soviet Foreign Minister Andrei Gromyko at the White House. Gromyko misleads the president about Soviet intentions. Kennedy does not inform Gromyko that the United States knows about the missile bases.
October 20	Warfare between China and India breaks out over border issues.
October 22	President Kennedy informs the U.S. public of the missile bases in Cuba and announces that the United States will impose a "quarantine" around the island.
October 24	Soviet ships approach but do not challenge the U.S. quarantine line.
October 26	Premier Khrushchev suggests in a letter to President Kennedy that he will withdraw missiles from Cuba in exchange for a public U.S. pledge not to invade Cuba.
October 27	In a second letter, Premier Khrushchev demands that the United States withdraw its missiles from Turkey. Without authorization from Moscow, Soviet forces in Cuba shoot down a U-2 over Cuba. Fidel Castro writes to Khrushchev predicting a U.S. invasion of the island and suggests that the Soviets respond with a nuclear attack against the United States.
October 28	Soviet Premier Khrushchev announces over Radio Moscow his decision to withdraw Soviet missiles from Cuba in exchange for a noninvasion pledge. He also accepts a confidential U.S. promise to withdraw missiles from Turkey.
November 8	The United States announces that the Soviets have dismantled missile sites.
November 20	President Kennedy announces the lifting of the naval quarantine of Cuba. He gives a qualified pledge not to invade Cuba.
November 20	China unilaterally ends the war with India and declares victory.
December 23	Cuba begins to release prisoners taken during the Bay of Pigs invasion in exchange for food and medicine.

1963

January 2 — At the battle of Ap Bac, Viet Cong forces administer a telling defeat on South Vietnamese forces who are supported by the U.S. military.

May 8 — South Vietnamese government forces attack and kill Buddhists protesting a government edict banning the flying of Buddhist flags.

June 10 — President Kennedy makes conciliatory remarks about the Soviet Union in a commencement address at American University. He proposes banning the atmospheric testing of nuclear weapons.

June 11 — A Buddhist monk in Saigon burns himself alive, protesting the government of Ngo Dinh Diem.

June 11 — President Kennedy gives a national address calling for civil rights legislation. He notes that the struggle against communism requires full racial integration in the United States.

June 19 — President Kennedy, aka "Higher Authority," approves a CIA program of propaganda, economic denial, and sabotage designed to bring about the "eventual liquidation" of the Castro regime.

June 20 — The United States and the Soviet Union agree to establish a communications link, or "hot line," between Washington and Moscow.

June 26 — President Kennedy visits Berlin and denounces the Berlin Wall in a speech to Berliners.

June 30 — President Kennedy, in a meeting in England with Prime Minister Harold Macmillan, demands that the United Kingdom delay the independence of British Guiana.

August 5 — The United States, Soviet Union, and United Kingdom sign the Limited Nuclear Test Ban Treaty.

August 21 — South Vietnamese government troops raid Buddhist pagodas, arresting 1,400 Buddhists.

August 24 — President Kennedy approves a cable informing South Vietnamese generals that the United States was prepared to abandon President Diem if he did not carry out fundamental reforms.

September 2	In a televised interview, President Kennedy emphasizes that only the South Vietnamese can win the war in Vietnam.
September 11	President Kennedy discusses with Taiwanese officials the possibility of attacking Chinese nuclear facilities.
October 2	President Kennedy gives tacit U.S. security guarantee to Israel in a letter to Prime Minister Levi Eshkol.
November 1	South Vietnamese military officers overthrow President Diem and then murder him and his brother.
November 12	President Kennedy approves the CIA plan to continue the sabotage campaign against Cuban economic assets.
November 14	In his last statement on China, President Kennedy says he is not "wedded to a policy of hostility" toward China.
November 18	President Kennedy pronounces the "Kennedy Doctrine," in a speech in Miami, vowing to prevent a second Communist regime in the Western Hemisphere.
November 22	CIA agents rendezvous in Paris with a Cuban official, code-named AM/LASH, and pass to him a poisonous hypodermic needle intended to produce Fidel Castro's instant death.
November 22	President Kennedy is assassinated in Dallas, Texas.
November 22	President Kennedy intended to tell his audience at the Trade Mart in Dallas that the United States would continue to defend South Vietnam.

CHAPTER 1

JOHN F. KENNEDY IN HISTORY

JOHN F. KENNEDY (1917–1963) served only two years and ten months, approximately 1,000 days, as president of the United States. His time in office, which lasted from January 20, 1961, to November 22, 1963, represents the sixth shortest presidential term in U.S. history. Presidents William Henry Harrison (1841), Zachary Taylor (1849–1850), and Warren Harding (1921–1923), all of whom died of natural causes, and James Garfield (1881), who was assassinated, served for shorter periods. Millard Fillmore (1850–1853) and Gerald R. Ford (1974–1977) also held office for a briefer time than Kennedy. None of these former presidents has ever evoked much discussion among scholars or the educated public. They are largely forgotten men, with perhaps only Warren Harding still alive in history, serving as the butt of history teachers' jokes because he was so pathetic and hapless in office. President Kennedy has not, however, been forgotten or reduced to farce. Since his assassination in late 1963, a stream of studies about the life and legacy of Kennedy have appeared. More than forty-five years after his death, President Kennedy remains a subject of fascination for both historians and U.S. citizens.

Notwithstanding the nostalgia that surrounds the Kennedy presidency and the lingering shock of his awful death in Dallas, Texas, historical interest in Kennedy reflects the judgment that he led the country during a momentous time. Kennedy perceived himself as a foreign policy president, and critical international developments marked his time in office. The United States and the Soviet Union had showdowns over the city of Berlin in 1961 and the island of Cuba in 1962. The threat of nuclear war and the prospect of the destruction of human civilization seemed to hang in the balance. Kennedy used the threat of force, good diplomacy, and sound judgment and kept the United States and the world from falling into the abyss. The U.S. public further associates President Kennedy with achievements for which they express continuing national pride. The president launched the United States on a journey to the moon and space exploration. His program to send volunteers abroad to help the poor of the world—the Peace Corps—remains a source of enduring satisfaction for U.S. citizens. Some scholars would point out, however, that the Kennedy record is not one of unalloyed achievement. His administration played significant roles in two fiascos in the history of U.S. foreign relations—the debacle of the Vietnam War and the failure of the Alliance for Progress, Kennedy's grand plan to transform Latin America. President Kennedy also proved very fond of using the Central Intelligence Agency (CIA) to destabilize sovereign countries, many of which had popularly elected, constitutional governments.

Popular Memories

The warm affection that the U.S. public has always held for President Kennedy can be attributed to the late president's colleagues and supporters. Laudatory accounts of the Kennedy years by administration officials began to appear soon after the president's death. Dozens of memoirs by friends and supporters would follow these initial insider accounts. In modern U.S. political history, it is not unusual for government officials and friends to publish accounts of their work or their relationship with a president, but these narratives are often critical of the president and his administration. Former officials of the George W. Bush administration (2001–2009), for example, wrote biting critiques of President Bush soon after they left office. But Kennedy's colleagues have lavished praise on President Kennedy. To be sure, the U.S. public has gradually learned from these memoirs that President Kennedy was not always faithful to his wife, Jacqueline Bouvier Kennedy, and that he took dubious medicines for his chronic health problems. Nonetheless, the insider histories and memoirs have promoted the Kennedy presidency, especially the president's conduct of international affairs. So remarkably loyal have been officials and supporters to their boss and friend that one scholar dubbed them "honorary Kennedys."[1]

John F. Kennedy, thirty-fifth president of the United States, January 20, 1961–November 22, 1963. (John F. Kennedy Presidential Library and Museum, Boston)

Historian and presidential aide Arthur M. Schlesinger Jr. set the tone for popular analyses of the Kennedy presidency with his worshipful memoir, *A Thousand Days: John F. Kennedy in the White House* (1965). Schlesinger worked in the White House and focused on relations with Latin America. As a scholar, he had written award-winning accounts of the presidencies of Andrew Jackson and Franklin Delano Roosevelt. Like Jackson and Roosevelt, Kennedy was a great Democrat who had changed history for the better. In less than a thousand days in office, "he had accomplished so much." He faced down Communist aggression in Berlin and Cuba. He made the world a safer place, negotiating a nuclear test ban treaty with the Soviet Union. He championed nationalism, identifying the United States with the emerging nations of Asia, Africa, and Latin America. And he reached out to the world's poor and needy with programs such as the Alliance for Progress, the Peace Corps, and Food for Peace. In Schlesinger's judgment, history had rarely witnessed a leader so capable of combining toughness and restraint. President Kennedy had also galvanized international diplomacy and dazzled citizens at home and abroad with his idealism and breathtaking eloquence. His inaugural address in 1961 and his declaration of solidarity with the people of Berlin in 1963 inspired "many to bear any burden" in the defense of liberty.[2] Other members of the president's staff sustained Schlesinger's testimony. Roger Hilsman, an assistant secretary of state for Far Eastern Affairs, wrote of working for a "leader" and a "hero." Theodore Sorensen, who composed many of the president's speeches, predicted that history would remember Kennedy not only for his grace, wit, and style but also for his "substance—the strength of his ideas and ideals, his courage and judgment."[3]

Schlesinger and his colleagues can perhaps be forgiven for abandoning scholarly restraint in their histories. They loved and admired the man that they served. Writing in the mid-1960s, they may also have been traumatized by Kennedy's assassination. But their memoirs have transcended time and place. Over the past five decades, their fellow citizens have agreed that President Kennedy represented the best that the United States had to offer. Kennedy had a narrow victory in the presidential campaign; he defeated Vice President Richard M. Nixon in November 1960 by less than 1 percent. Despite the close election, Kennedy always enjoyed solid job approval ratings from the public. Frequently 75 percent of the public approved of his job performance. Kennedy probably would have won a big reelection victory in 1964. By mid-1963, 59 percent of U.S. citizens claimed to have voted for him in 1960. After the assassination, that figure rose to 65 percent. In the twenty-first century, it would be difficult to find many elderly citizens who would admit to having favored Nixon over Kennedy in 1960. Beyond fibbing about their voting records, U.S. citizens have honored the memory of Kennedy by building monuments to him and naming airports, schools, and buildings after him. Monuments to President Kennedy abound throughout the world. Cities in Western Europe and Latin America have boulevards and avenues named after the president. A distinguished center of research on international relations and North American studies is the John F. Kennedy Institute at the Freie Universität (Free University) in Berlin.

U.S. citizens continue to believe that what the nation and the world needs is another John Kennedy. In 1996, a presidential election year, a *New York Times*/CBS News public opinion survey found that if voters could pick any former president to govern the country, they would choose Kennedy. He easily outpolled Franklin Roosevelt, the most influential political leader of the twentieth century. The survey's respondents preferred Kennedy over the sculpted faces on Mt. Rushmore—George Washington, Thomas Jefferson, Abraham Lincoln, and Theodore Roosevelt. When asked to explain their choice, respondents cited Kennedy's quality of leadership. A decade later, citizens still considered Kennedy one of the greatest leaders in U.S. history. In mid-2007 the polling firm Rasmussen Reports found that 80 percent of adults in their sample viewed Kennedy favorably. Only the Mt. Rushmore crowd and Franklin Roosevelt merited such high marks. George W. Bush and Richard Nixon, each with an approval rating of only 32 percent, earned the lowest grades.[4] Nixon's low favorability ratings added zest to Kennedy's joking question—"How did I manage to beat a guy like this by only a hundred thousand votes?"[5]

Scholars have speculated on the enduring popularity of President John Kennedy. Professor Alan Brinkley of Columbia University noted that Kennedy was a man of the television age—gifted, witty, and articulate. When contemporary citizens see him in old film clips, they are "struck by how smooth, polished, and spontaneously eloquent he was, how impressive a presence, how elegant a speaker." Kennedy also stands out by comparison. After the assassination, the United States endured the calamity of the Vietnam War and the lying, corruption, and abuse of power dubbed "Watergate" under President Nixon. Although well-intentioned politicians, neither President Gerald Ford nor Jimmy Carter overcame the national economic malaise engendered by the Vietnam War. The pleasant Ronald Reagan displayed Kennedy-style charisma and grace and had the good fortune to preside over the end of the Cold War. But Reagan nearly bankrupted the nation with his unwise tax cuts for wealthy citizens and even his closest advisers conceded that Reagan lacked intellectual depth. President Bill Clinton resolved U.S. federal budgetary problems and proved a tireless worker for peace in Northern Ireland, the Middle East, and southeastern Europe, but Clinton's lack of personal restraint tarnished the peace and prosperity he had achieved. Brinkley concluded that U.S. citizens believe that Kennedy's death "marked the end of an age of confidence and optimism and the beginning of an era of conflict and disenchantment." Kennedy's sense of mission and idealism stands, in Brinkley's judgment, "as an appealing contrast to what seems the emptiness and aimlessness of today's public world."[6] The disasters that have befallen the United States under President George W. Bush—the Iraq War, Hurricane Katrina, staggering federal budget deficits, and the collapse of the financial markets of Wall Street—only heighten that longing for an accomplished leader.

John Kennedy stands, as Brinkley observed, as "an important figure in our national imagination." His presidency set in motion powerful forces for change. Countless Americans, both old and young, dedicated themselves to public service, remembering Kennedy's inaugural day challenge to ask themselves what they could do for the country and the world. "Miss Lillian" Carter, President Carter's mother, joined the Peace Corps in 1966 at the age of sixty-eight, using her skills as a registered nurse to help people in India. Idealistic university students, black and white alike, risked their lives as they sought simple justice for African Americans who lived in the segregated "Jim Crow" South. When they marched in demonstrations, picketed segregated public facilities, and registered people to vote, students were responding to the young president's exhortation to "make a difference" and fulfill America's unfulfilled promises. Kennedy's "children" also included Lt. Philip Caputo, a young U.S. Marine Corps officer who landed in Danang, South Vietnam, in March 1965 as part of the first U.S. combat units sent to Vietnam. Caputo recalled that, as he marched through rice paddies, he was imbued by "the missionary idealism he [Kennedy] had awakened in us." Along with his rifle and field pack, Caputo carried with him the conviction that the Communist enemy would soon be beaten and that "we were doing something altogether noble and good."[7] Ironically, young people who left their university campuses and took to the streets to oppose the war in Vietnam similarly believed that they were upholding the idealism and commitment that John Kennedy expected of young Americans. The decision by Robert Kennedy, the slain president's brother and closest adviser, to run for the presidency in 1968 on an antiwar platform underscored the faith of the protestors.

Long after the tumultuous 1960s passed, the Kennedy spirit continued to infuse citizens, especially those who favored liberal, progressive policies. In 1992, at the Democratic Party's national convention, the delegates collectively gasped when they saw, in a campaign biography film, President Kennedy reach out into a crowd of young men and shake the hand of Bill Clinton. Clinton, almost seventeen, met the president while attending a leadership conference sponsored by the American Legion. To Democratic loyalists, however, it might have seemed as if the young Clinton had ascended to Camelot to be knighted by King Arthur! In the twentieth century, aspiring young leaders wanted, as Kennedy said in his inaugural address, for "the torch" to be "passed to a new generation of Americans." President Barack Obama, as the Democratic presidential candidate in 2008, received the coveted endorsement of the Kennedy family. Obama frequently appeared at campaign rallies with Caroline Kennedy, the president's daughter, and Obama appointed her to a committee to recommend a vice presidential choice.

Scholarly Analyses

U.S. citizens took up public service, becoming primary schoolteachers, university professors, elected officials, diplomats, U.S. Marines, community organizers, and Peace Corps volunteers, because they took seriously President Kennedy's inaugural day challenge to spurn self-indulgent careerism and to explore what they could do for their country, the world, and their fellow human beings. The United States is a more humane and progressive society because of this public service. Scholars are on solid ground when they assess the impact of Kennedy's idealism and stirring rhetoric on generations of Americans. Scholarly analysis must, however, transcend fascination with the man and a longing for the hope and promise of the 1960s. Scholars are enjoined to analyze the concrete domestic and international policies that Kennedy pursued between 1961 and 1963. Did he achieve his agenda or at least make good progress, during his limited time, toward that agenda? Can he be held responsible for failures? Were the challenges he faced extraordinary? Did he learn from his experiences? Scholars must further ask the ever-present historical question of change and continuity. Did President Kennedy alter the course and conduct of foreign policy? How did he change the U.S. approach in the Cold War? Did his decisions prolong or hasten the end of the Soviet-American confrontation? Finally, did President Kennedy preserve the national security of the United States and the West, and did he make progress toward global peace?

As a group, historians, political scientists, and presidential scholars rate President Kennedy in favorable terms. Like citizens, scholars enthusiastically participate in "rate the president" surveys. In professional surveys conducted in the 1980s and 1990s, historians rated Kennedy as an "above average" or "average (high)" president. Kennedy is the only president who served one term or less to receive such creditable ratings. Recent surveys have continued to place Kennedy in the upper ranks of presidents, although with some variation. In a survey of fifty-eight presidential scholars conducted on President's Day, February 21, 2000, by the public affairs cable channel, C-Span, Kennedy earned an eighth place rating out of forty-one presidents. In terms of presidential leadership, he finished just behind Woodrow Wilson and Thomas Jefferson and in front of Andrew Jackson and James Madison. On President's Day, February 16, 2009, C-Span released a new survey conducted among sixty-four scholars. John Kennedy had risen to sixth place, passing both Wilson and Jefferson. The scholars gave Kennedy especially high marks for his economic management skills and his commitment to equal justice. By comparison, in a survey published on October 1, 2000, the *Chicago Sun Times* asked scholars to rate presidents in five categories: leadership, foreign policy, domestic policy, character and integrity, and impact on history. In this survey, Kennedy earned only a nineteenth-place rating in the aggregate score. His leadership and foreign policy grades were strong, but his marks were only average for domestic policy and impact on history. The scholars gave Kennedy dismal ratings on character and integrity.[8] The respondents apparently took a dim view of Kennedy's incessant womanizing and his refusal to disclose the severity of his health problems, especially his Addison's disease, a disease of the adrenal glands.

John Kennedy by choice focused his energies on international affairs. He proved unable to persuade the U.S. Congress to pass his domestic agenda. Of the twenty-three bills he submitted to Congress early in his administration, only seven were enacted into law. Programs such as a tax cut to stimulate the economy and federal aid to education would not receive congressional backing until President Lyndon Johnson had the opportunity to employ his remarkable legislative skills. President Kennedy also belatedly embraced the central moral issue of his era—

the movement for freedom and justice for African Americans. He waited until 1962 to sign an executive order banning discrimination in public housing, and he nominated defenders of segregation laws to serve as judges in federal courts in southern states. Kennedy eventually responded to the civil rights movement and the courage and commitment of Dr. Martin Luther King Jr. and his followers. In mid-1963 he submitted a comprehensive civil rights bill to Congress, and he began to speak eloquently about the need for simple justice. His televised address to the nation on June 11, 1963, on civil rights ranks with his inaugural address and two other public performances in June 1963—his commencement address at American University on the Cold War and his speech in Berlin decrying the Berlin Wall.

Despite his thin domestic record, President Kennedy continues to merit his above-average rating from Professor James N. Giglio. Giglio's *The Presidency of John F. Kennedy* (2006) is a distinguished scholarly study of the Kennedy administration. Professor Giglio, whose expertise is in domestic political history, argues that a president should be judged on whether he met his stated goals and whether he improved the life of the country. Giglio sees a mixed record in international affairs for Kennedy. He enhanced U.S. global prestige and managed crises well but unwisely relied on counterinsurgency and intervention and left a dangerous problem in Vietnam. On the domestic side, Giglio credits Kennedy for boosting economic growth and reducing unemployment through judicious federal spending, job training, and improvements in the minimum wage and Social Security. Giglio judges that, having introduced a domestic reform agenda and with a growing economy, Kennedy would have had many of the legislative successes achieved by President Johnson. In 1964 he would have attained landmark civil rights legislation and a tax cut that would have stimulated rapid economic growth. In a second term, Kennedy would have likely won victories in health, education, and welfare. Giglio would also dispute the low marks that some historians assign to Kennedy on the issues of character and integrity, noting the Kennedy administration was remarkably free of corruption and scandal.[9] U.S. citizens still had faith in the early 1960s in the ability of government to do great things.

Robert Dallek in *An Unfinished Life: John F. Kennedy, 1917–1963* (2003) takes up Professor Giglio's theme that Kennedy simply needed more time. Kennedy had an "unfinished presidency." Dallek's eight-hundred-page biography is an influential recent study of Kennedy's life and is written in a style designed to appeal to the educated public rather than to scholars alone. Dallek, whose background is in the study of the history of U.S. foreign relations, considers Kennedy a great president because of his achievements and promise in international affairs. Dallek dismisses Kennedy's domestic record as "distinctly limited" and writes, "Foreign affairs, as Kennedy himself would have argued, were the principal concerns of his presidency." The Alliance for Progress, the Peace Corps, and the Apollo space program were "significant measures" of his foreign policy. But the "telling measures" of Kennedy's presidential leadership came during crises with the Communists over Berlin, Cuba, and Vietnam. During the Berlin and Cuba confrontations, Kennedy rejected military solutions that could have precipitated a nuclear war between the United States and the Soviet Union. The consequences of nuclear war in the early 1960s would be with us in the twenty-first century. Kennedy's decisions during the Cuban missile crisis served as "an imperishable example of how one man prevented a catastrophe that may yet afflict the world." Dallek finds evidence that Kennedy would have improved relations with the Soviet Union and Cuba in 1964 and thereafter and that he would have limited the U.S. military involvement in Vietnam and spared the country that disaster.[10]

Overviews of the Kennedy presidency, however insightful and influential, necessarily give little attention to potentially significant issues and questions. Proper assessments of the meaning and impact of an administration's foreign policy must not be limited to analyses of the "crisis-event," such as those in Berlin and Cuba. How an administration conducted relations with countries, leaders, and political movements that did not garner newspaper headlines and public attention can help provide a rounded, complete view of a leader's foreign policy. Kennedy's lofty Alliance for Progress and Peace Corps programs might be measured and weighed against the administration's nasty covert interventions in Latin America and Africa. In the 1980s and 1990s scholars published case studies or monographs of Kennedy's foreign policy in various regions of the world. In addition, Thomas G. Paterson, Diane Kunz, and Mark White edited collections of essays on Kennedy's foreign policies.[11] As historian Burton I. Kaufman noted in 1993, the scholarship portrayed a president who was "complex and ambiguous." In terms of the developing regions of Asia, Africa, Latin America, and the Middle East, for example, Kennedy showed sensitivity to anticolonial, nationalistic aspirations of third world people. But the historical literature suggested that Kennedy remained "an inveterate Cold Warrior whose dogmatic anticommunism often blinded him to the very forces that he championed."[12]

At the end of the first decade of the twenty-first century, an appraisal of John Kennedy's foreign policy seems appropriate. Foreign policy records of the Kennedy administration, including some CIA files, have finally been declassified. The end of the Cold War has also facilitated scholarship. The records of the former Soviet Union have become increasingly open to scholars. Scholars have gained access to meetings that Soviet leader Nikita S. Khrushchev had with his colleagues in the Kremlin. In a meeting held in late May 1961, for example, Khrushchev revealed his goals for his summit meeting with President Kennedy in Vienna in June 1961. China and Vietnam have also declassified Cold War records. These records from the Communist world broaden understanding of the character and nature of the Cold War.

This concise interpretative history of John Kennedy's role as world leader will first look at the president's foreign policy background, his core beliefs, whom he chose for his foreign policy team, and how he organized them. Subsequent chapters will analyze the administration's policies toward the Soviet Union, Cuba, and Vietnam as well as relations with key countries in Asia, Africa, Latin America, and the Middle East. A thorough examination of Kennedy's historic role must move beyond the obvious flashpoints of his administration—Berlin and Cuba—and consider his global impact. A final chapter will offer a reasoned judgment on Kennedy's significance in international affairs. This study can perhaps contribute to the debate about whether John Kennedy deserves the solid reputation he continues to enjoy with the U.S. public and many scholars.

CHAPTER 2

Background, Beliefs, People

John F. Kennedy brought to the White House a core of beliefs about the duties of the United States in the world, the challenges the United States faced in the international arena, and the role the president should play in directing the foreign policies of the United States. When he took command of the presidency on January 20, 1961, Kennedy became, at forty-three, the youngest president in U.S. history. Despite his relative youth, Kennedy had a number of experiences that had shaped his global outlook. Kennedy professed "internationalism." Like Presidents Theodore Roosevelt and Woodrow Wilson, he believed that the peace and prosperity of the United States depended upon peace and prosperity in the world. Given its size, wealth, and power, the United States had a natural obligation to take a leadership role in promoting international peace and prosperity. Kennedy further believed that the United States had the right to international moral leadership. The United States was an exceptional nation, with a historic role to serve as a model for other countries that aspired to freedom, liberty, and wealth.

John Kennedy was also a dedicated Cold Warrior. Like his contemporaries in the U.S. political and foreign policy world, Kennedy accepted the premise that the Soviet Union and the international Communist movement threatened the United States and its allies. Containment of the Communist menace had to be the essence of U.S. foreign policy. Kennedy confidently proclaimed, however, that he could wage Cold War far more effectively than had his predecessors, Presidents Harry S. Truman and Dwight D. Eisenhower. The United States would confront the Communists and defeat them. Winning the Cold War depended upon the president taking personal charge of U.S. foreign policies. Kennedy vowed to be an activist foreign policy president.

Early Career

Kennedy grew to be comfortable in the international arena. As a young man, he had the opportunity to travel abroad because he was a member of a wealthy and powerful family. Kennedy toured Europe during the time his father, Joseph P. Kennedy, served as President Franklin D. Roosevelt's ambassador in London. He attended Pope Pius XII's investiture in Vatican City in 1939. In 1941 Kennedy volunteered for military service, joining the U.S. Navy, even though he could have been exempted from service because of his various colon, stomach, and back ailments. He commanded a patrol-torpedo (PT) boat in the South Pacific during the war years. He acted courageously, saving men from drowning, after a Japanese destroyer rammed his PT 109, throwing Kennedy and his crew into the sea. His swimming efforts worsened his back problems. Kennedy admired individuals who risked all for a greater cause. His beloved older brother, Joseph, a Navy pilot, died during the war after volunteering to fly a dangerous mission.

Kennedy displayed intellectual interest in international affairs in 1940 with his senior thesis at Harvard University. The study, *Why England Slept*, asked why the United Kingdom had not immediately and forcefully confronted Adolf Hitler and Nazi Germany. Prime Minister Neville Chamberlain had tried to appease Hitler at a meeting in Munich in 1938 by permitting Hitler to seize part of Czechoslovakia. This appeasement only enhanced Hitler's military power and fed his appetite for further aggression, leading to World War II. Kennedy did not especially criticize Chamberlain in his senior thesis. Nonetheless, his thesis proved timely, for his study fit well into the intellectual consensus that developed in the postwar period. Foreign policy elites believed that two seminal historical lessons emerged from the interwar period. The United States, refusing to join President Wilson's creation, the League of Nations, had been foolish to isolate itself from the world, and the Munich conference taught the folly of trying to negotiate with expansionist dictators. U.S. leaders and citizens reasoned that the tragedy of World War II, and the destruction of European Jewry, could have been avoided if the United States had listened to President Wilson and if democratic leaders had stood up to Hitler. The United States needed to be actively engaged in international affairs, militarily prepared, and determined to resist criminal nations. The Soviet Union's domination of Poland and Romania in 1945, like Hitler's aggression in Austria and Czechoslovakia, could be the first hint of a master plan to conquer the world. The revised *Why England Slept* developed a good reputation for the young John Kennedy. Through his father's contacts he arranged for its publication and the book enjoyed good sales.

After the war, Kennedy entered politics, serving as member of the House of Representatives, representing Boston, from 1947 to 1953. Congressman Kennedy supported key Cold War initiatives designed to contain the Soviet Union—the Truman Doctrine (1947), the Marshall Plan (1948), and the North Atlantic Treaty Organization (NATO) (1949). He most certainly would have backed the central ideas in National Security Council Memorandum No. 68/2 (NSC 68/2), which the Truman administration secretly adopted in mid-1950. NSC 68/2 provided a blueprint for a Cold War strategy. The document claimed that the Soviet Union directed the international Communist movement and aimed at world domination. NSC 68/2 depicted the Cold War in apocalyptic terms, or, as Kennedy put it in 1960, "a struggle for supremacy between two conflicting ideologies: Freedom under God versus ruthless, godless tyranny." The United States needed to remember the lessons of Munich. Josef Stalin, the leader of the Soviet Union, had the same evil goals as Adolf Hitler. NSC 68/2 called on the United States to quadruple military spending and build a military power "second to none." The United States would contain the Soviet Union with hydrogen bombs, intercontinental bombers, nuclear-powered submarines, and a massive standing army sustained by a military draft. NSC 68/2 anticipated a globalist foreign policy; the United States must respond to the international Communist conspiracy.[1] In 1950 the Truman administration decided, for example, to aid the French in their colonial war against Ho Chi Minh and his Communist-led nationalist movement in Vietnam. When he became president in 1961, Kennedy asked Paul Nitze, a principal architect of NSC 68/2, to join his foreign-policy team.

Congressman Kennedy judged the Truman administration insufficiently vigorous in prosecuting the Cold War. He criticized his fellow Democrats for permitting the Communists to triumph in China and for not winning the Korean War. After the Soviets successfully exploded an atomic bomb in 1949, he decried the lack of civil defense in the United States to protect citizens from nuclear attack and radiation. As president, Kennedy would call for the building of fallout shelters. He also got along with Senator Joseph McCarthy, the Republican from Wisconsin, who recklessly charged that Communist subversives had infiltrated the Truman administration. His Democratic colleagues in the House perceived Kennedy as a moderate-liberal member on domestic questions and a moderate-conservative one on international issues. They did not judge him to be either hardworking or prominent. In 1951 Kennedy and his younger brother, Robert, and sister, Patricia, took a seven-week, 25,000-mile trip, visiting numerous countries in the Middle East and Asia. During the trip John Kennedy began to sense the power of nationalism in the postwar world. He questioned whether the United States should be linking itself to French colonialism in Vietnam.

Senator Kennedy (1953–1961) became a prominent political leader. His defeat of Henry Cabot Lodge for the Senate seat in Massachusetts gained him national attention because 1953 was a Republican year. Dwight Eisenhower won the presidency and Republicans gained control of the Senate and House. Kennedy began to travel the country speaking for the Democratic Party, and in 1956 he was nominated for the vice presidency when the Democratic presidential nominee, Adlai Stevenson, called on delegates at the Democratic Party convention to choose a candidate for him. Kennedy enhanced his national prestige when he graciously withdrew his name from the nomination fight. In 1957 he gained a coveted seat on the Senate Foreign Relations Committee. He began to make his mark on two international issues—national defense and anti-colonialism. He called for increased spending on defense and criticized President Eisenhower for shortchanging national defense. In a notable Senate speech in August 1958, Kennedy alleged that the Soviet Union had or would soon surpass the United States in nuclear firepower. The United States was fast approaching a "missile-lag period." President Eisenhower, Senator Kennedy charged, placed "fiscal security ahead of national security."[2] These allegations that the United States had fallen behind the Soviet Union would become a prominent part of Kennedy's 1960 presidential campaign. In the popular mind, Kennedy's call for increased military spending made sense because the Soviets had been the first to launch an artificial satellite, Sputnik, into earth orbit in 1957. In fact, President Eisenhower, the nation's only five-star general, knew, because of solid intelligence, that the United States had superior military technology. Eisenhower believed that an accelerated Soviet-American nuclear arms race would bankrupt both nations and increase the likelihood of a catastrophic conflict.

Kennedy also identified himself with nationalism and anticolonialism. He held that a key to a successful Cold War strategy was appealing to Asians, Africans, Latin Americans—the people of the developing world. The old order of European colonialism was collapsing; in 1960 alone eighteen new nations would appear. In July 1957 Kennedy gained national and international attention by denouncing a U.S. ally, France, on the Senate floor for its suppression of Algerian independence. He identified nationalism as "the most powerful force" in the world and Soviet and Western imperialists as the enemies of freedom. He proclaimed that "the single most important test of American foreign policy today is how we meet the challenge of imperialism" and that "on this test more than any other, this Nation shall be critically judged by the uncommitted millions of Asia and Africa and anxiously watched by the still hopeful lovers of freedom behind the Iron Curtain." Senator Kennedy gave substance to these words by subsequently sponsoring legislation to finance economic development in poor regions, with special assistance to India.[3] The speech boosted Kennedy's political fortunes. He had raised a vital issue, and he made himself more palatable to the liberal wing of the Democratic Party led by Adlai Stevenson and Eleanor Roosevelt. Liberals were suspicious of Kennedy because he had befriended Senator Joseph McCarthy and absented himself from the 1953 vote in the Senate to censure McCarthy for his outrageous behavior.

Kennedy's support for Algerian independence revealed an essential part of his character. He was a racial egalitarian who had a genuine concern for poor, oppressed people. As a legislator, he had supported legislation that assisted working-class people in Boston and Massachusetts. He and his brother Robert would be shocked by the appalling poverty they witnessed in West Virginia during the 1960 presidential campaign, and, as president, he would propose legislative remedies to poverty in the United States. His senatorial support for assistance to India presaged his $20 billion Alliance for Progress program for Latin America, which underscored Kennedy's belief that wealthy nations had a duty to help needy nations. Once, in 1963, while touring Costa Rica, President

Kennedy noticed an unoccupied hospital and instructed aides to find funds to staff it. Kennedy delighted in the company of Latin Americans and became fast friends with racially mixed Latin American leaders.[4] Although not passionate about the issue of civil rights, Kennedy considered racism, like colonialism, to be anachronistic, irrational, and unmodern. As president, he consoled African diplomats who encountered discriminatory treatment in states such as Maryland and Virginia. In deciding in mid-1963 to wholeheartedly back civil rights legislation, Kennedy knew that the abolition of segregation in the South would aid the United States in the ideological struggle with the Soviet Union for the hearts and minds of people of color throughout the world.[5]

Kennedy, however, qualified his fervor for nationalism and economic justice and his opposition to colonialism and racism. Anticommunism outranked equality and justice in his hierarchy of values. During his legislative career, Kennedy had established himself as a strident anti-Communist, what would be dubbed a "Cold War liberal." He implicitly accepted the premise of NSC 68/2 that the Soviet Union directed an international Communist movement driving to dominate the world. He professed that the United States would be more effective in countering the Communist menace if it built more weapons, expanded the size of U.S. military forces, and supported third world people in their struggle for freedom and economic development. The intellectual challenge for President Kennedy would arise when he encountered leaders and movements that fought against imperialism, racism, and economic injustice but held left-wing political and economic views, gave credence to Marxist critiques of capitalist societies, and accepted support from local Communist parties. Throughout his public career, Kennedy made fighting and winning the Cold War his paramount concern. His presidential record would demonstrate that he invariably chose anti-Communist dictators or colonialists over popularly elected leaders or nationalists who were not zealous anti-Communists.

Senator Kennedy further prepared himself for a run for the White House by enhancing his intellectual credentials. His book *Profiles in Courage* won a Pulitzer Prize for biography in 1957. The book told stories of political leaders in U.S. history who placed public needs over private concerns. In 1960 he released *The Strategy of Peace*, a compilation of his speeches on national security and international affairs. He also penned "A Democrat Looks at Foreign Policy," which appeared in the prestigious journal *Foreign Affairs*. Kennedy soberly reviewed the U.S. approach to global and regional issues, criticizing U.S. leadership for "a lack of decision and conviction." He charged that President Eisenhower had created a ponderous decision-making process within the NSC. The United States had "underestimated the capacity of the Russians to compete with us militarily and economically." Kennedy again reminded that the United States had to recognize the power and appeal of nationalism in the world and needed to be more generous with its foreign aid.[6]

Presidential Campaign

John Kennedy had the opportunity to present the foreign policy views that he had developed in his legislative career during the 1960 presidential campaign. Foreign policy issues dominated the debates between Kennedy and Vice President Richard M. Nixon. The focus on global affairs probably aided Kennedy's election because the U.S. public worried that the country's standing in the world had declined. After the successful launch of Sputnik in 1957, the Soviet Union continued to display its scientific prowess and rocket and missile technology with several impressive space missions. In 1958 Nixon toured South America and was greeted by protestors denouncing the Eisenhower administration's support for Latin American dictators. In Caracas, Venezuela, a howling mob surrounded Nixon's limousine and threatened the life of the vice president and his wife. In 1959 Fidel Castro triumphantly rode on a tank into Havana and transformed the Cuban Revolution into a bitterly anti-American movement. The next year, the Soviets shot down a spy plane, the U-2, and captured the U.S. pilot. The U-2 incident became an embarrassment for President Eisenhower, who had initially denied that the United States had intentionally violated Soviet airspace. The incident also wrecked the May 1960 summit in Paris between Eisenhower and Soviet leader Nikita S. Khrushchev. President Eisenhower had hoped to strike a bargain with Khrushchev banning the testing of nuclear weapons. The bad news marred the public image of the United States. A U.S. Information Agency (USIA) survey of world public opinion conducted in 1960 found that people believed that the Soviet Union was militarily superior to the United States and was closing the gap economically. The success of Sputnik had a dramatic impact on the stature of the Soviet Union. The classified "prestige" study was leaked to the Kennedy campaign, and Senator Kennedy made good use of it during the last weeks before the election. He repeatedly promised "to get the country moving again," both at home and abroad.[7]

Kennedy relentlessly criticized the Eisenhower-Nixon stewardship of U.S. foreign policy. During the 1952 campaign, the Republicans had accused Democrats of losing the Cold War, especially citing the "loss" of China to communism. Kennedy repaid the Republicans for the China issue by blaming the Republicans for Fidel Castro. He reminded an audience in Nashville, Tennessee, that the United States now faced "a Communist satellite ninety miles off the coast of Florida, eight minutes by jet." In a press release, he suggested he would take steps to assist the overthrow of Castro. The decline in U.S. prestige and the rise of Castro signaled that the United States was losing the Cold War. The enemy, "the Communist system itself," was, in Kennedy's words, "lean and hungry" and "implacable, insatiable, unceasing in its drive for world domination." Kennedy warned that the Communists might fulfill their master plan. He told an audience in Alexandria, Virginia, that history might judge "that these were the days when the tide began to run out for the United States. These were the times when the Communist tide began to pour in."[8] Senator Kennedy's rhetoric reverberated with the lessons of Munich and the omens of NSC 68/2.

The Soviet Union might soon overwhelm the United States militarily. Returning to a theme he raised in the Senate in 1958, candidate Kennedy charged that the Eisenhower administration had undercut U.S. military strength with niggardly defense budgets. A "missile gap" was developing with the Soviet Union gaining the capability of starting and winning a nuclear war with a superior intercontinental ballistic missile (ICBM) force. The stakes could not be higher, for "we are facing a gap on which we are gambling with our survival." In one of the televised presidential debates with Nixon, Kennedy predicted the missile gap would appear as early as 1961–1963. Kennedy rang a false alarm. He chose to believe unofficial estimates of the nuclear arms race. President Eisenhower accurately denied the existence of a missile gap. The majority of analysts in the intelligence community calculated that the United States had an overwhelming lead in nuclear weapons and delivery vehicles. The U-2 program, which ended in May 1960, never photographed a single deployed ICBM. Kennedy received three intelligence briefings on the issue during the 1960 campaign. Because

CIA Director Allen Dulles chose not to give a definitive answer to Kennedy on the missile gap issue, the candidate thought it fair to hammer away at the Eisenhower-Nixon team.[9]

Kennedy's narrow victory over Nixon in November 1960 can be explained in a variety of ways. He appeared presidential—cool, calm, analytical—during the televised debates. The debates helped undermine Nixon's central argument that he had more experience in the international arena. Republicans were also hurt by the memory of the sharp economic recession of 1958 and the ensuing slow economic recovery. By promising to increase defense expenditures, Kennedy appealed to working-class citizens who wanted employment in defense plants. President-elect Kennedy interpreted his victory as a mandate to restore U.S. power and prestige.

Foreign Policy Team

Presidential leadership was the key to victory in the Cold War. The organization of a foreign policy team would determine whether the president could carry out bold, decisive actions. As he had written in his *Foreign Affairs* article, Kennedy was convinced that President Eisenhower had produced an organizational scheme that guaranteed ponderous thinking and torpid foreign policies. Drawing on his military experience, Eisenhower had created an intricate staff system to recommend policies and monitor their execution. Eisenhower made critical policy decisions at lengthy NSC meetings. From 1953 to 1961, the NSC met 366 times, with Eisenhower presiding over 339 of the meetings. From President-elect Kennedy's perspective, this process guaranteed endless talk and little action. But Eisenhower supplemented the NSC conclaves with regular meetings in the Oval Office with his closest advisers, including his secretary of state. Eisenhower used these Oval Office meetings to coordinate national security policy with diplomacy, the daily conduct of international relations. Presidential scholars have concluded that Eisenhower's organizational scheme had merit, for it prevented rash action, allowed for a healthy exchange of ideas, and permitted the president to make the vital decisions.[10]

President-elect Kennedy thought in terms of people, not committee structures or organizational charts. He wanted to be a foreign policy president and his own secretary of state, or, as he put it, the presidency had to be "the vital center of action in our whole scheme of government."[11] He insisted on discussing his policy options and making his decisions in small, intense meetings. His appointment of McGeorge Bundy to direct the NSC signaled his intention to break from the Eisenhower model. Bundy centralized decision making in the White House and controlled the flow of information to the president. Bundy's appointment also demonstrated Kennedy's wish to consult brilliant, relatively young men who enjoyed making decisions. Bundy, forty-one, had been a professor of government and then dean of the faculty at Harvard University. Journalists would tag Kennedy's appointments as "action intellectuals" or the "best and the brightest."[12]

Beyond being intellectually able, Kennedy's appointments shared other characteristics. They were all males; Kennedy did not interview any women for key foreign policy positions. Most were combat veterans of World War II who had won medals for bravery. Kennedy's men shared the belief that the containment of communism had to be the core of U.S. foreign policy. Kennedy's secretary of state, Dean Rusk, had established his anti-Communist credentials as assistant secretary of state for the Far East during the Truman administration. Presidents Truman and Eisenhower had relied on their respective secretaries of state, Dean Acheson (1949–1953) and John Foster Dulles (1953–1959), for leadership. Kennedy wanted a loyal secretary of state who would serve him and not object if foreign policy emanated from the White House rather than the State Department. Rusk had impressive credentials—combat veteran, Rhodes Scholar, college professor, experienced diplomat. Rusk (1961–1969) served both Kennedy and President Lyndon Baines Johnson and remained remarkably loyal to both men.

Since he was going to be his own secretary of state, the president-elect judged his appointments to the Treasury and Defense departments as critical. C. Douglas Dillon, whose father had established an international banking house, became the secretary of treasury. Dillon, a medal-winning naval aviator, had been ambassador to France and undersecretary of state during the Eisenhower years and was a Republican. Kennedy appointed three Republicans to his cabinet to create an air of bipartisanship in foreign affairs and to indicate that he recognized that he had barely won the presidential election. Robert S. McNamara, the president of Ford Motor Company and a nominal Republican, accepted Kennedy's offer to be secretary of defense. McNamara, forty-four, had been the youngest assistant professor ever at Harvard's business school and then a lieutenant colonel in the Army Air Force during the war. He analyzed the efficiency and effectiveness of bombing campaigns. An expert in management control systems, McNamara, dubbed "an IBM machine with legs," was renowned for his quick, analytic mind.

Kennedy drew talent from the liberal wing of the Democratic Party. Adlai Stevenson, the former presidential candidate, became ambassador to the United Nations but wielded no real power. Chester Bowles, a former governor of Connecticut and ambassador to India, became undersecretary of state but lost the position at the end of 1961 because of perceived disloyalty to Kennedy. Bowles

President Kennedy is at ease here with two of his chief foreign policy advisers, Secretary of Defense Robert McNamara and Secretary of State Dean Rusk (nearest the president). Kennedy, who wanted to be a foreign policy president, made the key decisions, after consulting with his advisers, including McNamara, Rusk, National Security Adviser McGeorge Bundy, and Attorney General Robert Kennedy. (John F. Kennedy Presidential Library and Museum, Boston)

had disclosed to the press that he had opposed the invasion of Cuba—the Bay of Pigs operation. Bowles later became a roving diplomat, an ambassador-at-large, for President Kennedy. George Ball became the new undersecretary of state. Ball, a crusty, self-confident liberal, wanted the United States to promote free trade policies and focus its attention on the North Atlantic world. He would bluntly warn both Presidents Kennedy and Johnson not to entangle the United States in Vietnam. Kennedy also brought Arthur Schlesinger Jr., the famous historian and Harvard professor, into the White House. Schlesinger, who concentrated on relations with Latin America, wanted the United States to defeat international communism with foreign aid and economic development or what he called "enlightened anticommunism."

The president-elect reappointed two prominent conservatives, J. Edgar Hoover and Allen W. Dulles. Hoover, the longtime director of the Federal Bureau of Investigation (FBI), ostensibly protected domestic security. But Hoover and his agents meddled in international affairs, and they harassed citizens who held leftist and liberal political views on foreign affairs. The tawdry Hoover kept dossiers on the private lives of U.S. politicians, including Kennedy. Dulles, who was the younger brother of Secretary of State Dulles and the grandson of a former secretary of state, served as director of the CIA during the Eisenhower years. He oversaw covert interventions in Iran (1953), Guatemala (1954), Indonesia (1958), and elsewhere. Under his leadership, the CIA developed plans to assassinate foreign leaders. Dulles and his staff resigned in September 1961 after the Bay of Pigs fiasco. Kennedy appointed John A. McCone, a Republican and the chair of the U.S. Atomic Energy Commission, to replace Dulles.

Other notable appointments included Gen. Maxwell Taylor, Paul Nitze, and Walt Whitman Rostow. The president-elect made Taylor his special military adviser and later recalled him to military service and appointed him chairman of the Joint Chiefs of Staff. Taylor, another military hero of World War II, had been Army chief of staff but resigned from active military service in 1959. He criticized President Eisenhower for not spending enough money on conventional, nonnuclear forces. Nitze, who wrote NSC 68/2, also wanted more military spending and became an adviser to Kennedy on nuclear forces. Rostow, a prominent economist from the Massachusetts Institute of Technology (MIT), had written a famous treatise, *The Stages of Economic Growth, a Non-*

Communist Manifesto (1960), on how newly emerging nations could achieve high rates of economic growth and modernization. The West could spur the development process with foreign aid. Rostow, who served in the NSC and State Department for Kennedy, also fancied himself an expert on counterinsurgency warfare. Rostow, a proponent of a maximum U.S. effort in Vietnam, replaced Bundy as head of the NSC in 1966.[13]

Vice President Johnson exercised little influence on Kennedy's foreign policy. Kennedy had selected Johnson as his running mate to help secure the votes of southern Democrats and to carry Texas, Johnson's native state. Throughout his legislative career, which included being majority leader in the U.S. Senate, Johnson had focused on domestic issues. Johnson attended important meetings, such as deliberations during the Cuban missile crisis, but often said little. Kennedy dispatched his vice president on fact-finding tours to countries such as Vietnam. Johnson oversaw the space exploration program. Kennedy hoped that successful manned flights into space, including becoming the first nation to reach the moon, would restore the nation's lost international prestige.

Robert F. Kennedy, surprisingly, became his brother's most trusted adviser on foreign policy issues. The president-elect appointed his strong-willed brother, who had directed his 1960 presidential campaign, as attorney general. Robert Kennedy, who had a law degree from the University of Virginia, had never actually practiced law. The Justice Department had plenty of work during the Kennedy years protecting civil rights activists from violence in the South. But Robert Kennedy increasingly involved himself in foreign policy decisions after the Bay of Pigs fiasco of April 1961. Robert Kennedy believed his brother had been badly advised during the administration's first months in office. He was prepared to discipline any U.S. official who challenged the administration's policies. He joined in decisions on counterinsurgency operations and covert interventions and oversaw the covert war against Fidel Castro's Cuba. Robert Kennedy, a fierce, often ruthless man, loved his older brother and would have sacrificed his own life to protect him.

The foreign policy team that President-elect Kennedy assembled made plain what the priorities would be for the new administration. John Kennedy would keep his campaign promises. He would be in "the vital center of action" in the making of U.S. foreign policy. He would confront the Soviet Union with expanded military power both in nuclear and conventional forces. He would fight the Cold War in Asia, Africa, Latin America, and the Middle East with foreign aid and counterinsurgency tactics. The United States would lead the world and promote the free trade and investment policies of international capitalism. The men who joined the Kennedy team identified with their leader. They were brilliant, were accomplished, and had heroic pasts. They expected to win the Cold War.

CHAPTER 3

Soviet Union

President John F. Kennedy made containing and ultimately defeating the Soviet Union his main foreign policy objective. He upheld the central goals of his predecessors, Harry S. Truman and Dwight D. Eisenhower. But President Kennedy argued that the United States needed to act boldly and decisively in the international arena. The Soviet Union allegedly wielded more military power than the United States and had taken the lead in the ideological struggle for the hearts and minds of the world's people. The United States needed to speak unflinchingly about the perils that loomed and to broadcast its political and moral superiority. It also had to defend its interests in critical areas like the city of Berlin. Kennedy vowed that the United States would protect its vital interests by embarking upon a vigorous expansion of its nuclear and conventional military forces. Kennedy's assertive foreign policy intensified the Soviet-American confrontation and escalated the nuclear arms race.

The conduct of Soviet-American relations during the Kennedy years proved deeply ironic. Both Kennedy and his Soviet counterpart, Nikita S. Khrushchev, hoped to improve relations and wanted peace. Both men feared war, dreaded the prospects of nuclear war, and hoped to tame the military buildup with nuclear test ban and disarmament treaties. Khrushchev actually favored the election of Kennedy in 1960, as he judged Vice President Richard M. Nixon an unreconstructed Cold Warrior. Both Kennedy and Khrushchev spoke words and took actions, however, that shocked the other and led to belligerent responses. After confrontations over Berlin and Cuba, both men seemed to have reflected upon and reassessed their positions. By mid-1963 the prospects for

Soviet-American cooperation, even a détente, had improved. Neither Kennedy nor Khrushchev would be in a position, however, to negotiate the peace that they both envisioned.

National Security Policies and the Nuclear Arms Race

The new president demonstrated that he was a politician who kept his campaign promises. During the 1960 presidential campaign, Senator Kennedy's constant theme had been that President Eisenhower and Vice President Richard M. Nixon had imperiled the security of the United States with lax, inattentive diplomatic and military policies. Eisenhower had allegedly denied the U.S. military the money and hardware it needed to counter the threat of the Soviet Union. Kennedy's inaugural address, with its call for duty, greatness, and national self-sacrifice, stirred the hearts of U.S. citizens. But the president's address to a joint session of Congress on January 30, 1961, ten days after the inauguration, set both the style and substance for the administration's approach to international affairs. The president revisited the apocalyptic language of his political campaign. The United States faced "the hour of national peril." The Soviet Union and the People's Republic of China sought global domination. The United States drew nearer to "the hour of maximum danger." The new administration would "reappraise our entire defense strategy," for "weapons spread and hostile forces grow stronger." Sounding the alarm, Kennedy warned, "I feel I must inform the Congress that our analyses over the last ten days make it clear that, in the principal areas of crisis, the tide of events has been running out—and time has not been our friend."[1]

To reverse the course of current history and to show the Communist forces that "aggression and subversion will not be profitable routes to pursue," the United States would rearm. In 1961 alone, in three separate budgetary requests, Kennedy asked for a 15 percent increase in military spending. By 1963 defense spending would be up to $54 billion, a nearly 20 percent increase over President Eisenhower's final defense budget of $46 billion. Overall, the Kennedy administration spent $17 billion more on military hardware and personnel than had been projected by Eisenhower's national security team. The new spending transformed the U.S. military. Between 1961 and 1964 the number of nuclear weapons increased by 150 percent. The delivery vehicles for the nuclear weapons, intercontinental ballistic missiles, increased from 63 to 424, with the administration setting a goal of 1,000 ICBMs. President Kennedy further authorized the expansion of Polaris submarines from six to twenty-nine. Each submarine carried sixteen nuclear-tipped missiles. The strategic bomber force, B-52s, increased by 50 percent.[2]

U.S. conventional military forces also grew in size and strength during the Kennedy years. The army divisions increased from eleven to sixteen, the number of ships in the U.S. Navy doubled, and tactical air squadron numbers increased by 30 percent. President Kennedy identified himself with counterinsurgency warfare. He ordered the Special Warfare Center at Ft. Bragg to accelerate training. The number of "special forces" personnel increased from under 1,000 troops to more than 12,000 by the end of 1963. Kennedy actually chose the green beret as the symbol of the Special Forces.

The United States projected power around the globe with its expanded military might. The nuclear firepower of the North Atlantic Treaty Organization increased by 60 percent between 1961 and 1963. By 1963 the United States had 275 major military bases in thirty-one countries. Sixty-five countries hosted U.S. armed forces, and U.S. military personnel offered training courses in seventy-two countries. More than one million U.S. military personnel were stationed abroad. The Kennedy administration also expanded military aid to anti-Communist friends. Between 1961 and 1964 U.S. military aid to Latin America, for example, averaged over $77 million a year, a 50 percent increase over the average of the Eisenhower years.[3]

The military buildup that President Kennedy had authorized repudiated the national security policies of President Eisenhower. Eisenhower had outlined his thinking on the Cold War in NSC 162/2 (1953) and implied that President Truman had not thought through the considerable implications of his national security document NSC 68/2 (1950). NSC 68/2 had called for a massive military buildup, predicted that 1954 would be the year of "maximum danger," and called on the United States to amass a preponderance of power. Paul Nitze, the major author of NSC 68/2, had suggested that the United States needed to take "increased risks of general war" in order to achieve a satisfactory relationship with the Soviet Union. Nitze, who Kennedy appointed as assistant secretary of defense for International Security Affairs, advised the president on nuclear weapons.

Kennedy had used Nitze's language of "maximum danger" in his January 30 address to Congress. Indeed, the new president seemed to be returning to the world of NSC 68/2 and unlimited military spending based on fears of impending disasters.

President Eisenhower had shared the anticommunism of Democrats, but he had rejected their doomsday scenarios. Eisenhower judged Soviet leaders as aggressive expansionists but also as rational men who loved their country, remembered the horrors of World War II, and understood the consequences of a nuclear conflict. The Soviets would respect firmness and resolve. Eisenhower believed that the United States needed a strategy that was sustainable and would not bankrupt the nation. As Eisenhower saw it, national defense was about protecting a way of life, which included a prospering domestic economy that enriched the lives and welfare of citizens. Excessive military spending would undermine "the American way of life." Federal tax money allocated to aircraft carriers inevitably meant that there would be fewer resources to spend on hospitals, schools, and national parks. National security included having a healthy economy and resources to assist allies and to woo nations emerging from colonialism. NSC 162/2 represented Eisenhower's thinking. The United States would avoid rash confrontations that could provoke general war. It would deter Soviet aggression with nuclear weapons and challenge Communist influence in Asia, Africa, and Latin America with military and economic aid policies.[4] Eisenhower also authorized covert interventions, as in Iran (1953), Guatemala (1954), and the Congo (1960) to counter perceived Soviet meddling.

Especially during his second presidential term (1957–1961), Eisenhower's diplomatic and military policies demonstrated his governing philosophies. Eisenhower foresaw that the military technologies such as ICBMs raised the prospects of catastrophic thermonuclear war. The successful launching of Sputnik I by the Soviets had demonstrated the accuracy and power of these new missiles. In October 1958 Eisenhower suspended the testing of U.S. nuclear weapons, and in 1959 he met with Nikita Khrushchev at Camp David, the presidential retreat, and had fruitful discussions on the nuclear arms race. The two old veterans of World War II spoke regretfully about how their respective military hierarchies pressured them to spend on military hardware. Eisenhower wanted to sign a treaty with Khrushchev that would permanently ban the testing of nuclear weapons and halt the nuclear arms race. The downing of a U.S. spy plane over the Soviet Union, the U-2 incident, ruined Eisenhower's summit meeting with Khrushchev in Paris in May 1960. Although devastated by his failure in Paris, Eisenhower persisted in his mission. He revisited his concerns about excessive military spending in his farewell address to the nation on January 17, 1961, when he warned citizens about the dangers of the "military-industrial complex."[5] President Kennedy's call to arms two weeks later stood in stark contrast to Eisenhower's plea for prudence.

In the 1950s politicians and military officers denounced Eisenhower for restraining military spending. In *Uncertain Trumpet* (1960), the newly retired Gen. Maxwell Taylor, the former Army chief of staff, charged that Eisenhower had shortchanged U.S. conventional forces and left the nation too dependent on its nuclear deterrent. President Kennedy would conspicuously appoint General Taylor as his special military adviser and, in 1962, recall him to military service and appoint him as chairman of the Joint Chiefs of Staff. As a presidential candidate, Kennedy had joined in the criticism of Eisenhower's military spending, alleging a "missile gap." With photographic evidence obtained by U-2 spy planes, Eisenhower knew the facts. Despite their success with Sputnik, the Soviets had technical failures with their first generation of ICBMs. The United States possessed an enormous strategic advantage over the Soviets, with 2,000 bombers, 100 ballistic missiles of varying ranges, and over 18,000 warheads in its nuclear stockpile. The United States had an "overkill" capacity—the power to end meaningful life in the Soviet Union. Despite his best intentions, Eisenhower had not succeeded in curbing the appetites of interest groups like the Joint Chiefs, Defense Department, and Atomic Energy Commission for nuclear technologies and more weapons. Eisenhower had confessed his frustration to Khrushchev at Camp David, and his "military-industrial complex" speech can, in part, be interpreted as an admission of failure.[6] Eisenhower declined, however, to point out publicly the disparities in the arms race. Boasts and threats would only heighten global tensions and encourage the Soviets to accelerate their nuclear weapons programs.

President Kennedy gained access to the classified intelligence on nuclear weapons that informed Eisenhower's thinking. On February 6, 1961, Secretary of Defense McNamara blurted out to correspondents, "There is no missile gap." The administration quickly backed off from the statement, realizing that it made its campaign charges seem false and misleading. President Kennedy qualified McNamara's accurate admission by noting that it would be "premature to reach a judgment." But throughout 1961, Kennedy received intelligence estimates that downgraded Soviet nuclear strength. Col. Oleg Penkovsky, a Soviet military officer who worked for the West, passed reports on Soviet military thinking to U.S. intelligence operatives. After the U-2 incident, the United States had replaced spy planes with the Corona spy satellite program. The photographic evidence in July 1961 showed the Soviets had only two ICBM sites between Leningrad (St. Petersburg) and the Ural Mountains, with a combined total of eight launching pads. By comparison, in September 1961 Kennedy received a briefing at the Strategic Air Command (SAC) headquarters in Omaha, Nebraska, that revealed the awesome power of the United States. The United States had the capacity with its missiles and bombers to hit nearly 4,000 targets in the Soviet Union with nuclear warheads. Kennedy nonetheless went forward with his massive military buildup. He justified his goal of 1,000 ICBMs by explaining that he did not want to signal weakness to the Soviets and that a buildup would leave the United States in a position of strength and capable of negotiating meaningful arms reductions in the future. Kennedy further believed that displaying awesome military power would enhance the global prestige of the United States and demonstrate to the world's people that the Soviet Union did not represent the wave of the future. Throughout the 1960 campaign, Kennedy had criticized Eisenhower and Nixon for projecting an image of weakness abroad.[7] Such a military expansion could, however, have the unfortunate effect of frightening the Soviets and forcing them into a crash expansion of their nuclear forces.

President Kennedy and his advisers publicly flaunted U.S. military prowess. In the fall of 1961, in news conferences and interviews, the president, Secretary of State Dean Rusk, and McNamara asserted that the United States had "nuclear power several times that of the Soviet Union." The president further authorized Roswell Gilpatric, the deputy secretary of defense, to provide specifics on U.S. nuclear power, enumerating U.S. bombers, ICBMs, and Polaris submarines. In his speech of October 21 to U.S. businessmen, Deputy Secretary Gilpatric proclaimed that the United States could survive a surprise nuclear attack and retaliate with a devastating blow. Put another way, the United States had achieved the capacity to begin, fight, and "win" a nuclear war. In the arcane world of nuclear-war-fighting doctrine, the United States possessed a "first-strike" capability. Gilpatric delivered the news at a time when Chairman Khrushchev was meeting with colleagues in Moscow at the Twenty-second Party Congress, the biggest event in the Communist world. Gilpatric seemed to be suggesting that the Soviet Union lacked the firepower to deter the United States.[8]

The Kennedy administration's massive military buildup and provocative public statements did not enhance U.S. national security or promote global peace. In retrospect, Secretary of Defense McNamara has conceded that the administration unthinkingly threatened the Soviet Union.[9] Looking at the U.S. arsenal and listening to U.S. officials, Soviet military planners could have surmised that the United States believed it could survive a nuclear war. The Soviets were further provoked by the administration's decision to deploy fifteen medium-range ballistic missiles, known as "Jupiters," in Turkey, a neighbor of the Soviet Union. President Eisenhower had authorized the Jupiters in 1959 but had delayed their deployment. The Soviets predictably responded to the U.S. nuclear threats. Khrushchev's decision in mid-1962 to send nuclear missiles to Cuba can be partially explained by his desire to gain the appearance of nuclear parity with the United States. In the 1960s, after the overthrow of Khrushchev, the Soviets under the direction of Leonid Brezhnev (1966–1982), would embark on their own rapid, gigantic expansion of nuclear weaponry to match the Kennedy-era buildup. By the mid-1980s both superpowers had the ability to hit over 10,000 targets with strategic nuclear weapons. By then, the United States and the Soviet Union together controlled nearly 50,000 nuclear warheads. On average, each warhead was thirty times more powerful than the atomic bomb that obliterated Hiroshima in August 1945.

The Kennedy administration coupled its nuclear buildup with another step that seemed to herald the onset of nuclear war. On July 25, 1961, the president gave an alarming address to the nation. This came a month after his stormy meeting with Khrushchev in Vienna, Austria, and with a Soviet-American confrontation over Berlin looming. Beyond announcing that he would ask Congress to add $3 billion to the defense budget, Kennedy said he would ask Congress to appropriate $207 million to begin a civil defense fallout shelter program. As the president said, he "hoped to let every citizen know what steps he can take without delay to protect his family in case of attack." He added, "The lives of those families which are not hit in a nuclear blast and fire can still be saved—if they can be warned to take shelter, and if that shelter is available."[10] The administration suggested building five to six million shelter spaces by early 1962 and more than fifty million spaces over the next several years.

The U.S. public ultimately rejected these macabre schemes. Kennedy's civil defense program received scant congressional or public support. To enter a shelter would be to enter a tomb. The firestorms generated by thermonuclear war would burn so fiercely that they would consume available oxygen and asphyxiate living things. Indeed, asphyxiation had been the fate of the residents of Dresden, Germany, when Allied planes firebombed the city in 1945. (The horrors of such attacks would be memorably described by Kurt Vonnegut, who experienced the incineration of Dresden, in his famous 1969 novel, *Slaughterhouse-Five.*) Even if a shelter program could save thirty to seventy million people, it would be in the context of over 100 million citizens perishing. The living would envy the dead in such a world. The U.S. public characteristically responded to this madness with biting humor. Comedians advised students, in case of nuclear attack, to "move away from windows, crouch under desks, put your head between your legs, and kiss your ass good-bye." Not to be outdone, Soviet citizens also sought solace in humor. Muscovites asked, "What should I do if a nuclear bomb falls?" The answer: "Cover yourself with a sheet and crawl slowly to the nearest cemetery. Why slowly? To avoid panic."[11]

President Kennedy's sympathetic biographers have fairly noted that the president would have been disturbed to learn that he had contributed to the escalation of the nuclear arms race. Kennedy, the father of two, a combat veteran, and one who lost his beloved older brother, Joe, during World War II, had no lust for war, especially nuclear war. As a presidential candidate, he wrote to Eisenhower, pledging his support for Eisenhower's search for a nuclear test ban as a way of bringing "us one step closer to world peace." He flatly rejected the concept of limited nuclear war. In 1959 he observed to an audience in Louisiana, "If we use them the Russians use them" and "inevitably, the use of small nuclear armaments will lead to larger and larger nuclear armaments on both sides, until the world-wide holocaust has begun." He worked to exert his authority over intemperate military leaders, like Adm. Arleigh Burke, the chairman of the Joint Chiefs, and Air Force Gen. Curtis LeMay, who served as the model for the crazed Gen. Buck Turgidson in *Dr. Strangelove* (1964), film director Stanley Kubrick's dark comedy about nuclear war. Kennedy made clear to the generals that he possessed sole authority over the use of any nuclear weapon.[12]

Like Eisenhower, Kennedy struggled against those who argued for more weapons and more confrontations with the Soviets. At a White House luncheon in October 1961, E. M. Dealey, the publisher of the *Dallas Morning News*, insulted Kennedy, saying that he headed an administration of "weak sisters." He called for "a man on horseback" and sneered that "many people in Texas and the Southwest think you are riding [daughter] Caroline's tricycle."[13] But Kennedy's policies cannot be explained away as reactions to pressures from right-wing political fanatics and overzealous admirals and generals. With his campaign promises and apocalyptic language, foretelling that "the complacent, the self-indulgent, the soft societies are about to be swept away with the debris of history," Kennedy made a war of words and a nuclear arms race more likely. Fear, suspicion, and distrust informed his attitude toward the Soviet Union. He blamed the Soviet Union for most of the world's troubles, telling Aleksei Adzhubei, Khrushchev's son-in-law, in an interview that Communist expansion was "the great threat to peace."[14] Kennedy would also react sharply to his counterpart Nikita Khrushchev's confrontational words and rash, often inexplicable, actions.

Nikita Khrushchev

Nikita Khrushchev also wanted peace between the United States and the Soviet Union. But as with the U.S. president, Khrushchev issued edicts and embarked on journeys that seemed to undermine his genuine desire for harmonious international relationships. Nikita S. Khrushchev (1894–1971), whose official title was chairman of the Council of Ministers of the Union of Soviet Socialist Republics, was a veteran Communist functionary. He came from a classic "peasant and workers" background. His father labored on a small farm, and Khrushchev worked for a time as a miner and metalworker. He had only a rudimentary education. In 1918 he joined the Communist Party and fought in the Russian civil war. Over the next decades, Khrushchev rose through the party ranks and became the boss of Ukraine, the Soviet Union's most prosperous agricultural region. He displayed enormous amounts of energy and an ardent commitment to Communist ideals. Khrushchev also related well with common people. The Communist system offered him opportunities to achieve a formal education, but Khrushchev chose to focus on building his career in the party.

Josef Stalin (1929–1953), the paranoid, murderous dictator of the Soviet Union, promoted Khrushchev's career. The distinguished biographer of Khrushchev, William Taubman, dubbed Khrushchev "Stalin's pet." Khrushchev socialized with Stalin, participating in the dictator's gross, drunken bacchanalias. He also applauded Stalin's purges of party rivals during the infamous "show trials" of the 1930s, and he ordered the arrests and signed the death warrants of Ukrainians accused of not being loyal to the Communist system. Millions of Soviet citizens perished during these periods of madness and terror. Khrushchev understood that he was up to his elbows in blood. As a general during World War II, he witnessed the ghastly suffering of soldiers and citizens. Twenty-seven million Soviet citizens died during the war, including Khrushchev's son, Leonid, an air force pilot. Khrushchev learned to hate war. After World War II, he could never bring himself to watch war movies or read the wartime memoirs of others. At the time of Stalin's death in 1953, Khrushchev was the leader of the Communist Party in Moscow. Although he remained slavishly loyal to Stalin, Khrushchev's experiences in Ukraine and during the war probably persuaded him of Stalin's mendacity, cruelty, and incompetence. After Stalin's death, Khrushchev used his party ties to become a national leader, and by 1957–1958 he had pushed aside rivals and taken full control of the Soviet Union.[15]

Khrushchev's assumption of power led to change in the Soviet Union. In a notable four-hour speech delivered to the Twentieth Party Congress in Moscow in 1956, he denounced Stalin for "a grave abuse of power." He held Stalin personally responsible for torture and murder, ordering interrogators to use methods "that were simple—to beat, beat, and once again beat." Innocent people had confessed to crimes "because of pressure, torture, reducing them to unconsciousness, depriving them of judgment, taking away their dignity." Khrushchev subsequently ordered the release of Soviet citizens rotting in Stalin's prisons. He relaxed censorship and promoted science. He gloried in his nation's historic scientific achievement—the launch of Sputnik in 1957. He also tried to curtail the country's military-industrial complex by devoting more resources to consumer goods. As he once instructed, "Comrades, you cannot put a rocket into soup." For socialism to succeed it was necessary "to toil, create material values, including bread, potatoes, cabbage, meat, butter—all that is necessary to man." Khrushchev fervently believed that the Communist system could demonstrate its superiority over international capitalism by producing the good life for common people. The Soviet Union would "bury" the West economically. He predicted that by 1970 the Soviet Union would match the economic output of the United States, and by 1980 surpass it. Khrushchev's dreams did not approach reality. The Soviet economy amounted to less than 30 percent of the U.S. economy. When he visited the United States in 1959, Khrushchev inspected a farm in Iowa and was astounded by the agricultural abundance. Back at home, Khrushchev mandated a variety of crazy schemes to increase agricultural output, especially corn production. His good intentions did not, however, improve the diets of his countrymen. Khrushchev, the authoritarian, refused to listen to agricultural experts, and he lacked the scientific and technical expertise to plan properly. His corn production scheme proved a spectacular failure.[16]

Khrushchev's international policies presented both challenges and opportunities for the United States. The Soviet leader initially suggested that he had an open mind toward various paths to socialism, and he made conciliatory gestures toward the independent Communist nation of Yugoslavia under Joseph Tito. But he sent Soviet tanks into Budapest in October 1956 to crush Hungarian patriots who fought to free their country from Soviet domination. Khrushchev thereafter kept a tight control over the Soviet empire in Eastern Europe created by Stalin. He also quarreled with the Chinese leader Mao Zedong about doctrinal issues in the Communist world and denounced him for not accepting the proposition that thermonuclear war would be catastrophic for global civilization. Khrushchev's ultimate international goal was to demilitarize the Cold War. He explicitly rejected the Communist doctrine that armed conflict with the capitalist nations was inevitable. Struggle between the capitalist and Communist worlds was historically justified but should be confined to the ideological and economic arenas. As the head of a powerful nation and the leader of the Communist movement, Khrushchev also believed that that the Soviet Union should expand its global contacts. He used economic and military aid to try to gain influence, with mixed success, with developing nations like Egypt and Indonesia. Khrushchev passionately trusted in the eventual peaceful triumph of the Communist model throughout the world.[17] He did not have, however, a "blueprint" for the destruction of the United States and the domination of the world—the premises of both NSC 68/2 and the ominous speeches delivered by President Kennedy throughout 1961.

U.S. leaders and citizens found it difficult to comprehend Khrushchev's objective of peaceful, competitive coexistence because he cloaked his goal in coarse behavior, crude language, and bullying threats. On January 6, 1961, just two weeks before Kennedy's inauguration, Khrushchev pledged to support "wars of national liberation." The Soviets presumably would mask their conspiratorial designs by infiltrating legitimate nationalist movements for freedom and justice. Kennedy took Khrushchev's speech as a personal affront and a direct challenge to the United States. Scholars have pointed out, however, that Chairman Khrushchev only briefly raised the issue in a lengthy speech and was probably addressing doctrinal disputes within the Communist world. Americans also tired of hearing the Soviet leader's nonstop boasting about Soviet achievements, which included putting a cosmonaut, Yuri Gagarin, into orbit around Earth in early 1961. Even Jacqueline Bouvier Kennedy, the soul of graciousness, told Khrushchev, who sat next to the First Lady at a state dinner in Vienna, to change the subject when he tried to regale her with statistics on teachers per capita in Ukraine. Americans were astounded when the Soviet leader punctuated an aggressive speech at the United Nations in October 1960 by taking off his shoe, waving it around, and apparently pounding the podium with it.[18] Khrushchev's decision to resume atmospheric testing of nuclear weapons on August 30, 1961, frightened U.S. citizens. In part, Khrushchev's move was a reaction to the Kennedy administration's massive expansion of nuclear weaponry. Over the next sixty days, the Soviets conducted fifty tests, including one 58-megaton (the equivalent of 58 million tons of dynamite) explosion. Khrushchev then bellowed that the Soviet Union might conduct a 100-megaton explosion, enough to consume the state of Maryland in a firestorm. Such warlike, reckless propaganda could not be made tangible because no country had delivery vehicles that could carry such massive bombs. President Kennedy responded by ordering the resumption of underground tests in September 1961. In the following March, atmospheric tests of nuclear weapons resumed. The two countries were again engaged in poisoning the atmosphere with radioactive particles that endangered the global population.

Mutual fear, mutual suspicion, and mutual distrust characterized the Soviet-American confrontation, especially during the Kennedy presidency. Neither superpower practiced the virtue of empathy. Indeed, in 1961 both Kennedy and Khrushchev privately referred to the other as "a son-of-a-bitch."[19] Khrushchev somehow seemed to think that uttering hostile propaganda and threatening war, as he did over Berlin, would put the two sides on the path to peace. He also apparently thought that Kennedy would figure out that his "wars of national liberation" speech of January 1961 was directed at the Chinese Communists. Kennedy inferred, however, that Chairman Khrushchev had declared war against the United States at the dawn of his presidency. Kennedy similarly must have thought that the Soviets would understand that his apocalyptic speeches were solely designed to appease extremist right-wingers in the United States. Soviet intelligence analysts were also presumably clairvoyant and knew that the president expressed deep skepticism in confidential discussions with U.S. civilian and military advisers about the concepts of "limited nuclear war" or "winning" a nuclear war. Khrushchev and his advisers predictably examined public statements by officials such as Roswell Gilpatric and became afraid that the United States was contemplating a preemptive nuclear strike against their beloved homeland. Fear and loathing served as the context for the Kennedy-Khrushchev argument in Vienna and the subsequent confrontation over Berlin.

Vienna Summit

President Kennedy and Chairman Khrushchev held lengthy discussions in Vienna, Austria, on June 3–4, 1961. It would be the only time the two leaders would meet, although they would later write to one another often. Kennedy went to Vienna hoping to exchange ideas on a nuclear test ban treaty. He had been warned by veteran advisers, including Averell Harriman who had negotiated with Stalin for President Franklin D. Roosevelt, that Khrushchev would be aggressive and try to rattle him. They advised Kennedy to avoid a debate over ideology, Khrushchev's favorite topic. Harriman further advised that Khrushchev would be keenly "aware of his peasant origins, of the contrast between Mrs. Khrushchev and Jackie."[20] Indeed, the two couples cut vastly different figures.

Beyond being handsome, wealthy, and well dressed, President Kennedy was twenty-three years younger and much taller than the short, fat, bald Khrushchev. Khrushchev's wife, the formidable Nina Petrovna Khrushchev, was also short and plump and plainly dressed. Jacqueline Kennedy exuded elegance. Harriman and others had been prescient in predicting Khrushchev's negotiating ploys. On May 26, 1961, Khrushchev had informed Soviet leaders that he would ambush Kennedy and issue an ultimatum over the future of East and West Germany and the city of Berlin. Khrushchev brashly predicted that he would overawe the young, inexperienced U.S. president.[21]

Chairman Khrushchev lived up to promises he made in Moscow. After opening pleasantries, the talks degenerated into the diplomatic equivalent of a food fight. President Kennedy began by noting that the two powers could be peaceful rivals, if they respected each other's basic strategic interests. But the Soviet Union, Kennedy averred, "was seeking to eliminate free systems in areas that are associated with us." Khrushchev denied that his nation promoted communism throughout the world, although he boasted, "what the Soviet Union says is that communism will triumph." Just as the French Revolution swept away feudalism, so communism, in a "victory of ideas," would overwhelm capitalism. The United States, Khrushchev implied, was like the Spanish Inquisition, which burned people who disagreed with it, "but ideas did not burn and eventually came out as victors." Right from the start, Kennedy had fallen into Khrushchev's trap by debating ideological differences.

Exchanges about allies and issues proved similarly unfruitful. Kennedy gave tortured defenses of why the United States worked with anti-Communist tyrants like Francisco Franco of Spain and the Shah of Iran. Khrushchev made the ludicrous point that Poland had freely chosen communism and that "its election system is more democratic than that in the United States." Hyperbole and distortion similarly characterized their arguments over Cuba, Vietnam, and nuclear testing.[22] The experience at the Vienna summit unsettled Kennedy. He later confessed to aides and friends that Khrushchev "beat the hell out of me" and that the older man had "treated me like a little boy, like a little boy." The memorandums of conversation reveal, however, that Kennedy did better than he thought and that he countered each accusation with his own allegation. The president also stayed calm, whereas Khrushchev, as was his manner, blustered.

During a stroll in a garden after a lunch, Khrushchev circled around Kennedy, snapped at him, and shook his finger at the president.[23]

The fate of Berlin, as Khrushchev intended, became the burning issue at Vienna. On the second day of the summit, Khrushchev stunned Kennedy when he demanded that the United States abandon its position in West Berlin by the end of 1961. He threatened to terminate wartime agreements and sign a separate peace treaty with East Germany. East Germany would then be in a position to cut off Western access to the city because Berlin sat entirely within East Germany, 110 miles from the border of West Germany. Khrushchev broke the bounds of diplomatic discourse, using the word "war." Kennedy noted that "he had gained the impression that the USSR was presenting him with the alternative of accepting the Soviet act on Berlin or having a face to face confrontation." Khrushchev responded "that if the United States wanted war, that was its problem." He repeated his ultimatum—his "firm and irrevocable" decision to sign a peace treaty in December. President Kennedy concluded the menacing exchange "by observing that it would be a cold winter."[24]

Chairman Khrushchev left Vienna in a cocky mood. He had precipitated the Berlin crisis, and he was confident that Kennedy would not risk war to save the city. Imprisoned by his Communist ideology, Khrushchev had told his associates in Moscow that he doubted whether Kennedy even controlled the government. In Khrushchev's frenzied imagination, Wall Street, the CIA, or the Pentagon directed the U.S. show. He had rejected the warning that he had received in May from Deputy Premier Anastas Mikoyan, the experienced diplomat and Khrushchev supporter. Mikoyan, who knew the United States, predicted that Kennedy would react strongly to an ultimatum and would be prepared to save Berlin by fighting with conventional, nonnuclear forces. War would undercut Khrushchev's central desire to focus on domestic issues by demilitarizing the Cold War. Mikoyan proved prophetic. President Kennedy sensed that Khrushchev was bluffing and would not risk war.[25] He would develop a sensible policy that safeguarded the city and reduced the threat of nuclear war.

The Berlin Crisis

Competing visions of the past, present, and future encompassed the Soviet-American showdown over Berlin. Berlin's unique international standing

President Kennedy is talking with Nikita Khrushchev, the leader of the Soviet Union, in Vienna on June 3, 1961. The Vienna summit proved to be a difficult experience for the president. He and Khrushchev had heated discussions during their two days together. Khrushchev stunned Kennedy when he issued a near ultimatum, demanding that the United States abandon its position in Berlin. (John F. Kennedy Presidential Library and Museum, Boston)

resulted from the defeat of Nazi Germany and wartime agreements. The four Allied powers divided Germany and its capital city, pending a comprehensive settlement. The United States, the United Kingdom, and France merged their respective sectors, creating West Germany (Federal Republic of Germany) in 1949 and West Berlin. Bonn became the capital of West Germany. The Soviet sector became East Germany (German Democratic Republic) and East Berlin. The Soviets imposed a Communist system on East Germany. The four powers retained occupation privileges in both Berlins. Legally, Berlin was part of neither West nor East Germany. West Germany did not govern West Berlin, although West Berliners were citizens of West Germany, and the divided city and the nation maintained close ties.

By 1961 West Germany had largely recovered from wartime devastation. Through the Marshall Plan, the United States had reconstructed the defeated nation, made it prosperous, and turned it into a bulwark against communism. Chancellor Konrad Adenauer (1949–1963) gave West Germany determined leadership. Adenauer, who had opposed Adolf Hitler and the Nazi Party, tied his nation to the West and anticommunism. In 1955 West Germany became part of NATO, the military alliance against the Soviet Union. Adenauer also foresaw the day when Germany was reunified and had a democratic, capitalist system. He refused to acknowledge East Germany, deeming it an illegitimate state. The Western powers officially favored reunification, although some officials privately expressed misgivings about the restoration of a powerful, unified Germany. Memories of Nazi horrors, including the near annihilation of European Jews, still burned deeply in the memories of many.

Nikita Khrushchev adamantly opposed a unified Germany. Germany had twice invaded Mother Russia in the twentieth century. Nazi Germany's invasion and destruction of the Soviet Union, the slaughtering of millions of Soviet citizens, arguably represented the most barbarous act in the history of modern international relations. When, in November 1943, General Khrushchev toured the liberated city of Kiev, the capital city of Ukraine, he saw that the Nazis had torched Kiev University just before they left. "The barbarians themselves should be burned," Khrushchev shouted. This revulsion toward Germans persisted in the postwar years. At Vienna, Khrushchev spoke emotionally of losing his son in the war. With little exaggeration, he added, "There is not a single family in the USSR or the leadership of the USSR that did not lose one of its members in the war." As Khrushchev told a U.S. magazine editor, "We have a saying here: 'Give a German a gun; sooner or later he will point it at Russians.'" From the perspective of Khrushchev and his fellow Soviet citizens, their wartime sacrifices were being dishonored by U.S. policy. West Germany had become part of the anti-Soviet military alliance, and former Nazi officers served in the NATO command. A unified, anti-Communist Germany with access to nuclear weapons would undermine national security and signify that the Soviet Union had gained nothing from its victory during World War II. As Khrushchev put it, "this constitutes a threat of World War III which would be even more devastating than World War II."[26]

Khrushchev's nightmare had substance as East Germany was collapsing in 1961. In the 1950s more than two million East Germans had fled the country via West Berlin, with many then moving on to West Germany. In the first six months of 1961, 100,000 East Germans left the country. In July 1961 alone, the month after the Vienna summit, 30,000 East Germans entered West Berlin. East Germans left because they resented Soviet domination of their country, opposed communism, believed in parliamentary democracy, or wanted to work in the dynamic West German economy. They represented the best and brightest of society—doctors, engineers, students, skilled workers. Soviet officials jibed that German Communist leader Walter Ulbricht and his mistress would be the only people left in East Germany.

President Kennedy could not accede to Khrushchev's demands that the United States abandon West Berlin. The United States had a moral obligation to stand by the more than two million West Berliners and their exceptional leader, Mayor Willy Brandt. Previous presidents had made the defense of West Berlin a keystone of U.S. foreign policy. In 1948–1949 President Truman had defeated Stalin's attempt to blockade the city with a massive airlift of food and supplies. In 1958–1959, President Eisenhower rejected Khrushchev's first ultimatum on Berlin. Eisenhower conceded that Berlin's status was "abnormal" but declined to negotiate a substantive change. Eisenhower stayed calm and deliberate during the crisis, calculating that neither side wanted nuclear war. As Kennedy explained to Khrushchev at Vienna, defending Berlin had become essential to upholding U.S. international credibility. In Kennedy's words, "US commitments would be regarded as a mere scrap of paper," if the United States deserted Berlin. Western Europeans tied the defense of Berlin to the U.S. pledge to safeguard them. Both President Charles De Gaulle of France and Prime Minister Harold Macmillan of the United Kingdom expected Kennedy to stand up to Khrushchev. De Gaulle further advised Kennedy that Khrushchev would not go to war over Berlin. President Kennedy also knew that the U.S. public, as expressed in public opinion polls, expected him to defend Berlin. Kennedy agreed, believing that he would be violating his constitutional oath of office to preserve national security if he let Khrushchev have his way on Berlin.[27]

As he planned his response to Khrushchev in the weeks after the Vienna summit, Kennedy acted in the same cautious, prudent way that he conducted himself during the Bay of Pigs invasion of April 1961 and subsequently during the Cuban missile crisis of October 1962. A peculiar pattern of behavior characterized Kennedy's presidential leadership. He gave rash speeches and took provocative actions that helped precipitate crises. In the midst of such crises, however, he proved calm and careful. By mid-1961 Kennedy knew that the "missile gap" favored the United States. But nuclear weapons could not be compared in the same way as counting tanks or howitzers. Although outgunned in nuclear weaponry, the Soviets still had the capacity to obliterate major U.S. cities like New York and Washington. President Kennedy understood the awful consequences of nuclear war.

The U.S. war plans for defending the exposed, isolated city of Berlin included firing nuclear weapons because military planners feared the strength of Soviet conventional forces in Eastern Europe. Kennedy received advice to launch nuclear or "general war" against the Soviet Union. In June 1961 he had asked former Secretary of State Dean Acheson to review U.S. war plans to protect Berlin. Acheson, a powerful personality, dominated discussions about Berlin. In Acheson's view, the "very survival" of the United States depended upon protecting Berlin. The United States had "to increase his [Khrushchev's] fear that we would use nuclear weapons if necessary." To make the nuclear threat credible, the United States had to make a "decision to accept nuclear war." Assistant Secretary of Defense Nitze later advised Kennedy to consider launching a preemptive nuclear attack on the Soviet Union if conflict broke out over Berlin. Nitze reasoned, "we could in some real sense be victorious in the series of nuclear exchanges." Secretary McNamara challenged Nitze's optimism and Secretary of State Rusk reminded the president, "the first side to use nuclear weapons will carry a very grave responsibility and endure consequences before the rest of the world." The president agreed with McNamara and Rusk and rejected war plans that saw nuclear war as inevitable in a struggle for Berlin. In a precisely worded letter to Gen. Lauris Norstad, Supreme Commander Allied Powers Europe, Kennedy ordered that the United States defend Berlin by developing "the capacity and readiness to fight with significant non-nuclear forces."[28]

Kennedy also rejected other rash options presented to him. Acheson wanted Kennedy to declare a "national emergency" and display U.S. mettle by dispatching a division of U.S. troops from West Germany along the highway, or *autobahn*, through East Germany. The angry Acheson grumbled, "This nation is without leadership." The president, however, received sound advice from

President Eisenhower, who told him not to overreact to Khrushchev's blustering. On July 25, 1961, Kennedy delivered a tough address to the nation, calling for a $3.5 billion increase in military spending, the mobilization of military reservists, and his mindless plan for fallout shelters. Kennedy was strengthening U.S. conventional forces and was signaling to Khrushchev that he would fight with nonnuclear forces. He also rallied the U.S. public with stirring language about the epic battles of World War II. He observed, "I hear it said that West Berlin is militarily untenable. And so was Bastonge. And so, in fact was Stalingrad. Any dangerous spot is tenable if men—brave men—will make it so."[29]

Khrushchev had badly miscalculated. He had opined that only a "stupid statesman" or an "idiot" would go to war for West Berlin. He should have listened to his friend, Anastas Mikoyan, who had predicted the U.S. reaction to his ultimatum. The Soviet chairman had backed himself into a corner. He barked, after reading Kennedy's speech, that "Kennedy had declared preliminary war on the Soviet Union."[30] But Khrushchev did not want war. And a sober analysis of Kennedy's speech showed the president had not provoked the Soviets. He refrained from calling for a unification of Germany or the right of East Germans to flee to West Berlin. Kennedy declined to place U.S. military power behind the nationalist agenda of Chancellor Konrad Adenauer. The president simply vowed to preserve surface access from West Germany to West Berlin, to maintain a military presence in the city, and to defend West Berlin. These were the treaty rights of the West.

A revolting end to the Berlin crisis came within weeks after Kennedy's national address. On July 30, 1961, Senator J. William Fulbright, the respected chair of the Senate Foreign Relations Committee, publicly suggested that the Communists treat the flight of East Germans as a domestic issue. Fulbright said, "I don't understand why the East Germans don't close their border, because I think they have a right to close it." Kennedy privately agreed, noting that Khrushchev had to do something because "East Germany is hemorrhaging to death." Kennedy offered, "Perhaps a wall."[31] Khrushchev had already come to a similar conclusion. During the night of August 12–13, 1961, uniformed East Germans closed the border between East and West Berlin, tearing up roads and installing roadblocks and barbed wire. On that last day, 4,000 East Germans had fled the country. East Germans thereafter constructed what would be known forever as the "Berlin Wall," a permanent installation of concrete, barbed wire, and watchtowers, bordered by minefields. The Berlin Wall, which reached 100 miles in length, surrounded West Berlin, sealing it off from East Berlin and neighboring parts of East Germany. Approximately 15,000 East German troops guarded the wall.

President Kennedy did not challenge Khrushchev's decision to build an "iron ring" around Berlin. As he told an aide, "A wall is a hell of a lot better than a war."[32] He kept silent about the Wall for a week, and thereafter, until June 1963, he mentioned it only three times. To signal his concern, he dispatched his vice president and Gen. Lucius D. Clay, the hero of the Berlin airlift of 1948–1949, to West Berlin. He also ordered a small battle group of 1,600 U.S. troops to travel on trucks down the autobahn through East Germany to West Berlin to ensure that the West preserved its access to the city. The battle group received a tumultuous welcome from Berliners when, on August 20, it rolled down the *Kurfürstendamm*, the glittering shopping street of Berlin. Vice President Johnson greeted the troops. Johnson had doubts about his assignment, thinking he might be caught in the middle of shooting. But with relief and joy in Berlin, Johnson reverted to his larger-than-life, Texas style. On the previous day, hundreds of thousands of Berliners had turned out for Johnson's arrival. The vice president plunged into the crowds, "pressed the flesh," and handed out ballpoint pens.

The Berlin crisis wound down gradually, without an effective settlement. Kennedy toned down his rhetoric, most notably at a speech he gave at the United Nations in September, when he spoke eloquently of the dangers of nuclear war. He memorably said, "Mankind must put an end to war—or war will put an end to mankind."[33] He and Khrushchev began a personal correspondence about Berlin, and he authorized high-level discussions about the status of the city. The subsequent talks produced nothing of substance. For his part, Khrushchev, on October 17, 1961, retracted his ultimatum to sign a separate peace treaty with East Germany when he met with the Twenty-second Communist Party Congress.

Sweetness and light had not, however, broken out between the superpowers. A potential crisis erupted in late October, when East German guards refused to allow a U.S. diplomat and his wife access to East Berlin to attend the theater. Tensions had risen in the city because the Soviets and East Germans had learned that General Clay had ordered his troops to practice breaching the wall with bulldozers. General Clay had not informed President Kennedy of these maneuvers. U.S. and Soviet tanks faced one another at "Checkpoint Charlie," the famed border-crossing point along the wall. It appeared, as one analyst put it, to be "a nuclear-age equivalent of the Wild West showdown at the OK Corral." Through an intermediary, Kennedy suggested a face-saving formula to Khrushchev; both sides withdrew their tanks. President Kennedy telephoned General Clay and ordered him to withdraw the U.S. tanks immediately after the Soviet tanks withdrew.[34]

In the aftermath of the Berlin crisis, the Soviet-American confrontation continued. Both sides resumed nuclear testing, and President Kennedy authorized Roswell Gilpatric to announce U.S. nuclear superiority. The Gilpatric speech came four days after Khrushchev rescinded his ultimatum during the Communist Party conclave. Kennedy and Khrushchev would also come much closer to nuclear war almost exactly a year later during the Cuban missile crisis.

The Berlin Wall

The Berlin Wall preserved Communist East Germany for a time. East Germans continued to try to enter West Berlin, but only a few thousand ever managed to get over the wall or through the minefields over the next three decades. The border guards shot 600 East Germans trying to escape. In one appalling incident in August 1962, Peter Fechter, an East German, was shot by border guards and allowed to bleed to death at the foot of the wall.[35] Visitors to Berlin can now see photographs and plaques, near where the wall once stood, commemorating the bravery of those who died trying to escape East Germany.

The building of the Berlin Wall addressed Khrushchev's short-term political fears. If East Germany had collapsed, the Soviet empire in Eastern Europe would have been imperiled. But the Berlin Wall proved politically disastrous for the Soviet system. International observers admired both the Soviet Union's heroic struggle against Nazi Germany and its scientific achievements in outer space. They also applauded Khrushchev's denunciation of Stalin's monstrous crimes. But reasonable people judged the Berlin Wall, in the words of Mayor Willy Brandt, as "an offense not only against history, but an offense against humanity."[36] The hideous scar that stretched across the city separated families, divided husbands and wives, brothers and sisters, and kept a national people apart. The

President Kennedy addresses a massive crowd in West Berlin on June 26, 1963. More than half of the city's population turned out to listen to the president. That morning Kennedy had seen the Berlin Wall for the first time. In his address, the president famously boasted "Ich bin ein Berliner" (I am a Berliner). (John F. Kennedy Presidential Library and Museum, Boston)

wall came to symbolize the political and economic failures of communism. Many in the world decided that Stalin's gross violations of basic human rights were not particular to a paranoid megalomaniac but endemic to the Communist system. President Ronald Reagan articulated those judgments, when in 1987, at Berlin's historic Brandenburg Gate, he implored Soviet leaders to "tear down this wall." When jubilant Berliners pushed the wall over in November 1989, it heralded the end of the Soviet domination of Eastern Europe and the collapse of the Soviet Union two years later.

President Kennedy seized the propaganda bonanza that Khrushchev had handed the West only once, but in a stirring way. On June 26, 1963, he addressed a delirious crowd of West Berliners from a platform mounted on the steps of the *Rathaus*, or city hall. Sixty percent of Berliners had turned out to witness the president. That morning Kennedy had seen the wall for the first time. He sent the crowd into a frenzy, proclaiming, "Today, in the world of freedom, the proudest boast is *Ich bin ein Berliner* [I am a Berliner]!" His answer to anyone who questioned the moral superiority of the West was: "Let them come to Berlin!" The "Free World" had shortcomings, "but we have never had to put a wall up to keep people in, to prevent them from leaving us!" Kennedy told the crowd that he foresaw the day when Berlin and Germany would be reunited. When that day came, "the people of West Berlin can take sober satisfaction in the fact that they were in the front lines."[37]

Conclusion

President Kennedy skillfully managed the Berlin crisis and avoided nuclear war. He demonstrated the presidential leadership for which scholars and the U.S. public well remember him. He contained both Khrushchev and some of the belligerent members of his administration. But Kennedy's alarmist rhetoric and acceleration of the nuclear arms race did not make the world a safer place. Both the president and Chairman Khrushchev professed a desire for peace and an accommodation between the United States and the Soviet Union. Both leaders would have to manage another crisis over Cuba, however, before they began to develop the empathy and understanding necessary to find a path toward peace.

CHAPTER 4

CUBA

THE COURSE AND CONDUCT of relations with Fidel Castro's Cuba helped define the John F. Kennedy presidency. U.S. policy toward Cuba represented both the high and low points of the Kennedy years. President Kennedy achieved a notable triumph in October 1962, when he pressured the Soviet Union to dismantle and withdraw nuclear-tipped ballistic missiles from Cuba. This Cold War victory came a year after the president suffered the worst defeat of his public career. In April 1961 Fidel Castro's forces routed the U.S.-backed invasion force of Cuban exiles on the shores of Cuba at the Bay of Pigs. But the history of the Cuban missile crisis and the Bay of Pigs invasion can be measured in more than just success and failure. During the Cuban crises, President Kennedy displayed his leadership talents, decision-making abilities, and crisis management skills. The president's steadiness and judgment can also be examined, for his administration waged a campaign of sabotage and terrorism against Cuba and tried to assassinate Castro. John Kennedy seemed obsessed with Fidel Castro's Cuba.

The Cuban Revolution

Fidel Castro and his band of bearded guerrillas rode on tanks into Havana in January 1959. Their triumphant entry into the capital city, which was greeted with wild, delirious crowds, marked the culmination of Castro's six-year struggle against dictator Fulgencio Batista, who had dominated the island's political life for twenty-five years and had seized power in 1952. As a youth, Castro (1926–), the son of a prosperous sugar planter, had led a privileged life. He was a good athlete and an excellent student, earning a law degree from the University of Havana and becoming active in student politics. Castro first came to international attention on July 26, 1953, when he led a group of 165 students in a disastrous storming of the army barracks at Moncada, located in the Cuban city of Santiago. He received a fifteen-year sentence for his rebellion but was freed from prison in 1955 by the confident Batista. Castro and his brother Raúl fled to Mexico to plan another assault on the Batista regime. In 1956 Fidel Castro and eighty-one other men struggled ashore after their leaky ship, *Granma*, beached on Cuba's eastern shore. Within a few days, Batista's forces killed most of the insurgents. The survivors, including the Castro brothers and Argentine revolutionary Ernesto "Ché" Guevara, retreated into the Sierra Maestra, the mountains of southeastern Cuba. Castro steadily rebuilt his forces and launched hit-and-run attacks against Bastista's forces. The determination and courage of the guerrillas inspired other Cubans, and by 1958 the insurgency had spread from rural areas into the cities. By the end of the year, support for Batista had evaporated.

What Castro and the 26th of July Movement intended for Cuba was initially unclear. The manifesto of the movement was Castro's long, rambling "History Will Absolve Me" speech, which he gave at his trial and subsequently rewrote in prison. Castro promised agrarian and industrial reform, administrative honesty, and a liberal and progressive constitution for Cuba. During the two years he spent in the Sierra Maestra, Castro released letters and issued declarations that his movement was libertarian and democratic, but also reformist and perhaps socialistic. Although his statements were vague and ambiguous, Castro was probably not trying to deceive Cubans or the international community. Prior to 1959 Castro lacked a clear vision for a post-Batista Cuba, and he had not committed himself to an ideological doctrine. Castro was almost certainly not a Marxist-Leninist, an ally of the Soviet Union, or an agent of the international Communist movement. In fact, the Cuban Communist Party, which was one of Latin America's largest Communist parties with 17,000 members, provided no substantial aid to the 26th of July Movement. International Communists judged Castro a well-intentioned but naïve, romantic revolutionary.[1]

Like other educated Cubans, Castro held ambivalent views about the United States. He appreciated the wealth and technological prowess of the United States and wished the same for Cuba. He also enjoyed U.S. popular culture, playing baseball and following major league teams. But Cubans resented the role that the United States had played in Cuba's history. After assisting Cuba's struggle for independence in 1898, the United States attached the Platt Amendment (1901–1933) to the Cuban constitution, giving the United States the right to intervene militarily and oversee Cuba's internal affairs. The United States also created a permanent military base in Cuba at Guantánamo Bay. U.S. troops repeatedly landed in independent Cuba, and U.S. warships plied the waters in sight of Havana's harbor. The U.S. ambassador was usually considered the second most powerful figure in Cuba, after the Cuban president. With their money guaranteed by the bayonets of U.S. marines, U.S. investors came to dominate Cuba's economic life. With approximately $900 million invested in Cuba in 1959, U.S. investors accounted for 40 percent of the country's sugar production. U.S. companies also controlled public utilities, oil refineries, mines, railroads, and the tourist industry. Cubans took further offense that U.S. tourists considered Havana their playground for gambling, narcotics, and prostitution. The U.S. criminal underworld, "the Mafia," operated freely in Batista's Cuba. The popular movie *The Godfather: Part II* (1974) accurately portrays the pervasive influence of organized crime in Cuba in the 1950s.

Reforming Cuban society inevitably meant altering the overwhelming U.S. presence in Cuba. With a per capita income of approximately $500, Cuba was a wealthy Latin American country. But Cubans, who lived as close as ninety miles from Florida, interpreted their socioeconomic status within the context of the United States, not the Dominican Republic or Nicaragua. Cuba was significantly poorer than Mississippi, the poorest U.S. state. And Cuba was an unequal and unfair society, with Cubans of African heritage especially destitute. Cubans, including Castro, blamed the United States for Cuba's poverty and backwardness. Castro's agrarian reform law of April 1959 set the tone for U.S.-Cuban relations. The law expropriated farmland over 1,000 acres, with compensation to be paid in Cuban bonds and based on the land's declared value for taxes in 1958. Sugar barons, both foreign and domestic, had predictably undervalued their land in Batista's Cuba. Howls of protest from Washington, U.S. investors, and propertied Cubans seemed only to encourage the Castro government to limit further the prerogatives of the wealthy in Cuba. Tens of thousands of Cubans fled the island, landing in Miami, Florida. Cuban revolutionaries also drove the criminal underworld out of Cuba, closing down the narcotics rings, brothels, and gambling dens.

Between 1959 and 1961 the Cuban Revolution took on the tone and shape of a Communist revolution. On December 1, 1961, Castro publicly declared, "I am a Marxist-Leninist, and I will continue to be a Marxist-Leninist until the last days of my life." In moving toward communism, Fidel Castro joined his brother Raúl and Ché Guevara, both committed radicals. Castro probably concluded that communism provided solutions to Cuba's problems. The Soviet Union, given its impressive economic growth rate since 1917 and scientific triumphs in outer space in the 1950s, seemed a viable model for poor countries. As he faced domestic opposition, Castro also welcomed and embraced Cuban Communists. Communism may have also suited Castro's authoritarian personality. The Communist concept of the "dictatorship of the proletariat" would enhance Castro's drive for personal domination of Cuba. As his growing radicalism reaped mounting hostility from the United States, Castro turned to the Soviet Union for help. In February 1960 Castro hosted a Soviet trade fair in Cuba and signed a commercial agreement with the Soviets.[2]

The Bay of Pigs Invasion

By the end of 1959 the Dwight D. Eisenhower administration had decided that the Castro regime threatened U.S. national security interests. During the Cold War, U.S. policymakers considered Latin America a special preserve or sphere of influence of the United States. The United States needed a secure and stable region so it could focus its energies on containing communism in Asia and Europe. U.S. officials discouraged Latin American nations from having diplomatic relations with the Soviet Union and flatly opposed socioeconomic reforms judged "Communistic." In 1954 the Eisenhower administration destabilized the popularly elected government of Jacobo Arbenz Guzmán (1950–1954), because it judged the Guatemalan leader either a Communist, soft on communism, or oblivious to the Communist menace. President Arbenz was in the process of carrying out a massive agrarian reform program in Guatemala, expropriating holdings of the Boston-based company United Fruit. After the overthrow of President Arbenz, the CIA scoured Guatemalan archives, but it failed to find evidence of Guatemalan ties with the Soviet bloc. Nonetheless, the Eisenhower administration and the CIA considered the Guatemalan operation an unqualified success. The administration had confidence it could again dispose of another dangerous radical. In December 1959 the CIA official responsible for the Western Hemisphere recommended "thorough consideration be given to the elimination of Fidel Castro."[3]

On March 17, 1960, President Eisenhower gave formal approval to a "program of covert action against the Castro regime." The plan included launching a propaganda offensive, creating anti-Castro forces within Cuba, and training a paramilitary force outside of Cuba for future action. Through the rest of 1960, the administration attacked Cuba. The CIA broadcast anti-Castro tirades from a radio station on Swan Island, a dot of land off the coast of Honduras. The administration tried to strangle the Cuban economy, cutting off sugar imports and banning exports to the island. The CIA began to train Cuban exiles in Guatemala with the mission of carrying out an amphibious invasion of Cuba. The exile army would grow from 300 men to over 700 by the end of the year and eventually to 1,400 men in April 1961. The CIA, with the approval of Director Allen Dulles, also contacted criminal figures interested in carrying out "gangster-action" against Castro. The CIA presumably calculated that the Mafia wanted Castro dead so it could resume its nefarious activities in Cuba. At the gangsters' request, CIA technicians developed poison pills to place in Castro's food and drink. The CIA actually worked with Sam Giancana, who was on the attorney general's list of the "ten most wanted men" in America. Giancana, a successor to Al Capone of Chicago, was the "Cosa Nostra" boss of the mob's Cuban operations.[4] Finally, on January 3, 1961, President Eisenhower broke diplomatic relations with Cuba.

John Kennedy's attitude toward Cuba evolved rapidly. As a senator, he denounced the Eisenhower administration for supporting the Batista regime through the 1950s. Like many U.S. citizens, Senator Kennedy welcomed the overthrow of Batista and hoped that Castro was a moderate democratic reformer. But in 1960 Kennedy seized on the mounting tension with Castro and turned it into a major campaign issue. The radicalization of the Cuban Revolution and the growing relationship between Cuba and the Soviet Union corroborated his basic campaign issue—the United States was losing the Cold War. The president-elect received a briefing from CIA Director Dulles on the covert campaign against Castro. In two meetings with Kennedy, on December 6 and January 19, President Eisenhower emphasized the need to oust Castro, telling the president-elect that the United States was helping the exile army "to the utmost" and that their training should be "continued and accelerated." Eisenhower warned that "in the long run the United States cannot allow the Castro government to continue to exist in Cuba."[5]

President Kennedy carried out Eisenhower's policy. The U.S.-backed invasion of Cuba took place at the Bay of Pigs on the island's southwestern shores on April 17–19, 1961, less than three months after Kennedy took office. Castro's forces quickly routed the 1,400-man invasion force known as "Brigade 2506." His forces killed 114 and captured another 1,189 of the exiles. Castro took personal command of the Cuban military, directed the counterattack, and garnered domestic and international prestige for having defeated the United States. The debacle at the Bay of Pigs represented a signal U.S. policy failure and a mortifying political setback for President Kennedy. Why the president authorized the invasion and acted as he did during the crisis have been controversial questions.

The new president was pressured to authorize the invasion. If he had cancelled the invasion, he would have been rejecting the plans of the nation's most trusted military leader, Gen. Dwight Eisenhower. He would also have what Director Dulles called a "disposal" problem. The Cuban exiles training in Guatemala would return to the United States and loudly complain to journalists and politicians that President Kennedy feared Castro and that he lacked the fortitude to wage cold war. But aborting the invasion would have averted a disaster. Although not debated within the administration between January and April 1961, there was a politically expedient way for Kennedy to relieve the pressure. Newspapers and journals reported about the Cuban exiles training in Guatemala. The president privately grumbled that Castro did not need intelligence agents in the United States, for "all he has to do is read our papers."[6] Kennedy could have conceivably lamented this exposure and terminated the training. Instead, he asked editors to suppress the news.

President Kennedy also received misleading advice about the invasion from key advisers, especially Richard Bissell, the CIA's deputy director of plans. Bissell met frequently with Kennedy and sent him numerous memorandums. Bissell structured his arguments in a way to compel the president to authorize the invasion. Bissell assured the president that the invasion had a good chance of overthrowing Castro or sparking a damaging civil war in Cuba. If the invasion did not go forth, however, Bissell warned that Latin Americans would lose faith in the United States and that "David will again have defeated Goliath." Moreover, the failure to overthrow Castro in the near future would lead "to the elimination of all internal and external Cuban opposition of any effective nature." When Kennedy repeatedly demanded that the U.S. role be limited in the operation, Bissell assured the president that the invasion would succeed without overt U.S. support. Kennedy assumed that the exiles would be able to retreat into Cuban mountains, if they could not hold and expand their beachhead at the Bay of Pigs. Bissell failed to make clear that the nearest mountains were far away and the area around the Bay of Pigs was filled with swamps.[7] The Joint Chiefs of Staff also failed their president. The leading U.S. military men privately doubted whether the exile army could take on Castro's forces. Nonetheless, the Joint Chiefs told Kennedy that the invaders had "a fair chance of ultimate success."[8]

The counsel that President Kennedy received was not one-sided, however; he received strong advice to cancel Eisenhower's plan. Congressional leaders, such as Senator J. William Fulbright, the chair of the Senate Foreign Relations Committee, and State Department officers, such as Secretary of State Dean Rusk and Undersecretary of State Chester Bowles, raised philosophical, diplomatic, and practical objections to the unprovoked invasion of a sovereign country. Former Secretary of State Dean Acheson, an inveterate Cold Warrior, told the president that one did not have to be a certified public accountant "to discover that 1,500 Cubans were not as good as 25,000 Cubans [the size of Castro's army]."[9] Presidential aide Arthur Schlesinger dismissed the idea that the U.S. hand could be kept hidden in the invasion. Given the long U.S. history of military intervention in Caribbean countries, global observers would immediately assume that the United States controlled the Cuban exiles. The U.S. standing in the world would be harmed. Referring to the dreadful Soviet invasion of Hungary in 1956, Schlesinger warned, "Cuba will become our Hungary."[10]

In the end, President Kennedy authorized the Bay of Pigs invasion because he wanted Castro overthrown and because he thought the exile army could accomplish that goal with a minimal cost to the United States. Kennedy shared President Eisenhower's view that the United States could not permit the Castro regime to survive. In early April 1961 the president dispatched Col. Jack Hawkins to Guatemala to assess the fighting abilities of the brigade. Colonel

Hawkins impressed the president with his report, noting, "These officers are young, vigorous, intelligent, and motivated with a fanatical urge to begin battle." The exiles assured Hawkins that once the battle began all they wanted was supplies and would not need direct U.S. military support.[11] As Robert Dallek, a sympathetic biographer of Kennedy, has noted, the commitment of the Cuban brigade had a romantic appeal to President Kennedy. He embraced the idea of courageous, patriotic men prepared to die for their country's freedom. Kennedy loved to read about the adventures of James Bond in the Ian Fleming novels with Agent 007 single-handedly taking on the evil-doers of the world.[12] Kennedy had, of course, shown his own commitment, courage, and patriotism during World War II, when he commanded a PT boat.

More than romantic idealism, however, led Kennedy to give the signal to invade Cuba. He embraced the mass delusion that has existed in the United States since 1959 about political life in Castro's Cuba. Cubans allegedly suffered under Castro and prayed for their deliverance. The invasion supposedly would produce a "shock" in Cuba, triggering a mass uprising. Those who planned the Bay of Pigs understood from the outset that the exile brigade could not conquer Cuba. As the planners noted, "The primary objective of the force will be to survive and maintain its integrity on Cuban soil." Exile leaders predicted that thereafter Cubans would rush to the side of their liberators and Cuban soldiers would desert Castro. CIA analysts tossed around wildly inflated numbers, ranging from 1,000 to 7,000, of resistance fighters already in Cuba. But enemies of the Cuban Revolution were more likely to reside in Miami than in Havana. In a postmortem report on the Bay of Pigs, the inspector general of the CIA wrote, "We can confidently assert that the CIA had no intelligence evidence that Cubans in significant numbers could or would join the invaders or that there was any kind of effective and cohesive resistance movement under anybody's control."[13]

Critics have lambasted President Kennedy for undermining Brigade 2506 by refusing to provide adequate air and naval support on the day of the invasion. The criticism seems unjustified, for Kennedy had always made it clear to Richard Bissell that he would not permit the participation of U.S. forces in the invasion. In any case, implicit in this criticism of Kennedy's caution is the assumption that the brigade could have established a defensible beachhead at the Bay of Pigs. Castro and his forces had prepared for an invasion. Fidel and Raúl Castro built an army of 25,000 and a loyal self-defense force of over 200,000 Cubans, who were armed with weapons from the Soviet bloc. In April 1961 one battalion of troops patrolled every beach in Cuba. Castro's intelligence agents anticipated an invasion because, just like President Kennedy, they could read about the training base in Guatemala in U.S. publications. Cuban spies presumably had also penetrated the exile community of Miami. Finally, in Fidel Castro, the Cubans had an experienced military commander who had fought for three hard years in the Cuban mountains. Before and during the invasion, Castro acted decisively. A pre-invasion air strike by the exiles on April 15 had destroyed five Cuban airplanes. To forestall further losses, Castro ordered pilots to be prepared to take off at a moment's notice. The pilots actually slept underneath their planes. If President Kennedy had authorized additional air strikes, the bombers would have likely hit empty airfields. The Bay of Pigs should be counted as a Cuban victory.

In an ironic way, President Kennedy may actually deserve credit for his decisions during the invasion period. From April 17 to 19, he acted much as he would in subsequent confrontations with the Soviet Union over Berlin and missiles in Cuba. Once he had blundered into a confrontation, the president proved steady and cautious, rejecting options that could lead to wholesale conflict. If U.S. forces had joined Brigade 2506, it would have probably led to catastrophic losses for the uniformed and civilian populations of Cuba. The consequences of such a tragedy for the U.S. standing in Latin America and the world might have been grave and dire in 1961 and into the future.

Operation Mongoose

Although angered and embarrassed by the Bay of Pigs disaster, President Kennedy did not waver from the goal of destroying the Cuban Revolution. On May 5, 1961, he presided over an NSC meeting and ruled that U.S. policy would continue "to aim at the downfall of Castro." The United States would not invade Cuba now but neither would it foreclose the possibility of a future military invasion. Adm. Arleigh A. Burke of the Joint Chiefs noted that at the NSC meeting it was decided that "sooner or later" the United States would probably have to intervene in Cuba.[14] The president designated his brother to be his point man on Cuba. Robert Kennedy roughly informed U.S. military and intelligence officials that "the Cuban problem" was the top priority of the government and that "no time, money, efforts, or manpower is to be spared." The attorney general often berated senior CIA officers about their lack of success in Cuba. Richard Bissell recounted being "chewed out" by the Kennedy brothers at the White House "for sitting on his ass and doing nothing about Cuba."[15] Richard Helms, Bissell's successor at the CIA, was told in early 1962 by Robert Kennedy, speaking for his brother, that "the final chapter on Cuba has not been written."[16]

President Kennedy judged Castro's Cuba a dire threat to vital U.S. national interests. But his administration's assessment of the Cuban threat did not necessarily sustain those fears. In preparation for the NSC meeting of May 5, Paul Nitze of the Defense Department coordinated a lengthy evaluation of "Cuba's threat to the national interests." The report depicted Cuba as more a psychological than real threat to the traditional U.S. domination of the Western Hemisphere. The Cuban Revolution inspired radicals and militants throughout the region. Cuba assisted these potential revolutionaries through propaganda and perhaps the supply of funds. But the administration had "no hard evidence of an actual supply of arms or armed men going from Cuba to other countries to assist indigenous revolutionary movements." In any case, poverty and economic discontent, not Castro, generated social ferment throughout Latin America. The report also considered it "a remote possibility" that the Soviet Union would transform Cuba into a military base for a strategic attack on the United States. Castro's real crime was that "he had provided a working example of a communist state in the Americas, successfully defying the United States."[17]

While awaiting a new campaign for undermining Castro, President Kennedy brushed aside a Cuban peace offer. On August 17, 1961, Ché Guevara spoke late into the night with presidential aide Richard Goodwin. Both men were attending an inter-American conference in Uruguay. Guevara had previously sent Goodwin a handsomely designed box filled with the finest Cuban cigars. Guevara suggested that by discussing issues like U.S. expropriated properties, trade, and Cuba's role in Latin America the two countries could reach a modus vivendi—a way of living together. Goodwin informed his president of the conversation. Nothing developed from the Goodwin-Guevara exchange. President Kennedy's only tangible gesture was to smoke one of Guevara's cigars.[18]

In November 1961 the president launched a new war against Castro, "Operation Mongoose," under the direction of Gen. Edward G. Lansdale. Lansdale was a flamboyant Air Force officer who claimed expertise in counter-insurgency and guerrilla warfare based on his experience in the Philippines and Vietnam in the 1950s. He was the type of "action intellectual" in the James Bond mold that always impressed the Kennedy brothers. Armed with a $50 million budget, Lansdale assembled a team of more than 400 CIA employees and thousands of Cuban exiles who operated from headquarters near the University of Miami campus. The mission of the exiles was to make their way from Florida to Cuba in speedboats, infiltrate the island, collect intelligence, organize resistance fighters, and carry out sabotage on the island. As Robert Kennedy, who oversaw Operation Mongoose, noted, "My idea is to stir things up on the island with espionage, sabotage, general disorder, run and operated by the Cubans themselves."[19] Lansdale's plan was predicated on sparking a massive popular rebellion in Cuba that would prompt demands for a rescue mission. The U.S. military would then have the international legitimacy to invade the island and dispose of Castro. Like the Bay of Pigs planners, Lansdale denied Castro's political strength. In November 1961 a chastened CIA had conceded, "The great bulk of the population still accepts the regime and a substantial number still support it with enthusiasm." Lansdale continually pressured CIA analysts to modify their conclusions, as if changing things on paper in Washington would alter political realities in Cuba.[20]

The Kennedy administration applied other pressures to Cuba. It imposed a near total trade embargo on the island. It demanded that Latin Americans drive Cuba out of the inter-American community, the Organization of American States. The Defense Department drew up extensive plans to attack Cuba with air strikes, parachute drops, and an amphibious assault. In the spring of 1962 U.S. marines trained for an amphibious assault by invading Vieques Island, Puerto Rico. The military exercise carried the codename "ORTSAC," or "Castro" spelled backward. Attorney General Kennedy proposed staging a violent incident at the U.S. military base at Guantánamo Bay, thus providing a rationale for an attack on Cuba. Under pressure from the administration, the Joint Chiefs developed "Operation Northwoods" as a complement to Operation Mongoose. Among the schemes military planners suggested was sinking a boatload of Cuban refugees sailing for Florida or shooting Cuban refugees in the United States. Castro would then be blamed for the violence. The military planners also recommended that the United States be prepared to provide proof that Cubans were responsible for a disaster in outer space, if a manned flight exploded in space.[21]

The CIA's assassination efforts against Castro, which began under President Eisenhower, continued throughout the Kennedy presidency. Just before the Bay of Pigs operation, the CIA's underworld contacts managed to pass poison pills to anti-Castro Cubans in Havana. One plot failed when the pills, intended for Castro's ice cream dessert, allegedly froze to coils in an icebox. What precise knowledge President Kennedy had of these and subsequent conspiracies cannot be determined. Shortly after taking office, National Security Adviser McGeorge Bundy received a briefing on the CIA's assassination capabilities. In May 1962 Attorney General Kennedy received a thorough briefing about the CIA's contacts with gambling syndicate figures John Rosselli and Sam Giancana.[22] (Giancana's girlfriend was Judith Campbell, who was also President Kennedy's mistress during his White House years.) No document has yet appeared proving that either Bundy or Robert Kennedy told the president about the assassination plots. According to aides, President Kennedy asked for military intervention plans for the day when Castro might be removed from the Cuban scene. He also broached the subject of assassination with his good friend, Senator George Smathers, and with a journalist. Both men later said that the president expressed distaste for the idea. Biographers, including Arthur Schlesinger, have also claimed that a Roman Catholic like Kennedy could not countenance assassination. On the other hand, Richard Helms, who commanded the CIA's clandestine service, answered a journalist's question about whether President Kennedy wanted Castro dead. Helms replied, "There is nothing on paper, of course." He added, "There is certainly no question in my mind that he did."[23] All who have debated the assassination issue agree that John Kennedy dominated the foreign policy-making process. No document has yet appeared to show that the president ordered the end of assassination efforts against Castro.

Scholars and journalists have speculated about what led the Kennedy administration to engage in such bizarre and extreme behavior. Indeed, Secretary of Defense Robert McNamara would later lament that the administration was "hysterical" about Castro. Investigative journalist Seymour Hersh, who interviewed former CIA operatives, has charged that the Kennedy brothers had a personal vendetta against Castro and took a blood oath to make Castro and his Communist friends pay for the staining of the family's honor at the Bay of Pigs.[24] Although personal animus may have informed the administration's policies, no document or taped conversation has appeared in which the Kennedy brothers vowed revenge against Castro. Both in private conversations with U.S. officials and foreign leaders and in confidential memorandums, President Kennedy insisted that communism in the Western Hemisphere threatened the United States, impeded the U.S. ability to act elsewhere, and threatened to become a divisive domestic political issue.

The Cuban Missile Crisis

President Kennedy's worst fears about Cuba came true on October 16, 1962, when National Security Adviser Bundy informed the president that the Soviets were building sites in Cuba for ballistic missiles equipped to carry nuclear weapons. Scholars have labeled the Cuban missile crisis "the most dangerous event in human history," pointing to the potential for a nuclear holocaust and the destruction of civilization.[25] Nikita Khrushchev and Fidel Castro bear significant responsibility for the crisis. President Kennedy had publicly warned that "the gravest issues would arise," if the Soviets sent "ground to ground missiles" to Cuba. Soviet and Cuban officials assured the United States that the Soviet Union would not base offensive weapon systems in Cuba. Soviet Foreign Minister Andrei Gromyko warned Khrushchev, "Putting missiles in Cuba would cause a political explosion in the United States." Indeed, the CIA calculated that the Soviets understood the risk and would not send missiles to Cuba.[26]

President Kennedy and his advisers share responsibility with Khrushchev and Castro for the ominous confrontation. The United States had undertaken a massive buildup of nuclear weapons and boasted of nuclear superiority over the Soviet Union. The administration had also committed acts of war against Cuba. The president did not think about the consequences of his anti-Castro policies. At the beginning of the crisis, Kennedy conceded he did not understand the motives behind missiles in Cuba, blurting out, "It's a goddamn mystery to me."[27] From the Soviet and Cuban perspective, all evidence—assassination plots, the rejection of Ché Guevara's peace offering, Operation Mongoose, the trade embargo, military training exercises in the Caribbean—pointed to the conclusion that the United States wanted to invade Cuba and murder its leader. General Lansdale, the head of Operation Mongoose, conceded that the Soviet Union might respond to U.S. aggression by building a military base in Cuba. In retrospect, Secretary of Defense McNamara reasoned that the Soviets could have concluded that the United States planned to invade Cuba.[28]

Scholars have extensive knowledge about the course and conduct of the Cuban missile crisis. Participants have published memoirs, and U.S., Soviet, and Cuban officials have attended conferences in Havana and exchanged "war stories" about the confrontation. Most important, President Kennedy secretly taped many of the secret deliberations he and his advisers carried out during the thirteen days of crisis. Kennedy taped conversations because he believed that advisers had misled the news media about their roles during the Bay of Pigs debacle. The president met regularly, almost continually, with a special group known as the Executive Committee of the National Security Council, or the "ExComm."

The basic outline of the Cuban missile crisis can be readily summarized. After extensive discussions in Moscow with Cuban leaders and with Castro's approval, the Soviets began their military deployment, code-named "Operation Anadyr," in the summer of 1962. Khrushchev had authorized a formidable force to protect Communist Cuba and rectify the military imbalance with the United States. The Soviets planned to send thirty-six medium-range missiles, twenty-four intermediate-range missiles, and forty-eight light IL-28 bombers. The Soviets could hit cities throughout the United States with the missiles and bombers. The missiles were capable of carrying warheads that were fifteen to seventy times more powerful than the bomb that annihilated Hiroshima in 1945. The Soviets further planned to deploy up to 50,000 military personnel. These forces would be equipped with more than 100 tactical nuclear weapons, which could be used to repel an invasion of the island.

President Kennedy met with the ExComm, beginning on October 16, for almost a week. Kennedy did not inform the Soviets that U-2s, U.S. reconnaissance planes, had photographed the military buildup. The president immediately vowed, "We're going to take out those missiles." Initial discussions focused on a military response, perhaps an air strike on the missile sites. The president decided, however, to postpone the military solution advocated strenuously by the Joint Chiefs of Staff and advisers such as former Secretary of State Dean Acheson and to impose a naval blockade, labeled a "quarantine," around Cuba. Kennedy feared that a surprise attack on Cuba would remind the international community of Japan's sneak attack on Pearl Harbor and dubbed such an attack "a Pearl Harbor in reverse."[29] On the evening of October 22, in a televised address, a somber president informed the nation of the crisis, announced the quarantine, and demanded that the Soviets remove the missiles. Over the next week, tensions mounted between the two superpowers. On October 24, as Soviet ships approached the quarantine line, Robert Kennedy thought, "We were on the edge of a precipice with no way off." On Saturday, October 27, Secretary of Defense Robert McNamara wondered whether he would live to see another Saturday. But on October 28, the president and Soviet Chairman Khrushchev struck a deal. The Soviets would remove the missiles, and, in turn, the United States would pledge not to invade Cuba. The United States also confidentially promised to dismantle Jupiter missile sites in Turkey. By November 20 Kennedy announced the end of the crisis, as the Soviets had withdrawn the missiles and bombers from Cuba.[30]

President Kennedy garnered international and domestic prestige after his diplomatic triumph in the fall of 1962. He had forced the Soviet missiles out of Cuba, while simultaneously avoiding a catastrophic clash. The president now seemed the natural, gifted leader of the Western alliance. As measured in public opinion surveys, his approval rating from the U.S. public rose to 74 percent and remained high for the rest of his presidency. His triumph has fueled the popular admiration and enthusiasm for Kennedy that has persisted for more than four decades. Scholarly reviews of the president's management of the crisis have, however, been more mixed. Neither the criticism nor the praise Kennedy has received is mutually exclusive.

Scholarly questions about Kennedy's performance have centered on his decision to issue a public ultimatum to Soviets instead of trying to resolve the crisis quietly and diplomatically and for failing to make explicit his terms of settlement in his ultimatum. To be sure, no serious student of the crisis questions whether President Kennedy had to challenge the Soviet-Cuban action. The secret, deceptive nature of Khrushchev's actions generated international alarm. Kennedy judged that he would be shirking his highest constitutional duty—to defend the security of the country—if he did not act. Moreover, the Soviets had lied to the president in reneging on their pledge not to introduce into Cuba weapons that threatened the United States. Foreign Minister Gromyko had a previously scheduled meeting in the Oval Office with Kennedy on October 18. Gromyko again assured the president that the Soviets would give the Cubans only "defensive" weapons. Kennedy had the photographic evidence of the missile buildup in the drawer of his desk. As the president told advisers, Gromyko "told more barefaced lies than I have ever heard in such a short time."[31] Whereas Gromyko's charade would have infuriated any reasonable leader, the question still remains, why did the president choose not to inform Gromyko of what U.S. terms would be in the looming confrontation?

On October 20, two days before the public ultimatum, Ambassador to the United Nations Adlai E. Stevenson, reiterating a position previously articulated by Secretary of Defense McNamara, argued to the ExComm that the president should tie the demand to remove the missiles with a public pledge not to invade Cuba, evacuate the military base at Guantánamo, and further promise to dismantle U.S. missile sites in Italy and Turkey. ExComm members, including the president, "sharply" dismissed the plan, implying that Stevenson lacked fortitude and courage. In Kennedy's view, Stevenson's plan "would convey to the world that we had been frightened into abandoning our position."[32] In fact, Stevenson's proposal, which emphasized negotiation and diplomacy, served as the basis of the settlement. ExComm members knew that the Jupiter missiles in Italy and Turkey were redundant because the United States was in the process of introducing nuclear-powered submarines equipped with Polaris nuclear missiles into the Mediterranean region. The United States actually dismantled its missile sites in Italy, along with those in Turkey, after the crisis.

For Kennedy to give diplomacy a first chance would not have jeopardized national security because the missiles in Cuba did not alter the nuclear balance of power. In terms of intercontinental ballistic missiles, the United States still retained overwhelming advantage over the Soviets. In any case, in an era of thermonuclear weapons, counting missiles, bombers, and warheads represented worthless arithmetic. Both the United States and the Soviet Union had the means to destroy the world. Missiles in Cuba might give the perception of a Soviet advantage. But Cuban missiles would soon also be redundant. ExComm

President Kennedy meets with Soviet Foreign Minister Andrei Gromyko (nearest the president) and the Soviet ambassador to the United States Anatoly Dobrynin (with eyeglasses) at the White House on October 18, 1962. By this time, the president knew that the Soviet Union was building medium- and intermediate-range nuclear missiles in Cuba. The president chose not to confront the Soviets with the photographic evidence that he had in the drawer of his desk. Gromyko lied to the president, assuring him that the Soviets would give the Cubans only "defensive" weapons. (John F. Kennedy Presidential Library and Museum, Boston)

members could anticipate that the Soviets would have submarines equipped with nuclear missiles along the Atlantic and Pacific seaboards and in the Gulf of Mexico.

The problem in international relations with choosing a public confrontation over quiet diplomacy is that, whereas a leader can initiate the course of events, the leader can easily lose command over them. The Cuban missile crisis had the potential to spin out of control. Both on the U.S. and Soviet sides, subordinates made decisions that shocked both President Kennedy and Chairman Khrushchev. U.S. military leaders resisted being controlled by civilian officials. Chief of Naval Operations Adm. George Anderson flaunted U.S. constitutional principles, telling Secretary of Defense McNamara that the Navy would run the naval quarantine its own way. The Navy forced Soviet submarines patrolling near the quarantine line to surface. In one case, the Navy chose the high-risk option of using light depth charges to force the submarine to the surface. The U.S. Air Force, in readying its forces for nuclear war, issued alert instructions in the clear, rather than in code, because it wanted to impress the Soviets with the awesome nature of U.S. power. A U-2 plane based in Alaska became lost and wandered into Soviet airspace; Soviet fighters scrambled to intercept it. The president assumed that such surveillance flights had been postponed. Attorney General Kennedy worried that Operation Mongoose attack teams in Cuba would inflame the situation with a spectacular raid or an attack on Castro.[33]

Khrushchev suffered similar command and control problems. On October 27, at the height of the crisis, the Soviet leader was surprised to learn that, against his standing orders, a Soviet surface-to-air missile had brought down a U-2 plane over Cuba. A Soviet military officer authorized the attack without the explicit approval of Gen. Issa A. Pliyev, the commander of Soviet forces in Cuba. A letter the Soviet chairman received from Fidel Castro shortly thereafter further unnerved Khrushchev. Warning that an attack on the island was imminent, Castro urged Khrushchev not to "allow the circumstances in which imperialists could launch the first nuclear strike." Alarmed that Castro wanted the Soviet Union to launch a preemptive nuclear strike, Khrushchev took the unusual step of going on Radio Moscow to announce the end of the crisis. Thereafter, Khrushchev unilaterally decided to withdraw the tactical nuclear weapons from Cuba. He was troubled by Castro's erratic behavior after the missile crisis and his rash talk about nuclear war.[34]

Historians can also find much to praise in Kennedy's leadership during the missile crisis. His establishment of the ExComm demonstrated that he had learned from the haphazard way he had approached planning for the Bay of Pigs invasion to have his key advisers meet and debate options in front of him. Kennedy deserved further credit for standing up to the Joint Chiefs of Staff, who demanded a surprise air attack on Cuba. Air Force Gen. Curtis E. LeMay insulted Kennedy, saying to him in the cabinet room that, if he did not order direct military action, it would be "almost as bad as the appeasement at Munich." President Kennedy remained coolly professional, noting that aggression toward

Cuba could jeopardize U.S. positions in other areas such as Berlin.[35] By October 27 discussions in the ExComm were becoming unfocused and disorganized; the advisers, exhausted and under extreme stress, rambled and expressed incomplete thoughts. As revealed in the tapes and transcripts of the meetings, Kennedy remained poised and lucid and capable of analytic thinking.

Kennedy chose a peaceful path out of the crisis. Disastrous consequences might have ensued if he had authorized air strikes or an invasion. As the Soviet military personnel on the island suffered casualties, pressures would have mounted on Khrushchev and General Pliyev to unleash tactical nuclear weapons. And as Kennedy once noted, "Inevitably, the use of small nuclear armaments will lead to larger and larger nuclear armaments on both sides, until the world-wide holocaust has begun." Khrushchev also grasped that shooting between the superpowers posed, in his words, "the danger of war and of nuclear catastrophe,

President Kennedy meets with his advisers, the Executive Committee of the National Security Council, or the "ExComm," on October 29, 1962, during the Cuban missile crisis. On the previous day, Soviet Premier Khrushchev had announced that he would dismantle the Soviet missiles in Cuba. The president's brother, the attorney general, can be seen hovering over the meeting. President Kennedy relied on his brother for advice. (John F. Kennedy Presidential Library and Museum, Boston)

with the possible result of destroying the human race."[36] His decision to accept U.S. terms helped Kennedy keep the Joint Chiefs of Staff at bay. Both leaders had precipitated the Cuban missile crisis. Kennedy and Khrushchev, using separate methods, found a way out of it. The most dangerous event in human history became something for historians to analyze rather than the end of civilization.

The Last Year

Whereas Soviet-American relations improved in the aftermath of the crisis, U.S. relations with Castro's Cuba remained hostile. In the year after the missile crisis, the Kennedy administration continued to pursue an aggressive, belligerent policy toward Cuba. In his October 27 letter to Chairman Khrushchev, Kennedy directly and concisely offered a pledge not to invade Cuba in order to remove missiles. But after October 27, the administration always conditioned its pledge with the provisos that Cuba must cease being a source of Communist aggression, that the United States reserved the right to halt subversion from Cuba, and that the United States intended for the Cuban people to gain their freedom one day.[37] Because it judged that Castro's Cuba would never conform to U.S. standards, the administration considered itself free to attack Cuba, for-swearing only an unprovoked military invasion of the island.

Between December 1962 and November 1963, the administration renewed its war against Castro on all fronts. The Agriculture and State departments investigated whether the United States could damage the Cuban economy by manipulating sugar prices on world markets. The State Department pressured U.S. allies to curtail trade with Cuba. The administration also began the process of ejecting Cuba from the International Monetary Fund. The president coupled economic warfare with new military preparations. In April 1963 he urged his national security team to prepare for an invasion of Cuba, asking, "Are we keeping our Cuban contingency plans up to date?"[38] Kennedy wanted to send troops to Cuba quickly in case of a general uprising.

The administration's fury against Castro mounted when the Cuban spent the entire month of May 1963 in the Soviet Union. Khrushchev soothed Castro's hurt feelings over the missile crisis with a package of economic and military aid for Cuba. In April Kennedy had personally approved the sabotage of cargoes on Cuban ships and the crippling of ships. He also authorized inciting Cubans to harass, attack, and sabotage Soviet military personnel in Cuba, "provided every precaution is taken to prevent attribution." After Castro's trip, the president demanded and received an integrated program of propaganda, economic denial, and sabotage against Cuba.[39] On June 19 Kennedy, dubbed "Higher Authority" in CIA parlance, approved a sabotage program against Cuba, expressing "a particular interest" in external sabotage operations. The CIA was subsequently authorized to carry out thirteen major sabotage operations in Cuba, including attacks on an electric power plant, an oil refinery, and a sugar mill. On November 12 Higher Authority conducted a major review of his anti-Castro program and received an upbeat assessment from the CIA. The president was also informed that the CIA would launch new attacks, including the underwater demolition of docks and ships.[40] The memorandums of record state that "Higher Authority" rather than President Kennedy attended these meetings. This was to give the president, again in CIA language, the option of "plausible denial." U.S. officials wanted the president of the United States to be able to deny that he had authorized terrorism and sabotage.

Nikita Khrushchev protested these attacks on Cuba, averring that the United States had reneged on the agreement that ended the missile crisis. President Kennedy deflected the complaints, charging that the Cubans were fomenting revolution throughout the Western Hemisphere.[41] In fact, the United States lacked hard evidence to sustain those charges. Havana certainly exhorted revolutionaries throughout the region and invited political radicals to come to Cuba to study and train. But Cuba did not supply arms or troops to insurgent groups, and U.S. intelligence analysts knew that Khrushchev had made clear to Castro in May 1963 that the Soviet Union would not support armed insurrection in Latin America. One student of Cuban foreign policy has estimated that only forty Cubans fought in Latin America in the 1960s. This included Ché Guevara's ill-fated guerrilla-war mission to Bolivia in 1967.[42]

The evidence the United States wanted surfaced on a Venezuelan beach in early November 1963, when Venezuela announced that it had discovered a cache of Cuban arms, allegedly left for leftist radicals determined to disrupt upcoming elections. This detection of the purported Cuban intervention raised many questions. Former CIA agents have subsequently written that they believed that their colleagues planted the arms in Venezuela. In May 1963 the CIA sent an anti-Cuba plan to the NSC that included the idea of placing caches of arms from Communist countries in selected regions of Latin America, "ostensibly proving the arms were smuggled from Cuba."[43]

Assassination plots against Castro also continued after the missile crisis. On November 22, 1963, the day of the president's death in Dallas, CIA agents rendezvoused in Paris with a traitorous Cuban official, Rolando Cubela Secades, code-named AM/LASH. The agents passed to Cubela a ballpoint pen rigged with a poisonous hypodermic needle intended to produce Castro's instant death. In the previous month, the CIA had assured Cubela that it operated with the approval of Attorney General Kennedy.[44] Former CIA operatives have also alleged that the president signaled encouragement to AM/LASH through a speech. On November 18 in Miami, in what turned out to be his last address on inter-American affairs, Kennedy referred to Castro as a "barrier" to be removed.[45]

Scholars have suggested that Kennedy showed interest, during his last months in office, in improving relations with Castro, even predicting that a U.S.-Cuban "détente" would have developed during Kennedy's second presidential term.[46] In the fall of 1963, the Kennedy administration authorized intermediaries to speak with Cuban officials. However, the administration attached stringent conditions to these preliminary discussions, insisting that Cuba would have to break ties with the Soviet Union, expel Soviet troops from the island, and end subversion in Latin America. The United States also wanted Castro to renounce his faith in communism.[47] In short, President Kennedy was prepared to accept Castro's surrender.

The Kennedy Legacy in Cuba

The Lyndon Johnson administration also refused to accept the legitimacy of the Cuban Revolution, maintaining the diplomatic and economic isolation of Cuba. But President Lyndon Johnson made one significant change in his predecessor's policy. He gradually shut down the campaign of assassination, sabotage, and terrorism directed at Castro's Cuba. Johnson, who as vice president had not been actively involved in the covert war against Castro, received his first comprehensive briefing on CIA activities on December 19, 1963. CIA officials reviewed the various sabotage and terrorism attacks that President Kennedy had personally approved in June and November 1963. At the briefing, President Johnson asked pointedly "whether there is any significant insurgency within Cuba." Desmond Fitzgerald, the CIA official who directed the covert campaign, admitted, "There is no national movement on which we can build." Thereafter at the briefing, President Johnson ruled that the CIA's next attack on a major target—the Matanzas power plant—would be cancelled.[48]

Over the next eighteen months, President Johnson shut down the covert war against Fidel Castro. The United States stopped sponsoring raids on Cuban targets, terminated the funding of Cuban exile groups who planned to attack Cuba, and severed its contacts with potential assassins. By June 1965 the United States no longer waged covert, violent war against Cuba. Johnson overruled powerful bureaucracies, including the CIA and the Joint Chiefs of Staff, that wanted to continue to attack Cuba.[49]

President Johnson had several reasons for reversing the Kennedy policy of attacking Cuba. The new president disliked Attorney General Robert Kennedy, the person most identified with the anti-Castro campaign. He wanted to improve relations with the Soviet Union and did not want another Soviet-American confrontation over Cuba. Johnson wanted to be perceived as a man of peace during the 1964 presidential campaign. In any case, Johnson already had his share of foreign policy challenges, especially in Vietnam. His decision to invade the Dominican Republic in late March 1965 in order to forestall an alleged Communist takeover only compounded his international problems. President Johnson also apparently objected to some U.S. actions, such as assassination plots, against Castro's Cuba. Shortly after taking office, he told CIA Director John McCone that he no longer wanted his CIA chief to have the image of a "cloak and dagger role." After he left office, Johnson revealed in an interview, "We were running a damned Murder Incorporated in the Caribbean."[50]

Perhaps the key reason for Johnson's decision to halt the war against Castro was that he concluded the CIA's war would not work. Attacks on Cuba's economic infrastructure and maritime raids on coastal targets were designed to spark a mass uprising in Cuba against Castro. However grudgingly, Johnson and his advisers conceded that Fidel Castro enjoyed widespread popular support on the island.[51]

The United States thereafter pursued "containment" policies against Fidel Castro. The administration authorized the CIA to disseminate propaganda, covertly collect intelligence and counterintelligence, and wage economic warfare against Cuba. The United States would make life hard for Cubans, hoping either that the Communist system would collapse in Cuba or that Castro would die. Notwithstanding the palpable failures of Castro's brand of communism, this policy of perpetual antagonism has contributed to misery and malnutrition in Cuba for over forty years. John and Robert Kennedy created this futile foreign policy.

CHAPTER 5

Latin America

President John F. Kennedy once remarked to an aide that "Latin America's not like Asia or Africa. We can really accomplish something there."[1] During his three years in office, the president focused on relations with the Soviet Union, the nuclear arms race, and Cold War confrontations over Berlin and Cuba. But he probably hoped that his historical legacy would center on his efforts to improve the lives of Latin Americans. The crowing achievement of the Harry S. Truman administration was that it rebuilt Western Europe with the Marshall Plan (1947–1952). President Kennedy similarly hoped that he could modernize and transform Latin America with his grand program, the Alliance for Progress.

An examination of President Kennedy's policies toward Latin America offers an opportunity to assess the complex, conflicted nature of the president's approach to the world. He brought high ideals and noble purposes to his Latin American policy. He pledged to transfer U.S. wealth to uplift the conditions of Latin America's poor. His answer to political extremism was representative democracy and socioeconomic progress, and he was prepared to deploy the awesome power of the United States to reach those enlightened goals. When it came to Latin America, Kennedy displayed remarkable presidential leadership. But the president held exaggerated fears of Communist expansion and displayed a persistent inability to separate nationalism from communism. Kennedy's Cold War ethos led him and his administration to compromise and even mutilate his magnificent goals for the Western Hemisphere.

Alliance for Progress

ORIGINS

President Kennedy unveiled his reform program for Latin America in an impressive White House ceremony on March 13, 1961. After hosting an elegant reception for 250 people, including the diplomatic corps of the Latin American republics and congressional leaders, the president and his wife, Jacqueline Bouvier Kennedy, directed guests to move to the East Room. They seated themselves on gilt-edged chairs arranged in semicircles on both sides of the rostrum. President Kennedy's speech was simultaneously broadcast by the Voice of America in English, Spanish, French, and Portuguese, the languages of the Western Hemisphere. Kennedy thrilled his attentive audience, telling Latin Americans what they had been waiting nearly two decades to hear. The United States would underwrite the region's social and economic transformation. The United States would join in a "vast cooperative effort, unparalleled in magnitude and nobility of purpose, to satisfy the basic needs of Latin American people for homes, work and land, health and schools—*techo, trabajo y tierra, salud y escuela*."[2] Dubbed the Alliance for Progress—Alianza para el Progreso—the new program would be Latin America's "Marshall Plan."

Kennedy delivered over $600 million in emergency economic aid to Latin America in early 1961. His administration, however, gave real substance to his noble rhetoric at an inter-American economic conference held in August 1961 at the Uruguayan seaside resort of Punta del Este. Secretary of the Treasury C. Douglas Dillon informed Latin American delegates that they could count on receiving $20 billion in public and private capital over the next ten years, "the decade of development." With this influx of foreign money combined with an additional $80 billion that Latin Americans could reasonably expect to generate in internal savings, Latin American nations would achieve a real economic growth rate of 2.5 percent a year. Administration officials chose to be publicly cautious; they actually expected that growth might reach 5 percent a year. Marvelous changes would flow from foreign aid and economic growth. The Charter of the Punta del Este Conference enumerated over ninety lofty goals. Latin Americans would witness a five-year increase in life expectancy, a halving of the infant mortality rate, the elimination of adult illiteracy, and the provision of six years of primary education to every school-age child.

The Alliance for Progress meant more than improvements in health, education, and welfare. Political freedom and social reform would go hand-in-hand with material progress. Archaic tax and land-tenure structures would be dismantled and self-serving tyrants cast aside. President Kennedy vowed that North and South Americans would "demonstrate to the entire world that man's unsatisfied aspiration for economic progress and social justice can best be achieved by free men working within a framework of democratic institutions."[3]

The Kennedy administration decided to embark on a campaign to underwrite change and social development in Latin America because it perceived that the region was vulnerable to radical social revolution. President Kennedy characterized the region as "the most dangerous area in the world."[4] If poverty and injustice were preconditions for upheaval, then Latin America was indeed ripe for revolution. In several countries—Bolivia, the Dominican Republic, El Salvador, Guatemala, and Haiti—malnutrition was widespread, with a grossly inadequate daily per capita consumption of 2,000 calories or less and a daily intake of fifteen grams of animal protein. In eight other countries, daily per capita consumption approached only 2,400 calories, the bare minimum necessary to sustain people who toiled in fields and factories. By comparison, in 1961 U.S. adults on average consumed over 3,000 calories and sixty-six grams of animal protein daily. Hungry people had predictably poor health records. Guatemalans had a life expectancy of less than fifty years, twenty years less than for a U.S. citizen. In the Andean nations of Ecuador and Peru, approximately 10 percent of newborns died during their first year of life. The poor of Latin America also lacked education and skills. Adult illiteracy rates ranged from 35 to 40 percent in relatively prosperous nations such as Brazil and Venezuela. This misery was concentrated in the countryside, with *campesinos* working tiny plots of land and a rural oligarchy operating vast estates or *latifundia.* In Colombia 1.3 percent of landowners controlled over 50 percent of the land, and in Chile 7 percent owned 80 percent of the land. Desperate rural people were fleeing to urban areas, moving into squalid shantytowns that surrounded cities such as Bogotá, Caracas, and Rio de Janeiro.[5]

A sense of urgency informed the new administration's approach toward Latin America because inter-American relations had deteriorated during the postwar period. Latin Americans repeatedly complained that the United States took the region for granted. Between 1945 and 1960 the small countries of

Belgium, Luxembourg, and the Netherlands had received more economic aid than had all of Latin America combined. Bitter Latin American leaders recalled that their nations had stoutly supported the United States during the Second World War but had received nothing tangible in return, whereas the defeated enemies—Germany and Japan—had been rebuilt. Latin American democrats further resented that the Dwight D. Eisenhower administration had lavished medals and military support on right-wing dictators because they professed to be anti-Communist. Appalled Latin Americans watched as Eisenhower bestowed the Legion of Merit, the nation's highest award for foreign personages, on Manuel Odría (1950–1956) of Peru and Marcos Pérez Jiménez (1952–1958) of Venezuela, two of the region's notorious tyrants. Informed Latin Americans also knew that the CIA had destabilized the popularly elected Guatemalan government of Jacobo Arbenz Guzmán. Latin Americans visibly expressed their anger with U.S. policies in 1958, when Vice President Richard M. Nixon toured South America. Protestors hounded Nixon in Argentina, Peru, and Uruguay, and in Caracas, Venezuela, a mob tried to assault the vice president. Kennedy quipped that he liked to think that "those people who threw rocks at Nixon" objected to the vice president's "personality." But in fact, they were sending the message that "we can't embrace every tinhorn dictator who tells us he's anti-communist while he's sitting on the necks of his own people."[6]

The administration further believed that the United States had a stark choice to make in 1961. In a series of popular upheavals, ten Latin American military dictators fell from power between 1956 and 1960. Middle-class reformers, such as Rómulo Betancourt (1959–1963) of Venezuela, replaced the military men. They vowed to rule democratically and to reform the region's archaic social structures. Betancourt and influential political leaders, including Arturo Frondizi of Argentina, José "Pepe" Figueres of Costa Rica, and Juscelino Kubitschek of Brazil, pleaded for U.S. help in building progressive societies. They unabashedly played on the U.S. fear of communism. Latin America's poverty and injustice, they warned, was a fertile breeding ground for the Communist contagion to fester and spread. A second, third, and fourth "Cuba" might be on the horizon. Indeed, the Argentine revolutionary, Ernesto "Ché" Guevara, Fidel Castro's comrade, actually attended the conference at Punta del Este and debated Secretary of the Treasury Dillon. Guevara boasted that Latin America's "new age" would be under "the star of Cuba," not the Alliance for Progress.

The Kennedy administration perceived the Cuban Revolution as part and parcel of Soviet Premier Nikita Khrushchev's "wars of national liberation strategy." Ambassador to Brazil Lincoln Gordon, who helped design the Alliance for Progress, decided that Khrushchev had signaled his intention to use Cuba as "a base for military and intelligence activities against the United States and for further "opportunistic conquests in Latin America."[7] President Kennedy drew similar conclusions from his unpleasant meeting with Khrushchev in Vienna in June 1961. Upon returning home, the president soberly reported to the nation that his Soviet adversary predicted that in the developing countries "the revolution of rising peoples would eventually be a Communist revolution, and that the so-called wars of liberation, supported by the Kremlin, would replace the old methods of direct aggression and invasion." Kennedy added that it was "the Communist theory" that "a small group of disciplined Communists could exploit discontent and misery in a country where the average income may be $60 or $70 a year, and seize control, therefore, of an entire country without Communist troops ever crossing any international border." Secretary of State Dean Rusk followed the president's public warning with a confidential alert to U.S. diplomats in Latin America. Khrushchev was targeting Latin America.[8]

Not to oppose the alleged Communist master plan for Latin America would imperil the national security of the United States. The United States would be surrounded if Communists came to power in Central and South American nations. U.S. officials also believed that they had to maintain U.S. credibility "in our own backyard." Since the late nineteenth century, the United States, constructing a sphere of influence, had dominated the Western Hemisphere. The U.S. ability to act on the global stage would be impeded if it could not maintain order and stability in Latin America. Secretary Rusk once noted to Argentine diplomats that the Communist adversaries measured the resolve of the United States in the Western Hemisphere. "A lack of determination on our part," Rusk warned, might encourage Soviet aggression in Berlin.[9]

Not only national security anxieties but also domestic political calculations informed President Kennedy's approach to the region. The president was loath to face in his 1964 reelection campaign the same charge—losing a Latin American country to communism—that he had thrown at the Eisenhower-Nixon team in 1960. Throughout his tenure, Kennedy predicted disaster in Latin America. In January 1961 he told an aide "the whole place could blow up on us." In November 1962 he cautioned Argentina's Gen. Pedro Eugenio Aramburu to be alert, observing "that the next twelve months would be critical in Latin America with respect to renewed Communist attempts at penetration." In October 1963, a month before his death, he warned that Latin America posed "the greatest danger to us." A few months earlier, in a meeting with Prime Minister Harold Macmillan, Kennedy demanded that the United Kingdom postpone the independence of its South American colony, British Guiana. Kennedy alleged that British Guiana might become a Communist state. British Guiana would then join Cuba as a major campaign issue and jeopardize the president's reelection. The British ultimately succumbed to Kennedy's extraordinary pressure and postponed the colony's independence.[10] As presidential adviser and biographer Arthur Schlesinger put it, it was his boss's "absolute determination" to prevent a second Communist outpost in the Western Hemisphere.[11]

Although motivated by Cold War imperatives, the president and his team approached the task of building a prosperous, democratic, anti-Communist Latin American with supreme confidence. They thought they knew how to "modernize" Latin America. They fashioned the Alliance for Progress on contemporary social science theories espoused by intellectuals, including Ambassador Gordon and presidential assistant Walt W. Rostow. In the postwar period, social scientists had enunciated formal theories on political and economic development. They posited a universal, quantitatively measurable movement of all societies from a "traditional" situation toward a single ideal form or "modern" organization. Traditional societies, as they presumably existed in Latin America, had authoritarian political structures; rural, backward economies; and a lack of faith in scientific progress and the entrepreneurial spirit. A modern society, which would look remarkably like the United States, would be characterized by a competitive political system, a commercialized and technologically sophisticated economic system, mass consumption, high literacy rates, and a geographically and socially mobile population.

The mission of the United States was to accelerate the modernization process before the Communists could subvert it. The United States would identify and support urban, middle-class leaders in Latin America who favored democracy, universal education, and state policies that promoted economic development and social welfare. These modern Latin Americans presumably wanted to replicate superior U.S.-style institutions and inculcate Anglo-American values in their societies. The United States would assist these leaders with substantial amounts of economic aid until these Latin American societies could generate enough internal capital to underwrite their own economic development. At that point, presumably within ten years, Latin American nations would have reached the "takeoff stage," as outlined in Rostow's famous treatise, *The Stages of Economic Growth, a Non-Communist Manifesto* (1960). The modernization theory further held that democratic structures would flourish in nations that could sustain their own economic growth.

The lessons of history affirmed the administration's faith in the modernization process. U.S. leaders were justifiably proud that the past Democratic administration of Harry Truman had rebuilt war-torn Western Europe and Japan. John Kennedy's new Democratic team wanted to get the United States and the world moving again—to replay the success of the 1940s. The Alliance for Progress would be the "Marshall Plan for Latin America." To borrow Arthur Schlesinger's phrase, the United States would pursue a policy of "enlightened anti-Communism." The United States would win the Cold War in Latin America by doing noble things. The United States would build sturdy, progressive societies that uplifted the poor and dispossessed of Latin America. These modernized societies would naturally align themselves with the United States and reject the false promises of Khrushchev, Castro, and their fellow Communist travelers.[12]

President Kennedy displayed the enthusiasm, confidence, and empathy inherent in the Alliance for Progress. During his abbreviated presidency, he toured Colombia, Venezuela, Mexico, and Costa Rica and received tumultuous welcomes. The massive crowds that greeted him understood that he wanted to help poor people. He participated, for example, in a land redistribution ceremony in Venezuela. Kennedy also opened the Oval Office to Latin American presidents; former presidents; foreign, finance, and labor ministers; ambassadors; generals; trade unionists; and economists. The memorandums of these conversations with Latin Americans reveal an articulate, educated, refined man who had studied his briefing papers. Kennedy was unfailingly polite with his Latin American visitors, never patronizing or condescending toward them. He enjoyed the company of Latin Americans, especially friends such as Venezuela's Betancourt. Latin Americans left the White House both amazed at the depth of the president's understanding of their countries' problems and gratified by his eagerness to help. A telling example of the president's commitment occurred during his visit to Costa Rica. He noticed an unoccupied hospital and told aides to find funds to staff it. The U.S. Agency for International Development subsequently granted $130,000 for a children's hospital in San José.[13]

RESULTS

The enthusiasm, energy, and optimism that infused the Alliance for Progress did not result in meaningful political and social change in Latin America. The Alliance proved to be one of the notable U.S. policy failures of the Cold War. During the 1960s, sixteen extra-constitutional changes of government rocked Latin America. During the Kennedy years alone, military officers overthrew six popularly elected Latin American presidents. Latin American economies hardly reached the "takeoff stage," registering an unimpressive annual growth rate of about 2 percent. Most of the growth took place at the very end of the 1960s. Annual economic growth in Latin America during the Kennedy presidency barely reached 1 percent. The Alliance failed to reach any of its ninety-four numerical goals in health, education, and welfare. The number of unemployed Latin Americans rose from 18 million to 25 million during the decade.

U.S. officials misled themselves trying to apply dubious social science theories and misleading historical analogies like the "Marshall Plan for Latin America." Latin America was not Europe. Western European countries had been devastated by war, but they had financial and technical expertise, familiarity with industrial forms of organization, institutionalized political parties, strong national identities, and, except for Germany, a robust democratic tradition. The Truman administration had helped "rebuild" countries whose social fabrics, political traditions, and economic institutions were notably similar to those of the United States. On the other hand, the Spanish-Portuguese (Iberian) and Amerindian political heritages emphasized planned economies, strong central governments, and the organization of society into corporate groups. Latin Americans traditionally gave greater significance to the group than to the individual. Latin Americans further believed that national progress came from a unified government rather than one slowed by a mixed form of power sharing with checks and balances. In his last address on inter-American affairs, President Kennedy conceded that the Alliance for Progress should not be compared to the Marshall Plan, for "then we helped rebuild a shattered economy whose human and social foundation remained. Today we are trying to create a basic new foundation, capable of reshaping the centuries-old societies and economies of half of a hemisphere." Yet Kennedy assured his audience that idealism, energy, and optimism would bridge the vast cultural gap and bring about the "modernization" of Latin America.[14] Although recognizing the challenges ahead, Kennedy was still assuming that Latin Americans wanted their modernized societies to replicate the social structures of the United States.

The United States also lacked the power to force change in Latin America that it wielded in Germany and Japan in the postwar years. The United States militarily occupied both countries, ordering change. Gen. Douglas MacArthur, for example, directed the writing of the Japanese constitution, requiring the redistribution of land and limitations on military expenditures. The Kennedy administration repeatedly meddled and intervened covertly in Latin America. But it could hardly invade a Latin American country because the government wasted resources, abused *campesinos*, or discriminated against citizens of African or Native American heritages. Kennedy could not, as both he and President Johnson did in the U.S. South, dispatch troops to protect the civil rights of oppressed people who suffered racial discrimination. In any case, the Kennedy administration forgot some lessons of history that were relevant to the U.S. role in Latin America. During the first third of the twentieth century, the United States had militarily occupied countries, including Cuba, the Dominican Republic, Haiti, and Nicaragua. The history of these occupations suggested that the United States could not readily export its values to Latin America. Dictators, like Rafael Trujillo of the Dominican Republic (1930–1961), not democrats, had emerged in the aftermath of those occupations.

The Alliance for Progress also proved far less generous than the Marshall Plan. President Kennedy regretfully had to inform Latin American leaders in private that the United States "could not give aid to Latin American countries in the same way that it helped to rebuild Europe with the Marshall Plan."

Through his eloquence and spectacularly successful trips to Latin America, he had galvanized public and congressional support for the Alliance. But with its global containment policy and Kennedy's large increase in military spending, the United States had shouldered heavy financial burdens, curbing U.S. generosity. Most Marshall Plan aid was in the form of grants, whereas the Alliance offered loans, which eventually had to be repaid. In the 1960s the region received about $15 billion of the promised $20 billion. Even then, with Latin American nations being required to repay principal and interest on pre-1961 and Alliance loans, this meant that the actual net capital flow to Latin America during the 1960s averaged about $920 million a year. This was the equivalent of about $4 per Latin American per year. By comparison, Marshall Plan money, which did not have to be repaid, amounted to $109 a year in assistance for every person in the Netherlands.[15]

The Alliance money that Latin America received did have salubrious effects. Both Presidents Kennedy and Johnson could read upbeat reports about schools and hospitals being built and more people gaining access to potable water. Population growth, unfortunately, eroded many of the gains. With a 2.9 percent annual rate of increase, Latin America experienced the most rapid population increase in the world in the 1960s. Colombia saw its population increase from 15.6 million to 21 million, and Brazil added 25 million people, from 70 to 95 million. Alliance programs helped cut the percentage of Latin American children not attending school from 52 to 43 percent, but because of this population growth, the actual number of children not attending school increased during the 1960s. The Alliance for Progress did not place population control on its agenda. President Kennedy took no interest in population control, apparently believing it to be politically and medically impractical and morally dubious. He once disputed what proved to be the accurate prediction that the world's population of three billion in 1960 would double to six billion in 2000.[16] In truth, no Latin American leader raised population issues with the president. Oral contraceptives, an effective method of birth control, also became commercially available in the United States only in 1960.

Latin American leaders also bore responsibility for the Alliance's failures. Their governments often proved incapable of designing the long-range plans required for putting their countries on the path of sustainable economic growth.

They wasted U.S. money on short-term, politically expedient projects or directed the spending at enhancing the living standards of middle-income groups, rather than the poor. Latin American democrats also hesitated to attack traditional land tenure patterns, with 5–10 percent of the population, the landed oligarchy, owning 70-90 percent of the land. The rural regions were the locus of Latin America's poverty, underdevelopment, and population explosion. Ecuadorian agricultural laborers, for example, earned fifteen cents a day. During the 1960s, only Chile and Venezuela carried out anything more than token agricultural reform. Mexico continued to sustain its post-1940 economic growth in the countryside. In the aftermath of the Mexican Revolution (1910–1920), successive Mexican governments had redistributed over 100 million acres of land, often in the form of communal holdings, or *ejidos*. The Alliance for Progress, however, played a minimal role in Mexico.

In their defense, Latin American leaders pointed to the declining terms of trade as the cause for the region's economic stagnation. In order to generate the $80 billion of domestic savings mandated by the Alliance, Latin Americans needed to sell their primary products—coffee, sugar, bananas, copper, tin, lead, zinc, and oil—on the global markets. But the prices of these tropical foods and raw materials declined in the 1960s even as the prices of imported industrial machinery and finished goods—the very things needed for economic development—rose. The price of coffee, Latin America's chief export, fell from 90 cents a pound in the 1950s to 36 cents a pound in the early 1960s. The price of a barrel of Venezuelan oil fell from $2.65 in 1957 to $1.81 in 1969.[17]

As they surveyed the failures of the Alliance for Progress, admirers of President Kennedy blamed President Johnson. Given time, President Kennedy would have made his program work. In the interpretations of sympathetic biographers, the Alliance for Progress joins issues such as relations with Cuba and the war in Vietnam where progress would have ensued and tragedy would have been avoided, if Kennedy had enjoyed a second presidential term. The facts and the documentary record do not sustain the charge that President Johnson undermined the Alliance for Progress. President Johnson did not give Latin America the high level of attention that his predecessor had. His major regional interest was resolving boundary and water issues with Mexico, the neighbor of his native state of Texas. But money flowed to Latin America at the same rate in the late 1960s as it had in the early 1960s. Latin American economies also showed better economic growth in the second half of the 1960s than during the Kennedy presidency. President Johnson also waged Cold War in Latin America with the intensity that characterized President Kennedy's policies.

Interventionist Policies

The failure of the Alliance for Progress cannot be explained solely by structural problems or President Kennedy's unfortunate "unfinished life." If so, historians could limit their analyses to noting that Kennedy virtuously but unsuccessfully tried to end poverty and injustice in the hemisphere. They would further point to the president's determination in late 1963 to reorganize the administration of the Alliance for Progress. He repeatedly told aides that he had not given up on his cherished program. But a fair assessment of Kennedy and Latin America would emphasize that the president's Cold War initiatives undermined the Alliance for Progress. Kennedy judged regional governments on whether they affirmed the U.S. faith that Fidel Castro's Cuba represented the focus of evil. He demanded that Latin American nations break diplomatic relations with Cuba and enlist in the U.S. campaign to strangle Cuba's economy. He further required Latin American leaders to outlaw domestic Communists and to forswear establishing relations with the Soviet Union or the Communist bloc. Such leaders as Arturo Frondizi of Argentina, João Goulart in Brazil, Juan José Arévalo of Guatemala, and Cheddi Jagan in British Guiana failed Kennedy's Cold War test. These leaders respected constitutional processes and praised the Alliance for Progress, but they believed that the administration was obsessed with Castro. They also discounted the threat of Cuban communism to their counties and the hemisphere. The Kennedy administration would not, however, trust any progressive leader or group deemed suspect on the issues of Castro and communism. In less than three years, the Kennedy administration authorized 163 major covert operations, many of them in Latin America.[18] It successfully undermined the authority of Frondizi, Goulart, Arévalo, and Jagan. These destabilization campaigns produced ironic results. The authoritarian, anti-Communist successors who gained power in Argentina, Brazil, Guatemala, and British Guiana opposed free elections and disdained the idea of social reform, the essence of the Alliance for Progress.

President Kennedy signaled his views early in his tenure when he listed U.S. policy options in the aftermath of the May 30, 1961, assassination of the Dominican Republic's vicious, right-wing dictator, Rafael Trujillo. Both the Eisenhower and Kennedy administrations had authorized the CIA to make contact with Trujillo's enemies. The assassins carried pistols and carbines supplied by the CIA. They riddled the dictator's body with twenty-seven rounds of ammunition. Both administrations had pressured Trujillo, a longtime ally, to leave the country and seek a comfortable exile. U.S. officials worried that desperate Dominicans would turn to political extremism and communism if not released from Trujillo's tyranny. They foresaw history repeating itself, reasoning that Cubans had turned to Fidel Castro when they saw no end to the dictatorship of the U.S. ally, Fulgencio Batista. When the defiant Trujillo rejected the U.S. demands, the Eisenhower administration broke diplomatic relations, imposed economic sanctions on the island country, and contacted men prepared to eliminate Trujillo. President Kennedy continued that policy. However, chaos ensued in the Dominican Republic after Trujillo's death. The dictator's son, known as "Ramfis," seized power and captured and tortured his father's enemies. Kennedy speculated what policy he should now pursue. According to presidential aide Schlesinger, the president said, "There are three possibilities in descending order of preference: a decent, democratic regime, a continuation of the Trujillo regime, or a Castro regime. We ought to aim at the first, but we really can't renounce the second until we are sure that we can avoid the third."[19]

Kennedy's memorable remark about the descending order of possibilities on the post-Trujillo era proved to be a reliable guide to what choices the administration made in the Dominican Republic and throughout the hemisphere. In the case of the Dominican Republic, the administration used extreme pressure, which included shows of U.S. naval and air force, to force the Trujillo family out of the country in late 1961. Ramfis Trujillo slipped away on his yacht, bringing along his father's refrigerated body and bags full of money. Thereafter, the Kennedy administration arranged for a transition government and supervised a fair presidential election in late 1962, which saw the election of Juan Bosch, an intellectual and poet. President Bosch lasted only nine months in office, however, before being overthrown by a right-wing, reactionary coalition in September 1963. Whereas the Kennedy administration did not encourage this *golpe de estado*, or "blow to the state," it did little to save President Bosch and ultimately decided to recognize the Dominican junta. It was disappointed that Bosch had not outlawed the Communist Party and imprisoned Dominican radicals. President Bosch had reasoned that after three decades of tyranny, freedom of expression and association should be respected. President Kennedy's major priority for the Dominican Republic was not, however, safeguarding civil liberties. He repeatedly told aides, "We don't want to have another Cuba come out of the Dominican Republic." By November 1963 U.S. policy toward the Dominican Republic had come full circle. U.S. officials prepared to deal with men such as Col. Elías Wessin y Wessin, who trained under Trujillo, pilfered public funds, and indiscriminately condemned all opponents as "Communists."[20]

VENEZUELA

Kennedy's formula for descending order of possibilities can be further examined by looking at U.S. relations with Venezuela and Brazil. The president embraced a decent democrat in Venezuela in President Rómulo Betancourt (1959–1964), a social reformer and ardent anti-Communist. As Kennedy once proclaimed, President Betancourt represented "all that we admire in a political leader," and his reform program served as "a symbol of what we wish for our own country and for our sister republics." Kennedy exceeded diplomatic niceties because he trusted the Venezuelan, enjoyed his company, and knew that Betancourt believed in the Alliance for Progress. He also judged Betancourt a fellow Cold Warrior under assault from the international Communist movement. President Kennedy always found time and resources to support those types of Latin American leaders.[21]

Although rich in oil resources, Venezuela had deep social inequities and an authoritarian political past. Prior to 1959, it had only one brief experiment with democracy (1945–1948). Venezuelan political elites had not invested the nation's oil revenues, which became substantial in the 1920s, toward improving the health, education, and welfare of the population. Beginning in 1928, Betancourt, as a university student, led protests against the injustice and unfairness of Venezuelan society. Other than between 1945 and 1948, years known in Venezuela as the *trienio*, Betancourt spent much of the post-1928 period in exile in Latin America and the United States. His political ideas evolved over time. Once associated with the Communist Party, he became an evolutionary social reformer, founding Acción Democrática (Democratic Action), a secular political party dedicated to transforming Venezuelan society. While in exile in the 1950s, he associated with U.S. liberals in the Democratic Party. When mass protests toppled the Marcos Pérez Jiménez regime in 1958, Betancourt returned in triumph and secured an overwhelming electoral victory.

Betancourt presided over a turbulent Venezuela. Under assault from the political right and left, he suspended constitutional guarantees five times, 778 out of the 1,847 days he was in office. Betancourt especially focused on his leftist enemies, members of the Venezuelan Communist Party and the larger Movimiento de Izquierda Revolucionaria (Movement of the Revolutionary Left, or MIR). The MIR was inspired by the Cuban Revolution and covertly aided at times by Cuba. Nonetheless, a CIA study concluded that MIR members "ran their own shows," were a "home-grown revolutionary organization," and could be described as an "extreme-nationalist, revolutionary nationalist movement." MIR fighters, who numbered between 1,000 and 2,000, created havoc by waging guerrilla war in the countryside and carrying out urban terrorism. Betancourt and the Venezuelan military and police gradually suppressed the rebellion.

While fighting insurgents, Betancourt also performed within the spirit of the Alliance for Progress. He and his successor toiled diligently for the poor, resettling approximately 160,000 families on their own farms, allocating budgetary expenditures to health and education, and cutting unemployment. But Venezuela never hit the Alliance's target of 2.5 percent annual growth, and 75 percent of Venezuelan youth still did not complete the sixth grade. Economic growth stagnated because of the declining price of oil in the 1960s. Despite the uneven economic performance, Venezuelans participated in a political victory in the 1960s. On December 1, 1963, over 90 percent of the electorate voted, ignoring threats from leftists to shoot anyone who came to polling places. Raúl Leoni (1964–1969), Betancourt's political associate, secured a plurality of votes and was inaugurated on March 11, 1964. For the first time in its history, Venezuela had a peaceful transfer of power from one popularly elected leader to another.[22]

The Kennedy administration vowed to do anything "within reason" to support President Betancourt. Despite intelligence assessments showing that Venezuelan radicals acted independently, the administration judged Betancourt to

President Kennedy meets with a Venezuelan couple at a land redistribution ceremony in La Morita, Venezuela, on December 16, 1961. Also present is President Rómulo Betancourt (dark glasses) of Venezuela. President Kennedy took a personal interest in helping the poor of the world. The Alliance for Progress aimed at transforming the socioeconomic structure of Latin America. Venezuela was one of the few Latin American countries that achieved some Alliance goals during the 1960s. (John F. Kennedy Presidential Library and Museum, Boston)

be Castro's "number one target." During the early 1960s, Venezuela received over $200 million in loans and grants from the United States to finance public housing and public works projects. The administration further backed Venezuela's requests for an additional $200 million in loans from international agencies such as the Inter-American Development Bank and World Bank. President Kennedy also invited Venezuelan political and military leaders to the White House and urged them to respect constitutional procedures. He also frequently consulted with Betancourt on inter-American issues and established a direct telephone line between the White House and Miraflores, the Venezuelan presidential palace.

To help keep the Venezuelan military both loyal to Betancourt and busily fighting insurgents, the Kennedy administration authorized over $60 million in credits and grants for military equipment and training. Venezuelan military officers attended the Special Warfare School at Fort Bragg, North Carolina, and took counterinsurgency courses at Fort Gulick in the Canal Zone. The U.S. military mission, which was the largest in Latin America, trained men in anti-guerrilla tactics and, as in South Vietnam, assigned U.S. personnel to advise in combat operations against the insurgents.

President Kennedy admired President Betancourt's courage and commitment to the goals of the Alliance for Progress. But he especially appreciated Betancourt's fervent anticommunism. Betancourt reportedly knew of and supported the Bay of Pigs invasion. He broke relations with Cuba and supported the U.S. crusade to drive Cuba out of the Organization of American States (OAS). During the missile crisis, Venezuela held a seat on the UN Security Council. The Venezuelan ambassador firmly defended the military quarantine of Cuba, and Venezuela sent two destroyers to assist the U.S. Navy in enforcing it. Betancourt also permitted anti-Castro Cubans to operate in Venezuela. And he allegedly discussed with U.S. officials ways to arrange the assassination of Fidel Castro. President Kennedy always had time and found money for decent democrats who shared his loathing of Castro.[23]

Brazil

By comparison, President Kennedy turned against the Brazilian leaders, Jânio Quadros (1961) and his successor João Goulart (1961–1964). Both Brazilian presidents supported the Alliance for Progress. But the Kennedy administration condemned the constitutional leaders of Latin America's largest and most populous nation because Brazil refused to break diplomatic relations with Cuba and because it established commercial ties with the Soviet Union. Presidents Quadros and Goulart also tolerated domestic leftists. The Kennedy administration responded to Brazil's deviant behavior with a concerted effort to shape the international and domestic policies of Brazil. It organized non-democratic forces in Brazil. Controlling Brazil would help determine whether the United States maintained its sphere of influence in Latin America. As State Department planners once noted, "If U.S. policy fails in Brazil, it will become extremely difficult to achieve success elsewhere in Latin America." President Kennedy agreed, adding that "Latin America is critical to [the] West" and "Brazil is [the] key country in Latin America."[24]

The democratic leaders of the southern cone countries—Argentina, Brazil, Chile, and Uruguay—rejected the U.S. threat assessment of "Castro/communism." Castro ruled a small island country of impoverished sugar workers thousands of miles away from the glittering metropolises of Buenos Aires, Montevideo, Rio de Janeiro, and Santiago. Southern cone leaders stood firmly on the principle of nonintervention and argued that sanctions against Cuba "would only serve to push it irrevocably into [the] hands of the Sino-Soviet bloc." These leaders further worried that a Cold War confrontation with Cuba would exacerbate political tensions in their countries, exciting extremists on both sides of the political spectrum. As President Goulart once put it, Castro had become a "dramatic symbol of revolutionary aspirations of underprivileged masses throughout Latin America." If the United States were patient, the Castro regime would "deteriorate under its own weight." But the United States would do a great disservice by agitating the Cuban problem because "Latin American masses are instinctive[ly] on [the] side of tiny Cuba whenever it [is] menaced by [the] colossus of the North."[25]

The Kennedy administration, believing that South Americans were naïve about the Communist threat, dismissed such analyses. The administration also discounted other Brazilian facts. Brazil supported the United States during the Cuban missile crisis, and President Goulart proposed solutions to the crisis. Brazilians pointed out that there had been no known case of a Brazilian training in Cuba for subversive activities. To be sure, Brazil established relations with the Soviet Union in 1961, permitted the Soviets to stage a trade fair in Rio de Janeiro in 1962, and signed a commercial agreement in April 1963. Brazilian leaders defended these new ties by citing public opinion polls, which showed strong popular support for an independent foreign policy. In any case, Brazil had hardly become tied to the Soviet bloc. Soviet-Brazilian trade grew from five million to sixty-six million rubles between 1959 and 1963. But that commerce represented only 3 percent of Brazil's trade. The balance of trade favored Brazil because the Soviets offered goods of poor quality.

The Kennedy administration first tried to modify Brazil's international behavior by offering rewards. In March 1961 it proffered the new Quadros administration a $100 million gift to help it import capital goods and then asked for Brazilian support for the impending Bay of Pigs invasion. The U.S. emissary predicted an "early explosion" in the Caribbean. As outgoing ambassador to Brazil John Moors Cabot recalled, "It was obvious it was just a bribe. I mean that's what it amounted to. And Quadros, with increasing irritation, said no."[26] In May 1961 President Kennedy made his pitch. Meeting with the Brazilian finance minister, Kennedy observed that the United States had just agreed with the International Monetary Fund to give Brazil $335 million in credits. The president then lectured the Brazilian. In negotiating the loan, the United States "had completely avoided mention of political factors," but the Brazilians had to understand that "the United States was interested in the Castro regime because it is a weapon used by international communism in an effort to take over additional Latin American countries." Kennedy lamented that it would be impossible to drive Cuba out of the OAS unless the major Latin American nations agreed "on the basic analysis of the situation."[27] Quadros again refused to change Brazil's independent foreign policy, and he further irritated the United States by hosting Ché Guevara and awarding him Brazil's Order of the Southern Cross.

On August 25, 1961, Quadros unexpectedly resigned and his vice president, João Goulart, eventually succeeded him as president. A career politician, Goulart had served as vice president to President Juscelino Kubitschek (1956–1961) and as a minister of labor. A fiery speaker and populist, Goulart identified himself with the nation's powerless. He had various ties to leftist groups, including the Brazilian Communist Party. Brazilian conservatives, including military officers, distrusted Goulart and initially tried to block his ascension to power. Goulart took office on September 2, after the Brazilian Congress passed a constitutional amendment curbing the powers of the presidency. He regained full presidential powers in January 1963, however, as the result of a plebiscite.

The Kennedy administration shared the Brazilian military's suspicion of President Goulart, interpreting his political maneuvers through a Cold War prism. He sustained that suspicion by maintaining President Quadros's independent foreign policy and refusing to break relations with Cuba. He exasperated U.S. officials with his fickle and inconstant fiscal and monetary policies that swallowed up substantial U.S. aid, which amounted to over $700 million between 1961 and 1963. Other sins included expropriating the U.S. telecommunications giant International Telephone and Telegraph, arousing labor and student groups with inflammatory speeches, and appointing cabinet ministers with politically radical sentiments. He also called for higher prices for primary products, implicitly suggesting that better terms of trade, not the Alliance for Progress, would generate the economic growth that Latin America needed. In short, an irresponsible President Goulart seemingly opposed all U.S. objectives in Latin America and, at best, was indifferent to the international Communist conspiracy. The new U.S. ambassador in Brasília, Lincoln Gordon, predicted that Goulart intended to stay in power beyond his term and "take Brazil into the Communist camp."[28]

Kennedy administration officials had available to them other analyses of President Goulart's intentions. Juscelino Kubitschek, the former president, twice met with President Kennedy, assuring him that Goulart was not a Marxist, that he supported the Alliance for Progress, and that Goulart had a "genuine liking" for Kennedy. President Kubitschek, who spurred the building of the futuristic city of Brasília and had called for a Marshall Plan for Latin America, had credibility in the United States. Goulart himself tried to reassure Kennedy when he visited the White House in April 1962. CIA analysts also presented nuanced views of Goulart. They discounted the view that Goulart had a radical agenda for Brazil. The CIA essentially saw Goulart as an "opportunist" who was intent on preserving political power. Other administration officials argued that Goulart had to ally with political leftists because he accurately feared that conservatives, including military generals, plotted against him. These discerning interpretations of Brazilian politics failed to persuade the administration to abandon its Cold War verities. As President Kennedy remarked, the situation in Brazil "worried him more than that in Cuba."[29]

Several scholars have detailed how the United States destabilized the Goulart government. One scholar dubbed the covert campaign "the quiet intervention." In December 1962 President Kennedy dispatched his brother, the attorney general, to Brazil to confront Goulart over his "putting those leftists and Communists in positions of power." Although the three-hour meeting ended inconclusively, Robert Kennedy decided that the United States could not trust the Brazilian president. Beyond reprimanding Goulart, the administration manipulated the Brazilian political scene. In 1962 the CIA spent $5 million funding the campaigns of candidates for 15 federal Senate seats, 8 state governorships, 250 federal deputy seats, and some 600 seats for state legislatures. The CIA, working through U.S. labor unions, also covertly funded Brazilian trade union groups, encouraging them to organize strikes and demonstrations against Goulart. The U.S. unions coordinated their intervention with the U.S. embassy and the Brazilian military. The Kennedy administration's anti-Goulart campaign included undermining the cherished Alliance for Progress. The administration funneled Alliance funds to conservative state governors friendly to the United States and hostile to Goulart. These governors had records of ignoring the needs of the Brazilian poor.[30]

The Kennedy administration also tasked two study groups to explore ways to strengthen U.S. ties with the Brazilian military to prepare for a "more friendly alternative regime." The administration reached out directly to Brazilian generals when in 1962 it dispatched Col. Vernon Walters to Brazil as a military attaché in the U.S. embassy. Walters, who was fluent in Portuguese, had served with Brazilian officers during World War II, when Brazil sent an expeditionary force to fight in Italy. As Walters later recalled, somebody "high in the administration" briefed him that President Kennedy would not be averse to seeing Goulart overthrown and replaced by an anti-Communist who supported U.S. international policies. Walters's circumspect language belied the extent of his activities in Brazil. He developed a social relationship with Gen. Humberto de Alencar Castello Branco, who would lead the military conspiracy against Goulart. Walters was told of the military's plans in minute detail and passed the intelligence on to Ambassador Gordon and through Gordon on to the White House. Walters also relayed the Brazilian military's request for logistical support from the United States. After receiving the requests, Walters would tell his Brazilian friends that he "had no authority to discuss such matters."[31] Walter's playacting allowed Ambassador Gordon and officials in Washington to offer "plausible denials" that they had encouraged the Brazilian military to strike.

On April 2, 1964, Brazilian generals disposed of Goulart and established a military rule that would last until 1985. The new Johnson administration had prepositioned war matériel and readied a U.S. naval task force for duty off the coast of Brazil, in case the generals encountered resistance to the destruction of the Brazilian democracy. It granted diplomatic recognition to the new interim government eighteen hours after its installation. Although the overthrow of Goulart came about early in the Johnson presidency, it was the fulfillment of one of President Kennedy's policies. Robert Kennedy expressed satisfaction with the military action, noting that "Brazil would have gone Communist" if Goulart had not been deposed. National Security Adviser McGeorge Bundy emphasized that he, Lincoln Gordon, Dean Rusk, and George Ball, "all Kennedy men," supported the policy.[32]

The overthrow of President Goulart proved a momentous event in the history of Latin America in the Cold War. In the name of order, progress, and anticommunism, the generals gave Brazilians two decades of savage rule. Their dismantling of the Brazilian constitution polarized politics in the country. Strikes, demonstrations, bombings, terrorism, and guerrilla warfare broke out in the country. The generals responded brutally, murdering and torturing opponents. In December 1968 Gen. Arturo da Costa e Silva, who succeeded Gen. Castello Branco, issued Institutional Act (No. 5), which abolished Congress and transformed Brazil into a military dictatorship. Criticism of the government became a national security issue subject to military justice. The Brazilian military's seizure of power created an ironic "domino effect" in South America. By the mid-1970s, generals ruled throughout the continent. For about a decade, the generals oversaw good economic growth, known as "the Brazilian miracle." This "miracle," which vanished by the end of the 1970s, produced a grossly inequitable Brazilian society. Nonetheless, generals in Argentina, Chile, Uruguay, and elsewhere adopted the Brazilian model by abolishing democracy, smashing "Communists," and promising economic growth. In Argentina, the generals and their minions may have murdered as many as 30,000 Argentines in what was labeled "the dirty war" (*la guerra sucia*). In the early twenty-first century, South Americans are still trying to come to terms with these horrors.

As these gross violations of basic human rights unfolded, remnants of the Kennedy administration reacted with shock. Within a month after the attack on Goulart, Ambassador Gordon confessed "to considerable dismay" to learn that the generals he embraced displayed reactionary colors. One of their first acts had been to cancel for ten years the political rights of President Kubitschek. In 1965 Robert Kennedy, now a senator from New York, complained about U.S. friendship with Brazil. As the repression mounted, Washington comforted itself with the fantasy that Brazilians could not be expected to conform to the standards of Western civilization. Under the signature of Dean Rusk, one State Department officer told the embassy in Brasília, "We realize that Brazil's needs and performance cannot be measured against North American or northwest

European standards of constitutional democracy, nor even easily expressed in Anglo-Saxon terms."[33] Such a grotesque assessment represented a complete repudiation of the promise of the Alliance for Progress.

Conclusion

The course and conduct of U.S. policy in Brazil was not a unique feature of President Kennedy's approach to Latin America. The U.S. intervention in British Guiana represented another appalling story. The administration perceived Cheddi Jagan, the popularly elected leader of British Guiana, in the same way it judged President Goulart: he was either a Communist or blind to the international Communist conspiracy. Jagan and his wife were also friends of Fidel Castro. Jagan had strong electoral support from the majority community of Indo-Guyanese, whose ancestors came from contemporary India and Pakistan. The administration pressured the British to rig an election that would ensure that Forbes Burnham (1964–1985), the leader of the Afro-Guyanese community, would become the leader of an independent Guyana. Burnham created a vicious and venal dictatorship that lasted until his death. His misrule transformed Guyana into one of the poorest countries in the Western Hemisphere. A despicable racist, Burnham persecuted the majority Indo-Guyanese population. Many terrified Indo-Guyanese were forced to emigrate. In 1990 presidential aide and Kennedy biographer Arthur Schlesinger publicly apologized to Jagan for his hero's hostility. An intense fear of communism had warped the Kennedy administration's thinking. As Schlesinger admitted, "A great injustice was done to Cheddi Jagan."[34]

President John F. Kennedy offered an idealistic program for Latin America. His dogged determination to fight the Cold War in "the most dangerous area in the world" led him and his administration to undermine the noble vision of a democratic, economically progressive, and socially just Latin America.

CHAPTER 6

VIETNAM

FOR THOSE WHO LECTURE about the American experience in Vietnam (1945–1975), a question inevitably arises from the audience. Young students and adults ask, "If President Kennedy had lived, would he have plunged the United States into a full-scale war in Vietnam?" An answer would necessarily have to be speculative; historians cannot predict the future. Such uncertainty has not, however, prevented scholars from offering their learned opinions. Biographer Robert Dallek offered that John Kennedy was a "reluctant warrior" who could not imagine that more U.S. troops would die in the Vietnam War than in any other foreign conflict except World War II. Historian David Kaiser conceded that we can never know what Kennedy would have done about Vietnam, but that the president consistently rejected advice to send U.S. combat troops to Vietnam. Professor James Giglio, the author of a dependable study on the Kennedy presidency, echoed Dallek and Kaiser when he noted that it was "hard to imagine" that Kennedy would have sent over 500,000 troops to Vietnam. Giglio qualified that assertion by adding that Kennedy accepted the central premises of the containment doctrine. Fredrik Logevall, a scholar who has written sympathetically about Kennedy's Vietnam dilemma and critically of Lyndon Johnson's Vietnam decisions, has observed the Vietnam problem that Kennedy left behind "was much larger than the one he inherited." The distinguished historian of U.S. foreign relations Robert Schulzinger succinctly charged that Kennedy bequeathed a "terrible legacy" to Johnson. George C. Herring, author of *America's Longest War*, the most influential study of the United States and Vietnam, agreed with Logevall and Schulzinger that Kennedy handed down to his successor "a problem eminently more dangerous than the one he had inherited." Herring further asserted, "There is no persuasive evidence that he [Kennedy] was committed to withdrawal."[1]

Inherent in the question about Kennedy and Vietnam is the belief that Kennedy was a special leader and that he would have shown good judgment and spared the United States from disaster. The U.S. effort to build and secure an independent non-Communist South Vietnam represented the signal U.S. policy failure of the Cold War and one of the most dreadful episodes in U.S. history. U.S. marines and soldiers used the ironic term "wasted" to characterize the death in combat of one of their comrades in Vietnam. Precious blood and treasure were indeed wasted in Vietnam. Between 1961 and 1973, the United States suffered over 350,000 physical casualties in Vietnam, with approximately 58,000 servicemen and women dying. The names of the dead are etched in black marble on the haunting Vietnam Memorial in Washington, D.C.

Mental casualties also mounted in Vietnam. U.S. troops entered a world of horror. As Lt. Philip Caputo of the Marine Corps recounted in his acclaimed memoir, *A Rumor of War* (1977), the conflict in Vietnam "combined the two most bitter forms of warfare, civil war and revolution, to which was added the ferocity of jungle war. Twenty years of terrorism and fratricide had obliterated most reference points from the country's moral map long before we arrived." Caputo and his platoon witnessed and participated in atrocities. After a napalm attack, Caputo recalled seeing "pigs eating roast people."[2] Such experiences left veterans deeply troubled. The Veterans Administration has estimated that up to 400,000 Vietnam veterans have experienced some form of post-traumatic stress disorder (PTSD). The United States spent over $120 billion in Vietnam and incurred massive future expenses in caring for the physically and mentally disabled veterans and in servicing the principal and interest on the money borrowed to fight the war.

The Vietnamese suffered great pain also. Perhaps as many as two million people, civilian and military, died and another 4.5 million were physically wounded from 1945 to 1975. Over 200,000 Vietnamese are listed as missing. The fighting and violence created a wasteland in Vietnam. With bombing campaigns such as "Rolling Thunder," the United States dropped over fifteen million tons of explosives on Vietnam, the equivalent of forty Hiroshima bombs. During the "Christmas bombing" of 1972, U.S. bombers, principally B-52s, dropped more tonnage on Hanoi, the capital of North Vietnam, than Nazi Germany dropped on London between 1940 and 1945. U.S. planes also sprayed Vietnam with nineteen million gallons of defoliants, Agents Orange, White, and Blue, destroying 35 percent of Vietnam's hardwood forests. The toxins associated with the defoliants caused cancers, leukemia, and other maladies in both Americans and Vietnamese. And the dying and suffering continues. To their dismay and shock, international medical teams have discovered that Vietnamese who were not yet alive during the war years have deadly toxins in their bloodstreams because the toxins became rooted in Vietnam's ecosystem.[3]

The Vietnam War stands as a tragedy of epic proportions, considering the evolution of U.S. relations with Vietnam. In the first decade of the twenty-first century, Vietnam is a unified country under Communist rule. In 1994 the United States abandoned its trade embargo against Vietnam and the next year normalized diplomatic relations. Senators John Kerry (D-MA) and John McCain (R-AZ) led the movement for reconciliation. Kerry won combat decorations in Vietnam, and McCain had been a prisoner of war. In 1996 Douglas Peterson, another former prisoner of war, became the first U.S. ambassador to Hanoi. The United States subsequently extended "most-favored-nation" trading status to Vietnam and supported Vietnam's admission to the World Trade Organization (WTO). U.S.-Vietnamese trade amounted to $9.6 billion in 2006. Cold Warriors, such as Secretary of Defense Robert McNamara, attended scholarly conferences in Vietnam and traded war stories with former adversaries, such as Gen. Vo Nguyen Giap. As one of the last acts of his presidency, Bill Clinton visited Vietnam and received a tumultuous welcome. In 2001 Secretary of State Colin Powell, who served two combat tours in Vietnam, returned to the country and received a similarly warm reception. These official visits also reflected geopolitical concerns. Both countries are wary of the growing power of China, Vietnam's neighbor. That the United States and Communist Vietnam have developed a peaceful and prosperous relationship has given deeper meaning to the term "wasted" as a metaphor for death in Vietnam.

John F. Kennedy did not cause this death, destruction, and utter waste. The Johnson and Richard M. Nixon administrations bear prime responsibility for the U.S. war in Vietnam. But actions that Kennedy and his advisers took may have made it more likely that Johnson and Nixon would seek military solutions in Vietnam. Johnson and Nixon regularly defended their war policies by claiming they were upholding their predecessors' decisions, including those of Kennedy. Before musing about what Kennedy might have done in Vietnam during a second presidential term, it is essential to analyze the choices the president and his advisers made between 1961 and 1963. Any fair examination of the Kennedy presidency must assess Kennedy's role in precipitating the U.S. disaster in Vietnam.

Background

The U.S. decision to build, fortify, and preserve an independent, non-Communist South Vietnam preceded the Kennedy presidency. Both Presidents Harry S. Truman and Dwight D. Eisenhower had made Vietnam a national security issue. Since the end of World War II, the United States had opposed the revolutionary movement in Vietnam led by Ho Chi Minh, a patriot, a nationalist, and a Communist.

Since the mid-nineteenth century, Vietnam had been a colonial possession of France. The Vietnamese, who had a 2,000-year history of resistance to Chinese domination of their culture, fell under the control of the French because they lacked the technology and organizational prowess of their European occupiers. Ho Chi Minh and his followers, known as the Vietminh, would ultimately free the Vietnamese from colonialism. Ho (1890–1969) came from a traditional, patriotic Vietnamese family that resisted colonialism. His birth name was Nguyen Tat Thanh; he later took the pseudonym of Ho Chi Minh, meaning "he who enlightens." Encouraged by his father to learn French in school, Ho left Vietnam in 1911 and did not return for three decades. He traveled the world, often working on ships, and spent time in New York City. Ho became acquainted with doctrines that addressed issues of imperialism and socioeconomic inequality. In Paris during World War I, Ho joined the French Socialist Party and applauded Woodrow Wilson and his Fourteen Points (1918), which seemed to promise national self-determination. Ho wanted to discuss the devolution of French colonialism and actually tried to meet President Wilson during the Versailles Peace Conference (1919). Ho learned that French socialists and Wilson had only a theoretical interest in the liberation of the Vietnamese. A founding member of the French Communist Party, he went to the Soviet Union in the 1920s to study Communist doctrine. Ho became convinced that the Bolshevik Revolution of 1917, led by Vladimir Lenin and Leon Trotsky, would overthrow the imperial system. He also persuaded himself that communism offered solutions to Vietnam's poverty and backwardness. In exile, often in China, Ho organized the Vietnamese Communist Party, and in 1940 he slipped back into his homeland.[4] By any definition, Ho Chi Minh had become an "international Communist."

Ho's commitment to communism was intertwined with love for his country. During World War II, Ho organized the Vietminh movement to end Japanese and French domination of Vietnam. As part of their imperial drive through Asia, the Japanese militarists had pushed the French colonialists aside and taken control of the country. The French did not resist Japanese aggression and collaborated with the Japanese. Ho appealed to Vietnamese of all political persuasions to join the Vietminh in a political and military effort to secure liberation. The Vietminh agitated for independence and carried out sabotage activities against both the Japanese and the French. One of the many ironies of the U.S. experience in Vietnam is that the United States aided the Vietminh during the World War II. The Office of Strategic Service (OSS) infiltrated men into Vietnam. The U.S. officers trained Vietminh soldiers and provided arms and munitions. The officers reported favorably about Ho, the Vietminh, and their anti-Japanese campaign. Maj. Archimedes Patti of the OSS testified, for example, about the "gung-ho" spirit of the Vietminh soldiers.[5]

Vietnamese-American cooperation took another remarkable step in the immediate aftermath of World War II. With Japan defeated and the French discredited, Ho declared Vietnam's independence on September 2, 1945. OSS officers were guests of honor at the independence ceremony in Hanoi. Ho borrowed directly from Thomas Jefferson, affirming that "all men are created equal" and that they possessed the "unalienable rights" of life, liberty, and the pursuit of happiness. Ho's choice of words reflected not only idealism but also a realistic appraisal of the balance of power. The Vietminh needed U.S. support to secure Vietnam's independence and U.S. money for economic development. The United States had reaffirmed the Wilsonian vision of national self-determination in the Atlantic Charter (1941) and in the San Francisco meeting that organized the new United Nations (1945). As the ultimate winner of the war, the United States had the power to refashion the world.

As a matter of principle, the Truman and Eisenhower administrations opposed colonialism, but both administrations supported the French, who waged a pitiless, colonial war against the Vietminh from 1946 to 1954. The U.S. calculation of the balance of power differed from that of the Vietminh. France was a Cold War ally who could be used to contain the Soviet Union in Europe. Moreover, Ho and other Vietminh leaders, such as Pham Van Dong and General Giap, were Communists who demanded a revolution in Vietnam. Throughout the Cold War, U.S. leaders consistently rejected the argument that a political figure could be both a Communist and a nationalist. They assumed that triumph of communism in any country inevitably accrued to the benefit of the Soviet Union. And Ho had undeniable international Communist connections. Between 1945 and 1949, Ho repeatedly tried to convince the United States that he was an independent Communist not beholden to the Soviet Union. He sent a series of letters to President Truman, calling on the United States "as guardians and champions of world justice" to force the French out of Vietnam. He reminded President Truman that the United States had granted independence to its colony, the Philippines (1946), and "like the Philippines our goal is full independence and full cooperation with United States." In discussions with U.S. diplomats who came to Vietnam in late 1946, Ho assured them that Vietnam would welcome U.S. investment capital, that he understood the U.S. dislike of communism, and that national independence remained his primary goal. These diplomats accepted Ho's points. Abbot Moffat, the chief of the State Department's Division of Southeast Asian Affairs, reported that the Vietminh were "nationalists first" and "that an effective nationalist state is a prerequisite to any attempt at developing a communist state—which objective must for the time being be secondary."[6]

President Truman and his secretaries of state, George Marshall and Dean Acheson, did not respond to Ho's letters and rejected the advice of their subordinates, who were arguing that Vietnam be understood within its own historical context. By backing the French, the Truman administration was establishing a precedent that its presidential successors would follow, placing Vietnam, a regional issue, within the global context of the Soviet-American confrontation. The Truman administration initially provided diplomatic support to the French and, beginning in 1950, military aid. Between 1950 and 1954, the United States sent $2 billion in military aid, paying for 75 percent of the French colonial war. The Vietminh's acceptance of support and military aid from the Soviet Union and the new People's Republic of China (1949) solidified the U.S. conviction that the war in Vietnam, like conflicts in Greece (1947) and Korea (1950), was part of the global struggle against international communism.

U.S. military aid could not save the French. Resorting to guerrilla war tactics, the Vietminh gradually wore French forces down. The Vietminh also built a broad base of political support among the rural poor. By 1954 the Vietminh controlled perhaps 75 percent of the countryside. The exhausted French gave up, after suffering a severe conventional defeat at the battle of Dien Bien Phu in May 1954. Thereafter, at a conference in Geneva, the great powers—the United States, the United Kingdom, the Soviet Union, and Communist China—liquidated French colonialism. Under the terms of the Geneva Accords (1954), foreign forces would withdraw from Vietnam, the country would be temporarily divided at the 17th parallel, the Vietminh would withdraw its troops to the northern half of the country, and a unification election with international observers would be held within two years. At Geneva, Ho and his followers accepted less than they had won on the battlefield. They had been pressured by their allies to compromise. Both the Soviet Union and China pursued their own national interests rather than international Communist solidarity. China historically had opposed a strong Vietnam on its border. Nonetheless, informed international observers expected the Vietminh to dominate the forthcoming national election. The Vietminh had freed the Vietnamese from the ignominy of colonial rule.

The Eisenhower administration declined to sign the Geneva Accords, not wanting to be perceived as endorsing a Communist triumph. It saw a window of opportunity in the temporary division of the country. Pushing the French aside, the administration backed the installation of Ngo Dinh Diem (1954–1963) first as prime minister and then as chief of state in a new South Vietnam. Diem had first come to U.S. attention during the Truman years. He seemed the ideal leader from the U.S. perspective, for Diem professed to be an anti-French nationalist and an anti-Communist. Born in 1901, Diem was the son of a scholar–civil servant, or mandarin. His ancestors had converted to Catholicism, and Diem was a fervent Catholic. In the 1920s and 1930s Diem served in the French colonial bureaucracy. He proved efficient in rounding up local Communists, but he irritated his French masters because he called for local self-rule. During World War II, he lobbied for Vietnam's freedom but declined to join the Vietminh. The Vietminh subsequently imprisoned him. In 1946 Ho Chi Minh tried to persuade Diem to join his movement. The two Vietnamese quarreled, and Diem called Ho "a criminal who has burned and destroyed the country, and you have held me prisoner." During the colonial war, he went into exile in the United States. He won the backing of the influential Roman Catholic prelate, Cardinal Francis Spellman, a hard-line anti-Communist. Diem lived as a ward of Spellman in Maryknoll Seminary in New York. Through Cardinal Spellman, Diem met and impressed other prominent Catholics, including Joseph Kennedy, Senator Mike Mansfield (D-MN), and Representative Clement Zablocki (D-WI), the future chair of the U.S. House Foreign Affairs Committee.[7]

Diem became the U.S. man in Saigon, the capital of South Vietnam. Between 1954 and 1960, the Eisenhower administration supported Diem with $2 billion in aid, principally military assistance. By January 1961 there were 700 U.S. military advisers in South Vietnam working with Diem's troops. With the acquiescence of the Eisenhower administration, Diem rigged his own election, ignored the Geneva Accords call for a unification election, and launched a savage military campaign against South Vietnamese loyal to the Vietminh, communism, and the concept of national unification. Diem contemptuously referred to these opponents as the "Viet Cong." The Eisenhower administration judged Diem a peculiar person. He tended to answer questions with speeches that lasted for hours. Diem also had an elitist sense of government—the Vietnamese should trust in the rule of learned mandarins like himself. Nonetheless, the Eisenhower administration embraced Diem because he seemed patriotic and courageous. He also initially created a sense of order in Vietnam, suppressing criminal gangs and warlords. Between 1954 and 1961, the Eisenhower administration committed the United States to the preservation of an independent, non-Communist South Vietnam under the leadership of President Diem.[8]

Ngo Dinh Diem's regime had grave shortcomings, however. Diem commanded little popular support because he did not lower taxes or redistribute land to impoverished peasants—the majority of the population. He further alienated peasants with his "agroville" program, which forced them out of their ancestral villages into defended villages. To peasants it seemed as if they had been forced into concentration camps. Diem coddled Vietnamese landlords, including those who had sided with the French. His policies favored urban areas over the countryside. Diem also staffed his government with Catholics. Catholics represented only about 10 percent of the population. Most Vietnamese associated with Buddhism. A bachelor, Diem relied on his power-mad brother, Ngo Dinh Nhu, and his wife, Madam Nhu, a fanatical Catholic, for advice.

Diem had fostered the preconditions for the civil war that erupted in South Vietnam in the late 1950s. Ho Chi Minh and his Communist allies in the North had not vigorously protested the cancellation of the national election. The Communist Party initially focused on building communism in North Vietnam, through the forced, brutal collectivization of agriculture. But the South Vietnamese Communists, the Viet Cong, pleaded for Hanoi's help, fearing that Diem's U.S.-equipped army would annihilate them. In 1959 the North authorized its allies in the South to initiate armed resistance to the Diem regime. Southerners, who trained in North Vietnam, began to infiltrate back into their native villages. North Vietnamese troops did not, however, cross into South Vietnam. In 1960 Hanoi further instructed its southern brethren to form a political coalition with the non-Communist opponents of the Diem regime. Thereafter, the power of the Viet Cong and its political arm, the National Liberation Front (NLF), grew rapidly. The Viet Cong cadre won support in villages when it executed landlords and redistributed land. Nationalists also sided with the NLF because they yearned for unification and rejected Diem's authoritarian ways. Buddhists resented the growing U.S. presence, fearing the cultural pollution of the country.[9] By January 1961 the Diem government had only a shaky hold on power in South Vietnam.

Initial Decisions, 1961

President John Kennedy did not consistently focus on the insurgency in South Vietnam during his one thousand days in office. Relations with the Soviet Union, the crises over Berlin and Cuba, and the Alliance for Progress dominated his agenda. He did, however, make two fateful choices about Vietnam during his tenure. In November 1961 he authorized a significant expansion of U.S. military advisers and aid to Vietnam. And in August 1963 he approved a policy that would lead to the overthrow of President Diem on November 1, 1963. Both decisions had the effect of deepening the U.S. commitment to South Vietnam.

As a congressman and senator, Kennedy had gained knowledge and formed opinions about Vietnam. In 1951 he toured the region during the colonial war. He rejected the rationales of colonialism, and although he opposed communism, he questioned whether the United States should ally itself "to a desperate effort of a French regime to hang on to the remnants of empire." In 1953, like other leading Catholic politicians, he met with Ngo Dinh Diem in the United States. He thereafter supported Eisenhower's containment policy in South Vietnam. Senator Kennedy declared that South Vietnam represented "the cornerstone of the Free World in Southeast Asia, the keystone to the arch, the finger in the dike" and predicted that Asian nations would be endangered if "the Red tide of communism" flowed into Vietnam. In essence, he embraced the "domino theory" that President Eisenhower pro-nounced in 1954 in regard to Vietnam. Vietnam was vital to the defense of the non-Communist world. Kennedy also did not criticize the violation of the Geneva Accords by the United States and President Diem.[10]

During the 1960 presidential campaign, Vietnam was not a central part of the Kennedy-Nixon debate. President Eisenhower also did not raise the issue of Vietnam directly in his two briefings for the president-elect. But after reading analyses of the growing strength of the Viet Cong, President Kennedy realized that the United States had alarming military and political problems in South Vietnam. His first stop-gap measure was to approve on May 11, 1961, National Security Action Memorandum (NSAM) 52, which reaffirmed the Eisenhower policy "to prevent Communist domination of South Vietnam." Kennedy authorized U.S. support for increasing Diem's forces from 170,000 to 200,000 troops.[11] He also sent Vice President Lyndon Johnson to Saigon to signal solidarity with President Diem. Over the next twenty-seven months, Kennedy repeatedly sent fact-finding teams to Vietnam. After a few interviews and brief visits, the teams inevitably came back to Washington with recommendations that reaffirmed the existing viewpoints of the individual investigators. Once, when he received vastly different assessments from career diplomat Joseph Mendenhall and Gen. Victor Krulak, the president wryly asked, "Did you two gentlemen visit the same country?"[12]

In his own characteristically outrageous way, Vice President Johnson pointed to the fundamental dilemma of U.S. policy in South Vietnam. Johnson created a sensation in Vietnam, barnstorming the country as if he were running for reelection in the Hill Country of Texas, "pressing the flesh" on the surprised residents of Saigon. He fulsomely praised Diem, almost suggesting that his visage should be carved on Mt. Rushmore. In one toast, he called Diem "the Winston Churchill of Southeast Asia." In an off-the-record interview with correspondent Stanley Karnow, Johnson proved truthful, noting, "Shit, man, he's the only boy we got out there." Johnson's official report politely concluded that the "existing government in Saigon is the only realistic alternative to Viet Minh control." President Kennedy fundamentally agreed, observing in 1962, "Diem is Diem and the best we've got." Put another way, U.S. policy was "We must sink or swim with Ngo Dinh Diem," a ditty composed by a sarcastic but insightful *New York Times* journalist.[13] The United States had tied its international credibility to a leader who was patriotic, brave, and personally honest. But President Diem was remote, authoritarian, and insensitive to the suffering of Vietnamese peasants.

President Kennedy attached the United States to Diem in a tangible way on November 22, 1961. The president had received a report written by Gen. Maxwell Taylor and Walt W. Rostow, who had conducted an inspection mission in Vietnam in late October. Both men had well-deserved reputations for favoring military solutions to problems. Taylor had denounced President Eisenhower for limiting military spending in the 1950s. Rostow, who was identified with "nation building," had, in a speech to the Green Berets in June, confidently predicted that the United States could help Vietnam move through the "revolution of modernization." In their fifty-five-page report, the two presidential advisers predictably called for an intensive U.S. effort to save the embattled President Diem. They identified South Vietnam as a critical Cold War battleground, where the Communists were trying "a new and dangerous" technique. Soviet Premier Khrushchev saw Vietnam as a place for his "'wars of liberation' which are really para-wars of guerrilla aggression." The United States could, however, defeat this aggression and build a sturdy, self-reliant nation by offering a significant increase in aid and advice. U.S. advisory groups placed within the South Vietnamese government could identify and solve critical domestic problems, and U.S. military officers could teach the South Vietnamese army how to take the war to the enemy. Taylor and Rostow further recommended that the United States transfer sophisticated military equipment to South Vietnam. Most important, they called for dispatching 8,000 troops to the Mekong Delta, the southern region of the country, ostensibly to assist in flood relief. Once on the ground, U.S. forces would be available for combat against the Viet Cong.[14]

Both the Taylor-Rostow report and the spreading insurgency stimulated belligerent thinking within the administration. The Joint Chiefs of Staff, Secretary of State Dean Rusk, Secretary of Defense Robert McNamara, and National Security Adviser McGeorge Bundy called for building on the Taylor-Rostow report by publicly guaranteeing South Vietnam's survival and by preparing to send U.S. combat troops to the region. They spoke of deploying over 200,000 U.S. personnel. Rusk and McNamara also foresaw the day when the United States might strike at North Vietnam. As General Taylor had put it, the time may come "when we must declare our intention to attack the source of guerrilla aggression in North Vietnam and impose on the Hanoi Government a price for participating in the current war which is commensurate with the damage being inflicted on its neighbors to the south."[15]

President Kennedy loathed the options his closest advisers placed before him. Kennedy considered combat troops a "last resort," and he warned that the introduction of some U.S. troops would inevitably lead to requests for more troops. As he told an aide, it was "like taking a drink. The effect wears off, and you have to take another." The president further told the NSC on November 15, 1961, that "he could make a rather strong case against intervening in an area 10,000 miles away against 16,000 guerrillas with a native army of 200,000, where millions have been spent for years with no success." He rejected the idea of sending a formidable combat force. Nonetheless, Kennedy authorized a significant expansion of U.S. advisers and aid to South Vietnam.[16] His decision violated the Geneva Accords, which had called for the withdrawal of foreign forces from Vietnam.

Over the next two years, the U.S. military presence in South Vietnam persistently grew. As Kennedy had prophesied, the United States drained one mind-numbing drink after another. The administration established a formal military command and gave the commander, Gen. Paul D. Harkins, equal status with the U.S. ambassador in Saigon. The number of military advisers, which stood at 700 in January 1961, reached 3,200 by the end of 1961, grew to 9,000 in 1962, and reached over 16,000 by 1963. Operating advanced equipment such as helicopters, U.S. forces became directly involved in combat, and about 100 died from combat wounds during the Kennedy years. U.S. advisers taught South Vietnamese troops the tactics of helicopter envelopment and assisted them in carrying out covert raids against North Vietnam. The president authorized the use of defoliants to deny the Viet Cong ground cover and herbicides to destroy the food supplies of the enemy. The poison of Agent Orange began to enter the country's ecosystem. General Harkins held that he could terrify the Communists by bombing them with napalm.[17]

Scholars disagree over the rationale and meaning of President Kennedy's November 1961 decision. Some emphasize the president's oft-expressed misgivings and his rejection of his closest advisers' recommendation for a large U.S. military force in South Vietnam taking the fight to the guerrillas and North Vietnam. The Joint Chiefs, McNamara, and Bundy wanted the president to do in 1961 what President Johnson would do in 1965 with his massive military buildup in South Vietnam. President Kennedy, these scholars opine, should be applauded for keeping his options open and postponing disaster. He took a limited step in Vietnam because he assessed the political world in which he operated. The Bay of Pigs misadventure and the building of the Berlin Wall had left U.S. citizens alarmed that the Soviet Union was having its way in the world. To reject the Taylor-Rostow report might have fueled anti-Communist hysteria, a new McCarthyism, within the country.[18] Other historians find, however, that the president's decision to expand the U.S. investment in South Vietnam fit firmly within his conception of the world—the world of containment, NSC 68/2, and wars of national liberation. Khrushchev was again testing him, and he would press Soviet designs in Berlin, Cuba, and elsewhere, if the United States permitted Communist aggression to go unchecked in South Vietnam.[19]

Although President Kennedy received bad advice from his national security team and read unduly optimistic field reports, he received counsel from powerful friends and objective analysts who warned him of the Vietnam folly. The crusty, blunt George W. Ball, the future undersecretary of state, told Kennedy it would be a "tragic error" to accept the Taylor-Rostow analysis. The United States would repeat the French experience in Vietnam. Ball presciently predicted,

"Within five years we'll have three hundred thousand men in the paddies and jungles and never find them again." Kennedy did not engage Ball, other than to respond, "George, you're just crazier than hell. That just isn't going to happen."[20] Kennedy received similar advice from good friend Senator Mike Mansfield (D-MT), who concluded that his initial enthusiasm for Diem had been misplaced. In 1962, at the president's request, Mansfield went to Vietnam, where he was subjected to monologues from Diem that went on for hours. Meeting on the presidential yacht in November of that year, Mansfield told Kennedy that his policy of incremental escalation was trapping the United States in a civil war and that a non-Communist South Vietnam was not vital to U.S. national security. Kennedy argued with Mansfield and became red in the face, although he later privately admitted that Mansfield made good points.[21] Theodore White, author of *The Making of the President, 1960* (1961), wrote Kennedy, "Any investment of our troops in the paddies of the delta will be useless—or worse. The presence of white American troops will feed the race hatred of the Viet-Namese." Years earlier, White had correctly reported that the Franklin Roosevelt and Truman administrations had misplaced their trust in Chiang Kai-shek and the Chinese Nationalists.[22] Beyond listening to dissenters, President Kennedy, who was a voracious reader, could have read news accounts by young, energetic reporters such as David Halberstam of the *New York Times*, Neil Sheehan of United Press International, and Malcolm Browne and Peter Arnett of the Associated Press. They reported on corruption and nepotism within the Diem government, the utter incompetence of the South Vietnamese army, and the expanding reach of the Viet Cong. Weary of critical reports, Kennedy asked the publisher of the *New York Times* to transfer Halberstam out of Vietnam.[23] The publisher refused, and Halberstam went on to win the Pulitzer Prize for his reporting in Vietnam and to pen *The Best and the Brightest* (1972), his searing indictment of the men, like Bundy, McNamara, Taylor, and Rostow, who planned the U.S. war in Vietnam.

Through the end of 1962, President Kennedy apparently believed that his decision to expand the U.S. role in Vietnam was bringing positive results. At a news conference in December 1962, he cited the expanded U.S. military effort, lamented U.S. casualties, and acknowledged the challenges of fighting a guerrilla war in a difficult terrain. But he concluded with a note of cautious optimism, observing that "we don't see the end of the tunnel, but I must say that I don't think it is darker than it was a year ago, and in some ways lighter."[24] On the military level, Kennedy had the right to a bit of cheer. The increased U.S. military role hurt the Viet Cong in 1962. The Communists needed time to devise responses to counter tactics such as helicopter assaults on their positions. Kennedy deluded himself, however, if he thought the Diem regime was expanding its base of popular support. During the administration's debate over the Taylor-Rostow report, Kennedy had written to Diem suggesting that U.S. administrators help run the governmental machinery of South Vietnam. Ever the nationalist, Diem rejected the idea of making his country a protectorate. Without initial U.S. approval, Diem launched his new initiative to pacify the countryside—the "strategic hamlet" program. Having learned from the failures of the "agroville" effort, the Diem government pledged not to force peasants out of their villages. Instead the villages would be fortified and linked together in a common defense. In fact, many peasants were forced again to leave home. Villagers also resented being forced to labor without pay, building barriers and moats and stretching barbed wire. Once inside their strategic hamlets, they complained that they felt like they were in a prison. The government also did not deliver on the health, education, and welfare service it promised to the villagers. Diem's brother, Nhu, ran the strategic hamlet program, and he and associates pocketed the U.S. money allocated for social services. The Viet Cong also contributed to the disarray. One Viet Cong operative won Nhu's confidence, became an administrator of the program, and did everything in his power to transform peasants into Viet Cong sympathizers. Realizing how disgruntled the villagers were, the Viet Cong also began to target strategic hamlets in early 1963.[25]

Overthrow of Diem, 1963

President Kennedy received no good tidings from Vietnam in 1963. Both militarily and politically the U.S. position in Vietnam bordered on collapse. On November 2, 1963, the president received word of the assassination of President Diem. The overthrow of the Diem regime flowed from decisions the president had made in previous months.

The conduct of the battle of Ap Bac demonstrated that U.S. military advisers had failed to transform Diem's army into a lethal fighting force. The battle took place on January 2, 1963, in a village in the Mekong Delta, thirty-five miles southwest of Saigon. Government forces, numbering 3,000 men, took on about 320 insurgents. Diem's army had the 10-1 advantage popularly thought necessary for counterinsurgency operations. U.S. helicopters ferried South Vietnamese units to the battlefield. In support of the infantry were artillery, armored personnel carriers, helicopter gunships, and jet fighters. The Viet Cong had only handheld weapons. In the previous year, the Viet Cong had fled when confronted with the U.S.-made firepower. This time the Viet Cong held their ground, showing that they had learned how to counter modern military technology. They shot down five helicopters, killing three U.S. advisers and wounding eight other Americans. Displaying remarkable bravery, the Viet Cong attacked the armed personnel carriers on foot, throwing hand grenades. In the face of such boldness, the South Vietnamese forces refused to engage the enemy aggressively. Lt. Col. John Paul Vann, the U.S. military adviser who had designed the operation, surveyed the unfolding fiasco from his spotter plane. An enraged Vann threatened to issue an order to shoot the timid South Vietnamese commander. He later labeled the South Vietnamese fighting performance as "miserable," "just like it always is." The Viet Cong withdrew from the battlefield in good order. They had inflicted about 170 casualties in dead and wounded on Diem's men and had suffered perhaps 60 casualties.[26]

Delusional South Vietnamese military leaders claimed Ap Bac as a victory, for the Viet Cong had abandoned the village. The Viet Cong had, however, won a big political victory, discrediting the Diem regime and his pitiful army in the eyes of villagers living in the Mekong Delta. Peasants thereafter either began to support the Viet Cong or took a neutral stance in the civil war. Perhaps 300,000 South Vietnamese associated with the NLF. By the end of 1963, Viet Cong forces controlled up to 30 percent of the countryside.[27]

Political turmoil and religious intolerance by the Diem government further undermined the U.S. effort in Vietnam. Throughout his rule, Diem had favored his extended family and Catholics in government jobs and political patronage. But in 1963 the regime began to persecute Buddhists. On May 7, 1963, in the old imperial capital of Hue, Buddhists celebrated the 2,527th birthday of the Buddha by displaying religious flags. This violated a long-standing Diem edict banning such displays without government permission. The previous week Catholics had flown papal flags to celebrate the twenty-fifth anniversary of Diem's brother's elevation to bishop in the Roman Catholic Church. Buddhists demonstrated against the order to remove their flags. The next day, troops commanded by a Catholic officer attacked the protestors, hurling hand grenades at them. Nine Buddhists died and fourteen were wounded. Armored personnel carriers crushed two children. President Diem proved insensitive to this tragedy. He blamed the Viet Cong for the attack, refused to discipline his military officer, and subjected a Buddhist delegation to one of his typical harangues. Only after U.S. diplomatic pressure did Diem agree to offer financial compensation to the families of the victims. The amount offered—the equivalent of $7,000—was ungenerous.[28]

Over the next months clashes between Buddhists and Diem's forces mounted. An event that shocked the world ultimately sealed Diem's fate. On June 11, 1963, an elderly monk, Thich Quang Duc, immolated himself on one of Saigon's major boulevards in protest over the persecution of Buddhists. The monk, who was dressed in a flowing, saffron-colored robe, sat in the lotus position. He was surrounded by 350 monks and nuns, who chanted and prayed. One monk doused him with gasoline and then Quang Duc lit a match. He never moved or cried out, as his body burned for ten minutes. Alerted that a big event would take place, Malcolm Browne of the Associated Press took haunting photographs of the suicide. These images flashed across world wire services. Talking on the telephone to his brother, Attorney General Robert Kennedy, the president exclaimed, "Jesus Christ!" when he saw the image on television. He later remarked, "No news picture in history has generated so much emotion around the world as that one."[29]

The Diem family foolishly intensified tensions and violence in the country. Madam Nhu, the president's sister-in-law, used the word "barbeque" to characterize the monk's death. She later contemptuously offered to provide gasoline and matches for other monks. Riots and protests broke out throughout the country. More monks and nuns immolated themselves. After promising to resolve the crisis, President Diem further infuriated the Kennedy administration when troops, under the command of his brother, Nhu, raided 2,000 pagodas and arrested 1,400 Buddhists. Several hundred Buddhists also died during the August 21 raids.

Recognizing that U.S. citizens abhorred religious intolerance and that Diem was in the process of alienating the overwhelming majority of the population, the Kennedy administration began the process of removing the Diem family from power. On August 24, 1963, three days after the raid on the pagodas, President Kennedy casually approved a memorandum that gave wide latitude to his representatives in Saigon to support a coup d'etat. The president was not at his desk in the Oval Office at the time but rather vacationing at the family retreat in Hyannis Port, Massachusetts. South Vietnamese generals had secretly contacted U.S. officials in Vietnam, inquiring about the U.S. attitude, if they overthrew Diem and his brother. In the memorandum, the new ambassador, Henry Cabot Lodge Jr., was instructed to tell Diem to remove his brother from power. If Diem refused, the United States "must face the possibility that Diem himself cannot be preserved." The U.S. ambassador was further authorized to inform the generals that if Diem declined to reform his government, the United States would provide them with "direct support in any interim period of breakdown of central government mechanism."[30]

The momentous August 24 memorandum had not been analyzed by all members of Kennedy's national security team. Secretary of Defense McNamara and General Taylor especially resented not being consulted. And Kennedy would later regret not having the memorandum travel through the normal bureaucratic hierarchy. But the president subsequently allowed his key advisers to debate the new policy. Kennedy notably never repudiated the policy, albeit he also never issued a direct order encouraging South Vietnamese generals to strike. In effect, President Kennedy had decided to abandon Diem, if the South Vietnamese president did not follow U.S. orders.

Ambassador Lodge vigorously implemented the new policy. Kennedy had appointed the Republican and the 1960 vice presidential candidate to lend a patina of bipartisanship toward his Vietnam policy. Willful and self-confident, Ambassador Lodge spoke forcefully to Diem and refused to be subjected to his monologues. Within days after arriving in Saigon, Lodge decided that Diem had to go. He told the president, "We are launched on a course from which there is no respectable turning back." Lodge had a military officer, Lucien Conein, meet with South Vietnamese generals. Conein, who had been a CIA operative, had extensive experience in Vietnam, having led South Vietnamese commandos on

President Kennedy meets with Gen. Maxwell Taylor and Secretary of Defense Robert McNamara on October 2, 1963. Both General Taylor and Secretary McNamara were architects of the U.S. involvement in Vietnam. During the Kennedy presidency, U.S. military forces grew from 700 in early 1961 to over 16,000 by late 1963. The United States also played a role in the overthrow in early November 1963 of the South Vietnamese leader, Ngo Dinh Diem. (John F. Kennedy Presidential Library and Museum, Boston)

sabotage raids into North Vietnam. Known for his panache and swagger, Conein had a gangster nickname, "Black Luigi." He later admitted to a congressional committee investigating U.S. involvement in the Diem assassination, "I was part and parcel of the whole conspiracy."[31] Indeed like a Sicilian gangster, the United States was going to lay a dead fish at the doorstep of the presidential palace of Ngo Dinh Diem.

In September and October 1963 the Kennedy administration vacillated, wringing its hands over Diem's fate. The president sent more inspection teams to Saigon. As in the past, the teams came back with conflicting assessments of the political and military state of affairs. A frustrated president bemoaned, "This is impossible; we can't run a policy when there are such divergent views on the same set of facts." Kennedy further worried about being identified with a coup that failed. Recalling the lessons of the Bay of Pigs, Kennedy warned Lodge to be cautious. As the president observed, "I know from experience that failure is more destructive than the appearance of indecision. . . . When we go, we must go to win."[32] Indecision caused the mutinous South Vietnamese generals to wonder where the United States stood on Diem. In October the generals received the word from the Kennedy administration. The United States did not "wish to stimulate a coup." But it would not "thwart" a coup, and it would grant economic and military assistance to a new government that pursued the war and worked with the United States.[33] The South Vietnamese generals understood the meaning of this circumspect language.

On November 1, 1963, South Vietnamese generals attacked the Diem regime. The leader of the military junta was Gen. Duong Van Minh, known as "Big Minh." General Minh had a solid reputation as a brave patriot, having endured Japanese torture during World War II. He also had helped Diem establish order in the country in the 1950s. General Minh's forces quickly gained control of the government and shortly thereafter captured Diem and his brother. Just before his capture, a desperate Diem telephoned Ambassador Lodge, asking what the U.S. position on the rebellion was. Lodge feigned ignorance of Washington's attitudes but suggested to Diem that the generals would provide safe passage out of the country, if he resigned. Diem presumably deduced that Lodge had inside information on the coup and hung up. A comfortable exile did not await President Diem and his brother. Once captured, the two men had their hands bound and were murdered in the back of an armored personnel carrier. A South Vietnamese officer repeatedly bayoneted Nhu and shot President Diem in the head.[34]

News of the grisly murders stunned President Kennedy. General Taylor later recalled, Kennedy "leaped to his feet and rushed from the room with a look of shock and dismay on his face that I had never seen before."[35] A couple days later, the distraught Kennedy recorded on tape his own feelings about Diem. He summarized who in his administration favored and opposed the coup. He admitted to himself that "we must bear a good deal of responsibility" for the coup, beginning with the sloppy way the August 24 memorandum was approved. He expressed admiration for Diem for holding his country together and called him "an extraordinary character." He reiterated his shock over Diem's death and added "the way he was killed made it particularly abhorrent."[36] Whereas Kennedy's self-confession was surely heartfelt, he was not always true to himself. He could have remembered from the near misses and fiascos during the Cuban missile crisis the lesson that a president can initiate the course of events but cannot control it. Coups usually degenerate into violence and death. The president had previously approved covert interventions, such as in British Guiana, that had spurred ghastly violence and widespread death and destruction. And President Kennedy was not always squeamish about assassinations. His administration plotted against the life of Fidel Castro.

On the tape, Kennedy concluded his soliloquy on Diem and Vietnam with the observation, "The question now is whether the generals can stay together and build a stable government." The overthrow of Diem did not bring political order to the country or victory on the battlefield against the Viet Cong and the NLF. Big Minh lasted three months in power. In 1964 alone, several different governments tried ruling South Vietnam. The Communists and their supporters gained increasing credibility among South Vietnamese peasants. As one historian has noted, "The Diem government looked like a model of order and stability compared with the floundering, revolving-door regimes that followed in 1964–1965."[37] The Kennedy administration had encouraged the replacement of "bad leadership by no leadership at all." President Johnson found a terrible mess in South Vietnam. Without a functioning government in Saigon, he concluded that the now two-decade-long effort in Vietnam that stretched back to President Truman would collapse without a dramatic increase in the U.S. commitment. Johnson tried to compensate for Saigon's political weakness by defeating the enemy militarily with an overwhelming force of over 500,000 U.S. troops. President Johnson led the United States into what proved to be a catastrophe of "waste" for both Americans and Vietnamese.

The Past Versus the Future

The fact is that President Kennedy significantly expanded the U.S. presence in Vietnam. He increased the number of U.S. military advisers from 700 to over 16,000. These advisers became involved in perilous combat operations. The Kennedy administration also played a role in overthrowing President Diem. Political chaos ensued in South Vietnam and worked to the advantage of the Viet

Cong and North Vietnam. It was not, however, predetermined that Kennedy, in a second presidential term, would have followed the course that President Johnson chose. Americans, enchanted by the Kennedy mystique and the legend of Camelot, like to believe that Kennedy would have shown wisdom and judgment and avoided tragedy. One scholar has dubbed this the "Kennedy exceptionalism" approach.[38] Historians offer conflicting opinions on Kennedy exceptionalism. Their outlooks are based on analyses of Kennedy's statements and choices prior to November 22, 1963.

President Kennedy said many things about Vietnam during the last months of his life. His words were as inconsistent and contradictory as the many field reports from Vietnam that he read. In September 1963, in a televised interview with the CBS correspondent Walter Cronkite, he suggested that U.S. support for South Vietnam had its limits. The United States could provide military equipment and advisers, but "in the final analysis it is their war. They are the ones who have to win it or lose it." A week later, in an interview with the NBC correspondent Chet Huntley, the president seemed to reverse himself, suggesting that success in Vietnam was vital to U.S. national security. He reaffirmed his belief in the domino theory and warned that Communist China would be emboldened and would threaten neighbors if the Viet Cong and Hanoi took control of South Vietnam.[39] According to one presidential aide, Kennedy confidentially assured a worried Senator Mansfield that he now agreed with Mansfield that the United States should completely withdraw from South Vietnam. But this would have to wait until 1965, after he had won a second presidential term. Whether this represented a concrete plan or just a private musing cannot be ascertained. The president did not disclose such plans to his most trusted adviser, his brother. Robert Kennedy supported President Johnson's policies in Vietnam until 1966.[40] On the next to last day of his life, the president told an NSC officer to prepare at the start of 1964 a comprehensive review of U.S. policy in Vietnam, "including how to get out of there." But the text of the speech the president intended to deliver at the Trade Mart in Dallas reveals that he would warn the audience that the U.S. role in Vietnam was "painful, risky, and costly" but "we dare not weary of the task."[41] As he had in the interview with Chet Huntley, the president seemed to imply that Vietnamese Communists acted as surrogates of Communist China.

Those who profess Kennedy exceptionalism point to two decisions he made about Vietnam to support their case. In November 1961 Kennedy had declined to "Americanize" the war, rejecting the idea of sending over 200,000 U.S. combat troops. By November 1963 he also had second thoughts about the 16,000 advisers he had dispatched to South Vietnam. In October 1963 he approved NSAM 263, which called for a withdrawal of 1,000 advisers by the end of 1963 and further predicted that "the major part of the U.S. military task can be completed by the end of 1965." Other historians argue, however, that NSAM 263 represented little change. The withdrawal of 1,000 advisers was primarily a ploy to pressure Diem to reform his government. The goal of withdrawing most advisers at the end of 1965 was predicated on political stability in South Vietnam and an effective military campaign against the Viet Cong. Neither development occurred after the U.S.-encouraged overthrow of Diem.[42]

Kennedy had avoided one war in Southeast Asia, when he agreed in 1961 to the neutralization of Laos, Vietnam's poor, weak, and landlocked neighbor. President Eisenhower had emphasized the Communist menace in Laos, not Vietnam, when he briefed the president-elect. Early in his administration, Kennedy rejected military advice to send 140,000 U.S. troops to the country to support the U.S.-backed government. The Joint Chiefs also wanted the authority to use nuclear weapons as a last resort. Fresh off the disaster at the Bay of Pigs, Kennedy authorized veteran diplomat W. Averell Harriman to negotiate in Geneva for an agreement, which was struck in July 1962, to remove the country from the Cold War. Unfortunately for Laos, the country was dragged in the 1960s into the widening war between the United States and North Vietnam. In any case, Kennedy showed no such flexibility on Vietnam. He did not instruct diplomats to approach Hanoi or representatives of the NLF about initiating discussions. He also gave short shrift to a plan proffered in 1963 by French President Charles de Gaulle that called for the withdrawal of U.S. troops, the neutralization of South Vietnam, and the beginning of contacts between North and South Vietnam.[43]

Perhaps the strongest argument favoring the view that it would have been unimaginable for President Kennedy to go down the same road in Vietnam that President Johnson did is his prudent, cautious record during times of crisis and confrontation. He declined to rescue the Bay of Pigs invaders, choosing instead to pay a heavy domestic political price. He dismissed talk of saving Berlin with limited nuclear weapons, and he found a peaceful way out of the Cuban missile crisis. President Kennedy displayed poise and self-confidence and refused to be intimidated by belligerent advisers, like Gen. Curtis LeMay. One can imagine President Kennedy, with enormous international credibility, pursuing peace in his second presidential term. That optimistic view must be tempered by the knowledge that the president remained fond of covert interventions right to the end, as indicated by his campaigns against Brazil, British Guiana, and Cuba.

Debates over Kennedy's future course in Vietnam often seem abstract, failing to acknowledge that the Vietnamese Communists would present Kennedy with unpalatable choices. A critical question is whether the Kennedy administration would pay the geopolitical and domestic price and permit a unified Communist Vietnam. Hanoi did not relish a war against the United States. But the Vietnamese believed they had been denied their national aspirations at the end of World War II and at Geneva in 1954. They also had faith in their military prowess, as evidenced by their harassment of the Japanese and their defeat of the French. Ho Chi Minh felt obligated to his supporters in the South. In response to their pleas and demands, he had authorized the resumption of armed resistance and the formation of the NLF. In December 1963 Ho and the North Vietnamese politburo decided to pursue their "sacred war," by increasing their military support of the Viet Cong and by infiltrating regular North Vietnamese troops across the 17th parallel. This decision followed the assassination of Diem and the collapse of secret contacts between Hanoi and Saigon. Diem and Nhu had countered U.S. pressure to reform by discussing with the North Vietnamese a political settlement that would leave Diem in power and presumably force the United States to withdraw from Vietnam. Whether Nhu approached Hanoi with serious intent or was engaged in a ploy designed to deflect U.S. pressure on the Diem regime cannot be determined. But the commitment of Hanoi and the Viet Cong to revolutionary nationalism must be emphasized. A coalitional arrangement with Diem would, in the view of the Communists, be a step toward eventual control and triumph.[44]

President Johnson feared that the loss of Vietnam to communism would create a domestic uproar, imperiling his ambitious reform agenda, the Great Society. Democrats remembered that President Truman suffered political ruin and that McCarthyism flourished in the aftermath of the triumph of the People's Republic of China and the military stalemate in Korea. Beyond weathering a political storm, President Kennedy would also have to explain to U.S. citizens that the international Communist conspiracy was a figment of frenzied imaginations. Not all Communists took their orders from Moscow and Beijing. The Vietnamese had a storied history of patriotism and fierce independence. In any case, Hanoi did not want to become entangled in the confrontation between China and the Soviet Union. President Kennedy often said that he cared little about a country's socioeconomic system. He wanted to know whether a country followed an independent line in foreign affairs. His record in Africa, Asia, and Latin America revealed, however, that he often confused nationalism with communism.

Undersecretary of State George W. Ball deserves the last word on Kennedy and Vietnam. Ball also served on President Johnson's foreign policy team. Ball adamantly opposed Johnson's Vietnam policy, single-handedly taking on Dean Rusk, McNamara, Bundy, the Joint Chiefs, and the president himself. Ball questioned whether the United States had the means to resolve Vietnam's problems, and he did not consider Southeast Asia vital to U.S. national security. Ball believed the United States should focus its energies on protecting its Western European allies from the Soviet Union. Ball lost the debate on Vietnam. As he surveyed the damage the United States did to itself in Vietnam, Ball pondered in his memoir what President Kennedy meant when he told him in November 1961 that "you're just crazier than hell" when he warned that the Taylor-Rostow recommendations would lead to disaster. He wondered why the president had been so uncharacteristically short and abrupt with him. Perhaps Kennedy had shared his apprehensions but would not admit them even to himself. But Ball conceded that he had no answers to these questions. "I know no more than anyone else what would have happened to our Vietnam venture had President Kennedy not been killed." He had no opinion on the argument proffered by historians that Kennedy had a withdrawal plan. As Ball concluded, "Such speculation is inherently sterile; there are no answers in the back of the book."[45]

CHAPTER 7

ASIA

THE JOHN F. KENNEDY ADMINISTRATION planned to change the direction of U.S. foreign relations with the world's two most populous nations—the People's Republic of China and India. With a combined total of 1.1 billion people, the two nations represented more than one-third of humanity. The Kennedy administration hoped to lessen tensions with Communist China. The United States did not have diplomatic relations with China, and since 1949 the two nations had repeatedly confronted one another militarily. In the 1950s U.S. relations with India, the world's largest democracy, had been peaceful but difficult. U.S. policymakers disliked India's unwillingness to accept U.S. views on the Cold War and opposed India's friendship with the Soviet Union. By promoting India's socioeconomic development, U.S. policymakers believed that they could win India's allegiance to the West. President Kennedy and his team failed to achieve either objective. The Kennedy administration perpetuated, even intensified, the conflict with China. The administration made a significant contribution to India's development, but it did not persuade India to follow the U.S. lead on the global stage.

Sino-American Relations to 1949

The United States considered itself the special friend and protector of China. Sustained U.S. interest in China began in the late nineteenth century, when the United States became an industrial power and a major player on the global stage. The United States encountered a China that no longer controlled its own destiny.

China's imperial rulers, the Qing (Manchu) Dynasty, could not protect the Chinese people from the predatory designs of the European colonialists—the British, French, and Germans—or from the Japanese. China lacked the industrial might and technological sophistication to resist aggression. Japan visibly demonstrated China's weakness and Japan's new military and industrial power when it routed the Chinese in the Sino-Japanese War (1894–1895). The Europeans and the Japanese thereafter pounced upon China, carving it up like a ripe melon. They took parts of China for themselves, establishing European and Japanese spheres of influence within China. They also forced China to grant "unequal treaties" and "special privileges" to foreigners. The European colonialists and Japanese gained control over China's tariffs and trade and claimed "extraterritoriality" or immunity from Chinese law for their subjects living in China. In some port cities, such as Shanghai, the colonialists established neighborhoods reserved exclusively for Europeans. The Japanese especially pressed hard on China's sovereignty. In 1904–1905 they attained another military victory, smashing the forces of Czarist Russia in the Russo-Japanese War. Their victory left them free to establish a sphere of influence in Manchuria, China's northern region.

The United States opposed the dismembering of China and the humiliation of the Chinese and called for an "Open Door" policy for China. The William McKinley administration (1897–1901) issued "Open Door Notes" to the foreign powers. The United States stood for the territorial integrity and sovereignty of China. No foreign nation should have special privileges in China. Under the Open Door philosophy, all nations could compete fairly and peacefully for trade and cultural influence within China. The Open Door philosophy reflected the proud anticolonial heritage of the American Revolution. It also displayed the confidence that officials, businessmen, and Christian missionaries had in U.S. institutions. The United States favored a modernized, westernized, Christian China and professed that the Chinese wanted to adopt U.S. models of development and lifestyles and convert to Protestant Christianity. U.S. officials and citizens believed that the United States pursued a righteous, generous policy toward China, but neither the Chinese nor the foreign powers interpreted U.S. policy as disinterested or fair. The United States stationed troops in China, accepted "special privileges" like extraterritoriality, and demanded special rights for U.S. missionaries and Chinese who converted to Christianity.

Racism at home further undermined the U.S. commitment to China and its policies in Asia. Talk of a "yellow peril," of Asians coming to dominate U.S. life, entered public discourse. Beginning in 1882, the U.S. Congress prohibited Chinese immigrants from entering the United States. The ban lasted until World War II. Chinese Americans experienced discrimination in employment and housing, especially on the West Coast. After 1907 the United States also prohibited Japanese from entering the United States.

The Qing Dynasty collapsed in 1912, setting off a four-decade-long violent struggle among the Chinese for control of the nation's future. Warlords—generals with private armies—fought for control of the immense country. Two parties—the Nationalists and Communists—emerged as the dominant rivals. Generalissimo Jiang Jieshi (Chiang Kai-shek) led the Goumindang (Kuomintang/Nationalist) Party. Jiang's political strength was in the urban areas along China's coast. The Communists, led by Mao Zedong, promised sweeping land and tax reform and built a base of support among peasants in the interior of China. Peasants, many of them landless, composed the overwhelming majority of China's population. By the end of the 1920s, the United States decided to recognize Jiang and the Guomindang as the legitimate rulers of China. Jiang promised a constitutional, modernized China open to U.S. trade and investment. He had also married an impressive Chinese woman who had been educated in the United States, spoke excellent English, and professed Christianity. Madame Jiang Jieshi skillfully advanced China's interests in various forums in the United States. Her husband further cemented his ties to the United States when he converted to Christianity. Influential U.S. citizens, such as Henry Luce, the head of the *Time/Life* media empire, ceaselessly promoted Jiang and his party. Luce, the son of a Presbyterian missionary, had been born in China. Jiang and his wife appeared on the cover of *Time* magazine eleven times between 1927 and 1955. Businessmen and Christian missionaries would become the core of the powerful "China lobby" in the United States.

While still in the throes of civil war, China was beset by renewed foreign aggression in 1931, when Japan invaded Manchuria and established the puppet state of "Manchukuo." Full-scale warfare in China between the Chinese and the Japanese broke out in 1937. Beset by the economic depression of the 1930s and lacking significant military power, the United States initially did little to help the

Chinese. After September 1940, the United States began to back its Open Door policy with military aid to China and economic sanctions against Japan. Japan had joined the Axis alliance with Nazi Germany and Fascist Italy. In mid-1941 the United States issued the equivalent of an ultimatum to Japan, threatening to cut off vital oil exports unless Japan ceased its aggression in China. Japan responded by attacking U.S. naval forces at Pearl Harbor, Hawaii, on December 7, 1941.

The U.S. wartime alliance with Jiang's forces went badly. U.S. military leaders, such as Gen. Joseph Stillwell, found that U.S. military aid was squandered or misappropriated. Jiang was an authoritarian and his regime was riddled with corruption. Military officers won promotions for loyalty to Jiang rather than for courage and leadership on the battlefield. Jiang also seemed more concerned with keeping Mao and the Communists bottled up in the interior of the country than with waging war against the Japanese. U.S. generals and diplomats considered aiding the Communists, who seemed honest and ready to fight foreign aggressors. Mao's support in the countryside was also expanding rapidly. In the end, the United States fatefully stuck with Jiang, who had his influential American friends.

Civil war between the Communists and Nationalists resumed at the conclusion of World War II. The United States saw the vision it fought for in its war against Japan—an open, modernized, constitutional China—vanishing. U.S. officials tried unsuccessfully to mediate between the two parties. The Communists correctly sensed that the United States would always back Jiang no matter how unreasonably he acted. In any case, the United States could not countenance a thoroughgoing social revolution in China. From 1945 to 1949, the United States gave Jiang nearly $2 billion in military assistance, although U.S. officials implicitly understood they were backing a losing cause. U.S. military aid often ended up in the hands of Mao's army because Jiang's forces threw away their arms on the battlefield or sold them on the black market. By comparison, Mao's forces received little help from the Soviet Union. Josef Stalin kept the promises he made at the Yalta Conference (1945) and recognized Jiang as the leader of China. In 1949 Jiang and his loyalists fled to the large offshore island of Taiwan (Formosa) and reconstituted the Republic of China there. On October 1, 1949, Mao Zedong declared the People's Republic of China on the mainland. Mao and his Communist Party had won because they had built a powerful political and military force and had persuaded the people that they could end the century of humiliation and abuse that China had suffered.

The People's Republic of China

The Chinese Communists were predictably bitter that the United States had aided their enemy. A year after their victory, anger and bitterness evolved into hostility and warfare between China and the United States. The Harry S. Truman administration initially seemed predisposed to accept the Communist victory. It realized that Jiang and his army had lost the civil war because of their stupefying incompetence. They expected the Communists would soon launch an amphibious assault on Taiwan and end the Jiang regime. In a speech delivered in January 1950, Secretary of State Dean Acheson implied that the United States would not save Jiang. Acheson further suggested that the Communist giants, China and the Soviet Union, would eventually confront one another. In early 1950 the Communist nations had signed a treaty of friendship. The United States also did not develop a long-term strategy of preventing the People's Republic of China from taking China's seat on the Security Council at the United Nations. Communist North Korea's invasion of South Korea in late June 1950 radically changed the U.S. approach to China. President Truman dispatched the Seventh Fleet to the Formosa Straits to prevent warfare between China and Taiwan. This decision evolved into a guarantee for Jiang's survival. In November 1950 Chinese Communist troops crossed the Yalu River into North Korea and attacked U.S. forces led by Gen. Douglas MacArthur. China had previously warned the United States not to approach its border. Both China and the United States suffered horrific casualties during the Korean War. President Truman overruled General MacArthur's desire to attack China with nuclear weapons.

China, international communism, and the Korean War became major domestic political issues in the United States. Republicans blamed President Truman for losing China to communism. Senator Joseph McCarthy of Wisconsin charged that disloyal State Department officers had sold Jiang out. The Republicans further portrayed the Truman administration as being naïve for not comprehending that the Chinese Communist leadership acted out the dictates of the Soviet Union. General MacArthur should have been allowed to pursue victory in Korea by attacking China. These issues propelled the Republicans, led by Dwight Eisenhower, to political victory in 1952. Not all criticism of the Truman administration's dealings with China came from Republicans. Congressman John Kennedy also alleged that the United States had undermined Generalissimo Jiang Jieshi.

The Eisenhower administration treated China as the main enemy of the United States. Secretary of State John Foster Dulles characterized relations as "a virtual state of war." The United States refused to grant diplomatic recognition to China and imposed a trade embargo. Eisenhower and Dulles threatened China with nuclear war three different times. In 1954–1955 and 1958, confrontations erupted over offshore islands, especially the island groups occupied by Jiang's forces, Jinmen (Quemoy) and Mazu (Matsu). The CIA supported commando raids by Chinese Nationalists on the mainland. The Republicans had promised the "liberation" of Communist countries, and President Eisenhower suggested in 1953 that he might "unleash" Jiang and permit him to invade China. Dulles insulted the Chinese, dismissing the regime in Beijing as a "passing, and not a perpetual phase." The United States also used its influence with its anti-Communist allies to keep China out of the United Nations. The Republic of China continued to hold China's seat on the Security Council, which carried with it the veto power. These policies won strong support from the China lobby and the "Committee of One Million against the Admission of Communist China to the United Nations."

The Eisenhower administration privately pursued a more nuanced policy toward China than indicated by its public stance. It had no intention of permitting the Jiang regime to drag the United States into another major Asian war. It demanded that Jiang give secret pledges that he would clear any major attacks on the mainland with the United States. It also implicitly accepted that China had legitimate interests by opening talks with China in 1955 at the ambassadorial level, first in Geneva, Switzerland, and later in Warsaw, Poland. The administration knew that Taiwan was not China. President Eisenhower and Secretary Dulles understood that a nation with over 600 million people could not be excluded from the international community forever. What the administration wanted was for Mao Zedong and Jiang Jieshi to end the Chinese civil war by accepting the principle of "two Chinas." The Chinese rejected such a plan. There was only one China and the offshore islands, including Taiwan, were part of China. Whenever the Eisenhower administration inched toward a "two Chinas" approach, the Chinese precipitated a diplomatic incident with Jiang and the United States.[1]

Although Eisenhower and Dulles appreciated the realities of international politics, racism undercut their desire to move U.S. relations with China forward. U.S. officials still held old paternalistic feelings toward China and believed the United States was a special friend of the Chinese. But they drew on the "yellow peril" fears that had infected U.S. immigration laws toward Asians. The Chinese allegedly cared little about life and would try to overwhelm the West with their vast numbers. Eisenhower once noted that the "Red Chinese appear to be completely reckless, arrogant, possibly overconfident and completely indifferent as to human losses." The Chinese were "hysterical," "irrational," and "fanatical." The president agreed with CIA Director Allen Dulles's assessment that the Chinese Communists "would regard the loss of 50 million people as a gain."[2] President Kennedy and his advisers usually rejected such crude characterizations, although at a White House dinner Kennedy apparently told a French minister that the Chinese attached a "lower value" to human life. The Kennedy administration continued the implicit dehumanization of the Chinese by declining to speak about them as a national people with legitimate domestic and international aspirations. The "Red Chinese" lived in "Red China," "Communist China," or "Mainland China," never in the People's Republic of China. The bureaucratic shorthand, as expressed in memorandums and policy statements, was to denigrate the Chinese as the "ChiComs."[3]

In addition to racism, ideological convictions prevented U.S. officials from objectively analyzing China's role on the world stage. Both the Eisenhower and Kennedy administrations spoke about the international Communist movement. But Secretary of State Acheson's prediction in 1950 about an eventual Sino-Soviet split came to fruition in the late 1950s. The two nations clashed over doctrinal and leadership issues. Nikita Khrushchev complained that the Chinese wanted to play "first violin" in the Communist orchestra. The Soviets took an imperial attitude, arguing that the home of Vladimir Lenin knew what was best for the Communist world. The Chinese criticized Khrushchev for preaching "competitive coexistence" with the West. In turn, Khrushchev began in 1959 to withdraw Soviet advisers and technicians from China. Having been threatened with nuclear weapons by the Eisenhower administration, Mao Zedong had decided in 1955 that China must have a nuclear deterrent. Khrushchev reneged on his promise to help. At Communist Party conclaves, delegates from China and the Soviet Union hurled insults at one another.[4] Until 1962 U.S. officials did not begin to grasp the depth and significance of the enmity between China and the Soviet Union.

JOHN KENNEDY AND CHINA

International observers hoped that the election of John Kennedy would lead to a relaxation of the dangerous tensions, the "virtual state of war," between the United States and the People's Republic of China. Kennedy seemed to have moved beyond his House of Representatives days, when he joined in the chorus who recklessly charged that President Truman had "lost" China. In his article in *Foreign Affairs* in 1957, Senator Kennedy had defended the nonrecognition of China. But he added, "We must be very careful not to strait-jacket our policy as a result of ignorance and fail to detect a change in the objective situation when it comes." In the presidential debates, Kennedy criticized the Eisenhower administration for tying U.S. prestige and security to the defense of the offshore islands known at the time as Quemoy and Matsu. Chester Bowles, the future undersecretary of state, published an article in *Foreign Affairs* calling on the United States to recognize an independent Taiwan. In essence, Bowles, with his "two Chinas" approach, was making the heretical statement that Jiang Jieshi was not and never would be the legitimate ruler of China. Kennedy's appointment of Dean Rusk as secretary of state, however, seemed to signal little flexibility on China. In 1951, as assistant secretary of state for the Far East, Rusk had hurled the ultimate insult at China, labeling it a puppet state of the Soviet Union, a "Slavic Manchukuo." But during the 1950s Rusk had participated in study groups that discussed finding ways to normalize relations with China. In any case, Rusk accepted the view that the secretary of state served the president and would carry out his foreign policies.[5]

As he contemplated his China policy, the new president had to weigh domestic and international political realities. Kennedy was always acutely aware that he barely won the election and lacked a clear mandate for change. He had major issues and programs—Berlin, Cuba, Vietnam, the Alliance for Progress, a massive military and nuclear arms buildup—that he wanted to address first. He further understood the power of the China lobby. In mid-1961 the Senate voted 76-0 and the House voted 395-0 for a resolution opposing the diplomatic recognition of the People's Republic of China and its admission to the United Nations. Kennedy told foreign visitors that Eisenhower had informed him that he "would feel it necessary to return to political life if the Chinese Communists were admitted to the United Nations." In a private, unrecorded conversation held in May 1961, Secretary Rusk recalled that Kennedy had conceded that the United States was practicing an unrealistic policy in Asia. But Kennedy feared that "he could have been cut to ribbons politically by the China Lobby, the Republicans, and many members of Congress." He instructed Rusk to propose no new initiatives for China.[6]

Proceeding with a "two Chinas" approach also proved diplomatically impossible. The Chinese Nationalists continued to claim that they were the real Chinese and the 650 million people in China were imposters. Jiang and his retinue hatched crazy schemes for invading the mainland. Beijing also refused to accept Taiwan as an independent nation. On March 7, 1961, at the first U.S.-China ambassadorial meeting held in Warsaw during the Kennedy presidency, the United States proposed exchanging journalists with China as a confidence-building measure. Ambassador Wang Ping-nan responded that no progress could be made until the United States stopped militarily defending Taiwan. Although the sixteen ambassadorial meetings held between 1961 and 1963 were polite and business-like, the verbal abuse that China aimed at the United States and President Kennedy was not. The "ChiComs" saw the United States as the "foreign devil" and Kennedy was labeled a "100 percent imperialist gangster."[7]

Although the Kennedy administration had strong incentives not to reconsider U.S. policy in Asia, in 1961 it received advice from friends to change course. Prime Minister Keith Holyoake of New Zealand warned President Kennedy that the seating of China in the United Nations "would have to be faced." Except for Australia, members of the British Commonwealth unanimously agreed that China had to be a member of the United Nations. The United Kingdom had diplomatic relations and traded extensively with China. Prime Minister Harold Macmillan of the United Kingdom told Secretary Rusk that U.S. policy was "indefensible by any logic." In "vehement" tones, Macmillan observed that the United States "did not even admit that China existed." The prime minister added, "The United States had 'a fellow from Taiwan' sitting in China's seat in the UN." Macmillan wondered whether the United States had a long-range policy. The British, Macmillan noted, did "good business with the Chinese Communists."[8]

When confronted with such criticism, Kennedy tried to explain his political challenges at home. But more than a fear of the China lobby kept President Kennedy wedded to the impractical policies of the past. He rejected the option offered to him by Rusk to "work quietly behind the scenes for reconciliation" between China and Taiwan. John Kennedy came to office as a committed Cold Warrior who believed that Communist nations threatened the national security of the United States. He repeatedly spoke about the international Communist menace. In his second presidential news conference, he warned of the "increasing power of the Communist bloc, the belligerency which marks the bloc, particularly the Chinese Communists." Kennedy especially feared that the Chinese would be in the vanguard in promoting Khrushchev's theory of "wars of national liberation." He had read Mao Zedong's tract on guerrilla warfare and advised his aides to do the same. In his State of the Union Address in January 1963, Kennedy cast doubt on the significance of the Sino-Soviet split. The "Soviet-Chinese disagreement is over means, not ends," he told Congress. "A dispute over how best to bury the free world is no grounds for Western rejoicing."[9]

In 1961 the Kennedy administration's policy for China consisted of keeping it out of the United Nations. The United States had faced increasing difficulty in justifying its position to the UN General Assembly. New African nations emerging from European colonialism judged U.S. policy to be unreasonable, even "colonial." A year of diplomacy and lobbying succeeded when, on December 1, 1961, the General Assembly approved a resolution that any proposal to change the representation of China at the United Nations was an "important question." Prime Minister Macmillan complained that the United States had "bullied all the South Americans" into voting for the U.S. position. Knowing that it would be increasingly difficult to assemble majorities in subsequent years, the Kennedy administration took a step that the Eisenhower administration had declined to take. On October 16, 1961, President Kennedy instructed his ambassador in

Tapei, Taiwan, to meet with Jiang in private to "inform him orally of this private assurance from me. I wish to assure you that if at any time a US veto is necessary and will be effective in preventing Chinese Communist entry into the UN, the US will use that veto." Kennedy's pledge was a momentous step for the United States. During the Cold War, the United States made the point that the Soviet Union, not the United States, defied the will of the international community by exercising the veto at the Security Council. Kennedy noted to Jiang that he would issue a denial if the private assurance became public knowledge. Indeed, in the 1970s officials such as McGeorge Bundy tried to deny that Kennedy had made the veto promise. For Jiang, Kennedy's private pledge signaled that he would not have to consider a relaxation of tensions with China, as long as Kennedy remained president.[10]

Hardship and hunger in China did not motivate the administration to make a conciliatory gesture toward Beijing. In their "Great Leap Forward," launched in 1958 to spur industrialization, Chinese Communist leaders had shortchanged agriculture, leading to dire food shortages for the nation's vast, growing population. Chester Bowles, now an ambassador at large, suggested in a memorandum of February 6, 1962, to President Kennedy that the Chinese food crisis might offer an opportunity to lessen "the danger of Chinese expansionism" and develop some economic leverage with China. Bowles proposed in a private conversation with Kennedy that the United States sell surplus wheat to the Chinese. According to Bowles, Kennedy agreed but food assistance had to be tied to a change in China's behavior. By early April, the administration decided not to offer food or even inform the Chinese that the United States would consider selling wheat to them. The United States would wait for China to ask for help. As a Chinese diplomat put it, this meant that China would "need to be a beggar." Averell Harriman, the veteran diplomat who had worked for Franklin Roosevelt and now served as assistant secretary for Far Eastern Affairs, thought the decision was ungracious and the United States was missing an opportunity to move "our relationship from one of implacable mutual hostility." Harriman ventured that food aid might strengthen the hands of Chinese leaders who wanted to improve relations with the United States.[11]

The Kennedy administration's fear and loathing of China mounted when full-scale warfare broke out between China and India on October 20, 1962, over border issues. Disputes over the boundaries between the world's most populous nations went as far back as the nineteenth century. Scholars believe that both sides took provocative actions and bore responsibility for the violence. Brutal fighting at 14,000 feet took place in the Himalayan region. The Chinese forces routed the Indian army, and in late November 1962 China declared a unilateral cease-fire, having established its definition of the proper boundary. The Kennedy administration worried that China would seize vast areas of India. The administration responded to India's request for help by sending light firearms, artillery, and transport planes. Despite China's apparent restraint and limited war aims, the United States perceived the Sino-Indian war as another example of China's predatory nature. Kennedy administration officials no longer proposed conciliatory gestures such as food aid for China.

Although locked in perpetual conflict with China, President Kennedy, like President Eisenhower, did not want war with China. Like his predecessor, Kennedy rejected Jiang Jieshi's plans to embroil the United States in a major global conflict. In 1962 the Generalissimo of Taiwan began lobbying for using U.S.-supplied transport planes to drop hundreds, if not thousands, of Chinese Nationalists into China. Jiang argued that the failures of the "Great Leap Forward" left China ripe for rebellion. He further suggested that the Sino-Soviet split meant that the Soviet Union would not provide military assistance to the Chinese. Ray S. Cline, the CIA station chief in Taiwan, encouraged Jiang to plan for his return to China. Intelligence analysts in Washington rejected such optimism. In a "Special National Intelligence Estimate" of March 28, 1962, the intelligence community saw no prospect of a popular, widespread rebellion in China, and analysts predicted that the Soviet Union would come to the aid of China in a war.[12] In 1962–1963 President Kennedy in both personal letters and through emissaries to Jiang repeatedly reminded the Generalissimo of the pledges he had made to President Eisenhower not to launch major military operations without U.S. approval. Kennedy also reminded Jiang that he had learned a hard historical lesson from the failure of the Bay of Pigs operation. In June 1962 Kennedy took the additional step of informing China at the Warsaw talks that the United States had no plans to assist an assault on China.[13] In 1962 intelligence reports indicated that the Chinese were massing troops in Fujian (Fukien) Province on China's southeastern coast, the coastal area nearest Taiwan. The buildup was probably in response to the drumbeat of war from Taipei.

Although President Kennedy eschewed war, he approved commando raids on China. The commandos carried U.S.-supplied arms drawn from the $160 million a year that the United States gave to Taiwan in military assistance. The raids usually failed, with the Chinese killing or capturing and executing the commandos. A January 1963 intelligence report noted that the Chinese had recently slaughtered 172 commandos from nine teams. The CIA also continued the Eisenhower policy of carrying out spoiling operations, presumably terrorism and sabotage, in China and Chinese-occupied Tibet. In September 1963 the CIA concluded, however, that its efforts were "not especially productive."[14] Taiwanese pilots conducted U-2 spying flights over China. In September 1962, at the Warsaw talks, Ambassador Wang claimed that there had been 214 invasions of Chinese airspace since 1958. The Chinese had shot down a U-2 on September 9, 1962. On November 1, 1963, they brought down another U-2. From the U.S. perspective, these acts of war against China were justified because China remained an "unregenerate regime," as the State Department's Policy Planning Council put it.[15]

China and the Bomb

The U-2 spying missions pointed to President Kennedy's obsessive fear that China would develop an atomic bomb. Throughout his presidency, Kennedy sounded the alarm to friends, U.S. officials, and foreign dignitaries. In October 1961 he told Arthur Krock, a *New York Times* columnist and family friend, that when China developed a bomb all of Southeast Asia would fall under the sway of Beijing. In January 1963, at a state dinner for French Minister of Culture André Malraux, he predicted that a nuclear-armed China would be the "great menace in the future to humanity, the free world, and freedom on earth." Walt Rostow of the State Department related that Kennedy saw a Chinese nuclear test "as likely to be historically the most significant and worst event of the 1960s." According to William C. Foster, the director of the Arms Control and Disarmament Agency, Kennedy would "think out loud" about China and the bomb, saying, "You know it wouldn't be too hard if we could somehow get an anonymous airplane to go over there, take out the Chinese facilities—they've only got a couple—and maybe we could do it, or maybe the Soviet Union could do it, rather than face the threat of a China with nuclear weapons." Portuguese Minister of Foreign Affairs

Alberto Nogueira recalled that President Kennedy told him that the West would "have to decide whether to use the atomic bomb on China so as to prevent the Chinese from making atomic weapons."[16]

In the aftermath of the first offshore islands crisis in 1955, Mao Zedong had decided that China needed a nuclear weapon as a deterrent. He also believed that a nuclear capacity would enhance China's international prestige. Having been threatened again by U.S. nuclear weapons in 1958, the Chinese accelerated their program, building nuclear enrichment facilities deep in the interior of the nation. The U.S. intelligence community had difficulty discerning China's nuclear intentions. The U-2 spy planes flown by Taiwanese pilots undertook risky missions searching the interior of China. The development of spy satellite technology gradually gave U.S. officials knowledge of the Chinese nuclear program. Between January and June 1963, there were twenty-four Corona spy satellite missions over China.[17]

President Kennedy ordered his administration to find ways to derail the Chinese program. On January 11, 1963, McGeorge Bundy told CIA Director John A. McCone that "the President was of a mind that nuclear weapons in the hands of the Chinese Communists would so upset the world political scene it would be intolerable to the United States and to the West." Bundy's stark message made an impression on McCone. His memorandum of the meeting recorded that "it appeared to me that Cuba and the Communist China nuclear threat are two issues foremost in the minds of the highest authority [Kennedy] and therefore should be treated accordingly by CIA." On January 22, Kennedy reiterated his "great concern about the possibility of the Chinese Communist nuclear capability" to the NSC.[18] The administration thereafter focused on both a multilateral and a unilateral solution to the nuclear problem. The administration hoped it could engage the Soviet Union in a joint effort to pressure China. It also developed plans for a military strike against China.

The Kennedy administration thought that if it could negotiate a nuclear test ban treaty between the four nuclear powers—the United States, the Soviet Union, the United Kingdom, and France—then international pressure could be brought to bear upon the Chinese to abandon their program. At the January NSC meeting, the president explicitly made that point. Indeed, the Chinese saw a test ban treaty as being aimed at them. At the Warsaw talks, Ambassador

Wang of China protested that the nuclear powers wanted to consolidate their "nuclear monopoly" with a treaty.[19] Kennedy especially hoped that the Soviet Union wanted to deny China nuclear weapons. The Soviets had withdrawn their scientists and technicians from China in the late 1950s. Although it continued to downplay the meaning of the Sino-Soviet split publicly, the administration was beginning to grasp its significance. In early 1963 the CIA characterized the differences between Moscow and Beijing as "fundamental."[20]

In July 1963 Kennedy instructed Averell Harriman, his representative at the test ban negotiations in Moscow, to approach Chairman Khrushchev. He wanted Harriman to emphasize to Khrushchev that "relatively small forces in hands of people like ChiComs could be very dangerous to us all." Kennedy asked Harriman to gauge Khrushchev's "willingness either to take Soviet action or to accept US action aimed in this direction."

Khrushchev disappointed the administration. With France not participating in the negotiations, the Soviets would not isolate China. Khrushchev also played down differences with the Chinese and suggested that a nuclear-armed China would become "more restrained."[21] Scholars have speculated whether Kennedy was thinking about proposing a joint U.S.-Soviet strike against Chinese nuclear facilities.

Rebuffed by the Soviets, the administration discussed unilaterally attacking China. The Joint Chiefs of Staff submitted studies on the prospects and problems of attacking China, including hitting Chinese nuclear facilities with a nuclear weapon. The Joint Chiefs thought strikes would be effective if the United States could elicit the cooperation of the Soviet Union. The administration also analyzed whether Taiwanese sabotage teams could be dropped into China and authorized U-2 flights by Taiwanese pilots over China. A U-2 equipped with an infrared camera attempted to fly over a suspected plutonium plant to determine whether the reactor was "hot" and thus off limits to military attack. The Chinese shot the plane down.[22] President Kennedy participated in discussions about attacking China. On September 11, 1963, he had a lengthy meeting with Gen. Jiang Jingguo (Chiang Ching-kuo), the son of Generalissimo Jiang. The president asked if Jiang Jingguo thought it would be possible to send 300 to 500 men by air to such distant Chinese Communist atomic installations as that at Pao-t'ou, and whether it was not likely that the planes involved would be shot down. Jiang, who had met the previous day with Bundy and CIA officials, assured President Kennedy that "such an operation was feasible." CIA Director McCone subsequently established a planning group with the Taiwanese to study the viability of attacks by Taiwanese teams against Chinese nuclear sites.[23]

The question of whether President Kennedy would have authorized an attack on Chinese nuclear facilities in 1964 cannot, of course, be answered. The historical record suggests that Kennedy would have decided against any plan "to strangle the baby in the cradle," as one NSC staffer put it. Kennedy repeatedly refused to support Generalissimo Jiang's invasion plans. And in the midst of the Bay of Pigs, Berlin, and Cuban missile crises, he had rejected advice that would have led to war. Perhaps Kennedy would have been comforted by a State Department study of October 1963 that concluded that China's acquisition of the bomb would present diplomatic and political challenges to the United States but not military ones. The United States would retain overwhelming nuclear superiority. The study also ventured that China would use its weapon solely as a deterrent and would renounce the first-use of a nuclear weapon.[24] On October 16, 1964, China became the fifth nation to explode an atomic weapon.

THE KENNEDY LEGACY IN CHINA

Sympathetic biographers and former administration officials have offered the familiar prediction that President Kennedy would have pursued a peaceful policy toward China in a second presidential term. In his last public statement on China, at a November 14, 1963, news conference, Kennedy observed, "We are not wedded to a policy of hostility with Red China." Kennedy added the proviso that "Red China" would have to pursue peaceful policies before the United States changed its attitude.[25] In a speech delivered shortly after the president's assassination, Roger Hilsman, the State Department's new assistant secretary for Far Eastern Affairs, implied that the United States expected that once the revolutionary leaders of China retired a new "sophisticated" leadership would abandon "the present simple view with which the leadership regards the world." Using the hoary phrase of the late nineteenth century, Hilsman said that the United States wanted an "open door" policy toward "Communist China." In his memoir, Hilsman claimed that the president supported finding a flexible approach to China. But a few days after his speech, Hilsman wrote to UN Ambassador Adlai Stevenson and assured him that "the speech signifies no change in U.S. policy, no new departure."[26] In any case, China's descent in 1965 into the madness of the Cultural Revolution probably precluded any meaningful change in U.S. relations with China.

John F. Kennedy did nothing to change relations with the People's Republic of China. The United States remained locked in the "virtual state of war" with China that had existed since 1950. Also surprising for such a fair-minded person, Kennedy indulged in the contemporary fears of the "yellow peril" and the misguided assumption that Chinese leaders did not value life.

U.S.-Indian Relations to 1961

The United States did not have a long history of intense involvement with India. The United Kingdom had ruled the subcontinent since the mid-nineteenth century, and the United States had generally acquiesced to British imperialists on Indian matters. Contacts with India were limited to modest levels of trade and missionary activity. U.S. citizens traditionally opposed colonialism, and in the twentieth century, they followed the struggle by Indians for national self-determination led by Mohandas Gandhi, Jawaharlal Nehru, and the Indian National Congress. U.S. religious groups and intellectuals especially admired the tactics of civil disobedience and passive resistance that Gandhi and his followers used to garner international attention to their cause. Gandhi would later serve as a source of inspiration for Dr. Martin Luther King Jr. and the civil rights movement in the United States. Although he favored the end of European colonialism in Asia, President Roosevelt did not protest vigorously when Prime Minister Winston Churchill threw the leaders of the Indian National Congress in jail during World War II. Gandhi and Nehru launched the "Quit India" movement during the war and hoped for U.S. backing, but Roosevelt accepted his wartime ally's repressive approach in India.

The United States welcomed the end of British imperialism in India in 1947. The British partitioned "Mother India" into two states—India with a Hindu majority and Pakistan with a Muslim majority. Fighting broke out between the two new nations over the northern state of Kashmir. India secured control over most of the state, which had a Muslim majority. Indian leaders argued that Kashmir was an essential part of India's heritage and that India had a very large Muslim population. Pakistan refused to accept India's military victory over Kashmir. U.S. officials thought that the dispute should have been submitted to a plebiscite, permitting residents of Kashmir to choose their destiny. Under Nehru, who served as prime minister from 1947 to 1964, India established a parliamentary democracy and focused on uplifting the living conditions of its impoverished citizens. Pakistan proved less successful in maintaining political freedom. Gen. Muhammad Ayub Khan seized power in 1958 and ruled Pakistan until 1969.

The United States had better relations with authoritarian Pakistan than with democratic India during the early years of the Cold War. Pakistan supported the anti-Communist containment policies of the United States. In 1954 the Eisenhower administration awarded military aid to Pakistan and accepted Pakistan's membership in a regional anti-Communist alliance, the Southeast Asia Treaty Organization (SEATO). Pakistan supported U.S. efforts to preserve an independent non-Communist South Vietnam. Under Prime Minister Nehru, India took an independent stance in international affairs. Nehru preached nonviolence, called for the end of the nuclear arms race, and kept India out of the Cold War with his policy of neutralism and nonalignment. He became a world leader when he helped organize the first Asian-African conference in Bandung, Indonesia, in 1955. He condemned the United States for arming Pakistan and bringing the Cold War to the subcontinent. Nehru's policies infuriated Secretary of State John Foster Dulles, who famously labeled neutralism in the Cold War "an immoral and shortsighted conception." U.S. officials also thought that Nehru tilted toward the Soviet Union. In October 1956 he denounced the British-French-Israeli attack on the Suez Canal as "colonialism." India abstained, however, on a UN resolution denouncing the Soviet invasion of Hungary. Nehru also did not share the U.S. view on South Vietnam. At the Geneva Conference of 1954, India had been appointed as one of the three nations to supervise Vietnam's national unification election. India judged that the United States had violated the Geneva Accords with its military support of South Vietnam.

U.S. relations with India improved during Eisenhower's second term. At the end of 1956, Prime Minister Nehru had visited with Eisenhower at his farm in Gettysburg, Pennsylvania. The two elder statesmen enjoyed each other's company, and Eisenhower would enjoy a successful visit to India at the end of 1959. Nehru, who had a strong sense of nationalistic pride, observed that the amiable, easygoing Eisenhower treated even humble Indians with respect. Eisenhower quietly continued, however, to believe that Asians valued life less than Westerners did. In 1957 the president approved an NSC recommendation that the United States support India's economic development as "an alternative to Communism in the Asian context." If India succeeded, it would show the people of Asia and Africa that there was a better model for economic development than the authoritarian, Communist one offered by China. The Eisenhower administration was also reacting to a new Soviet challenge, for Khrushchev had begun to offer Soviet economic assistance in Asia and Africa. India carried out its development strategies through a series of five-year plans. During the First Five-Year Plan (1951–1956), India received $283 million in U.S. support. The Eisenhower administration increased U.S. aid to $875 million for the Second Five-Year Plan (1956–1961).[27]

As a legislator, John Kennedy had developed a strong impression of India. He had met Nehru in New Delhi in 1951, when he went on a tour of Asia and the Middle East. Nehru paid little attention to John and Robert Kennedy at dinner and chatted with their attractive sister, Patricia. Despite the snub, Kennedy came to see India as symbolic of the power of nationalism that could be used to counter the appeal of communism. In his *Foreign Affairs* article (1957), he denounced the Eisenhower administration's "ill-conceived and ill-concealed disdain for the 'neutralists' and 'socialists.'" Nations like India represented "the free world's strongest bulwarks to the seductive appeal of Peking and Moscow." In 1958 Senator Kennedy cosponsored the Kennedy-Cooper resolution, which called on the United States to assist India in its development plans. India represented "one of the few countries in this non-Communist zone which really believes in the importance of breaking stagnation and acquiring habits of growth." In the presidential campaign, Kennedy told U.S. citizens that it was essential that India win the "development race." India's victory would help convince "the doubting world . . . now precariously on the wall of indecision between the East and the West" that the United States, not the Communist nations, represented the wave of the future.[28]

ECONOMIC ASSISTANCE

President Kennedy gave immediate substance to his views on India's critical role in global affairs. In his initial State of the Union address, he paid tribute to Prime Minister Nehru's "soaring idealism." He also signaled his sensitivity to India's needs with his first appointments. Undersecretary of State Chester Bowles had been a successful ambassador to India during the Truman presidency. Phillips Talbot, the new assistant secretary of state for Near East and South Asian Affairs, had been an exchange student in India in the late 1930s and subsequently a scholar-journalist who specialized on Indian issues. Kennedy named the renowned Harvard University economist, John Kenneth Galbraith, to be his ambassador in New Delhi. Galbraith, the author of the best-selling book *The Affluent Society* (1958), had a high profile in the United States and experience in advising on economic development in South Asia. As self-identified liberals, neither Bowles nor Galbraith had philosophical objections to India's preference for state planning in economic development. President Kennedy made tangible that acceptance of the Indian approach when in early 1961 he authorized a $1 billion U.S. pledge for the first two years of India's Third Five-Year Plan (1961–1966). He further relaxed restrictions on how India could spend the aid. An overwhelmed Prime Minister Nehru thanked the new president for his "generous approach."[29]

As he did in Latin America, Kennedy continued to make good on his promises of economic aid for India. Beyond contributing to the Third Five-Year Plan, the Kennedy administration made additional pledges of bilateral development assistance, budgetary support, and food shipments that amounted to an additional $2 billion in aid. In the 1962 fiscal year, for example, the administration allocated $500 million of its developmental budget of $900 million for India alone. During the 1960s the U.S. food aid program, Public Law 480, or "Food for Peace," fed over 10 percent of India's population. At the end of 1961 Prime Minister Nehru welcomed the first twenty-six Peace Corps volunteers to India. By 1968 over 1,400 U.S. citizens would be serving as Peace Corps volunteers in India. Although fiercely nationalistic, Prime Minister Nehru welcomed the Peace Corps, appreciating that volunteers lived and worked in the poor rural villages of India.[30]

The U.S. plan for India's development resembled the Alliance for Progress for Latin America, with the ideas of presidential adviser Walt Rostow permeating the development approach. The United States would help India create a "modernized," urban industrial society that would by the 1970s enter the "takeoff stage" of self-sustaining economic growth. U.S. bilateral assistance focused on helping India build high-impact projects such as steel mills and nuclear power plants. Prime Minister Nehru agreed with this approach, believing that an industrialized India would be able to provide employment for India's burgeoning rural population. Over 80 percent of Indians worked in agriculture, yet India still could not feed itself. Ambassador Galbraith, who served two years in India, tried to encourage rural development and would later become critical in his scholarly writings of the emphasis on modernization and industrialization.[31] By the latter part of the twentieth century, international development agencies such as the World Bank preached that rural development and increased food production offered the best route to attacking problems of poverty.

President Kennedy took no position on debates about economic development but proved remarkably flexible in allocating funds to India. Congress resisted U.S. aid going to state-owned enterprises and to the concept of state planning. India asked the Kennedy administration to support plans to build the fourth state-owned steel mill at Bokaro in the state of Orissa. The plant would take fifteen years to construct at a cost of $1.5 billion. If the United States provided the $900 million in foreign exchange requirements that India requested, the Bokaro steel mill would be the largest single public sector project in the history of U.S. foreign aid. Kennedy eventually had to back down in the face of congressional resistance, but as he noted at a news conference in May 1963, "I think it would be a great mistake not to build it. India needs the steel."[32] President Kennedy generally promoted international capitalism and the principles of free trade and investment. But, as he also demonstrated in his negotiations with Latin Americans on economic issues, he favored economic development over ideological purity. The world's richest nation had an obligation to help poor countries. Throughout his life, John Kennedy showed sympathy to struggling people, both at home and abroad.

However flawed the 1960s approach to economic progress may have been, a reasonable case can be made that the Kennedy administration and its predecessors had aided India's development. Chester Bowles, who returned as ambassador to India in 1963, compared the India he knew in the early 1950s to the new India. National income had risen 42 percent, and India enjoyed a 10 percent annual rate of industrial growth. This growth benefited the people. India had increased life expectancy from twenty-seven years to forty-two years and eradicated malaria. India also continued to have a parliamentary democracy and a democratic civic life. Between 1951 and 1971, the United States provided India with over $10 billion in foreign aid, half of it in food aid. U.S. assistance sustained India until agronomists developed high-yield seeds, fomenting the "Green Revolution" and providing India with better resources to expand food production.[33]

INDIA AND THE COLD WAR

If relations with India were analyzed solely in economic terms, the Kennedy administration could boast of significant accomplishments. It had drawn the democratic nation closer to the United States and promoted India's development. As Vice President Lyndon Johnson noted to Kennedy after the vice president's successful visit with Nehru in New Delhi in May 1961, "This administration is highly regarded and well received in India." India and the United States now had "an affinity of spirit." Johnson cautioned, however, that it was "as unnecessary as it is improbable" that India could be drawn into "our sphere."[34] But President Kennedy dedicated himself to winning the Cold War. He often said that he respected neutralism and nonalignment, but the historical record demonstrates he expected nations that he befriended to support the United States, whether it be populous India or minuscule British Guiana. U.S. distress over India's unwillingness to back U.S. policies undermined the goodwill created by economic cooperation.

President Kennedy hosted Prime Minister Nehru in November 1961. The state visit turned into a fiasco. Kennedy would later characterize Nehru's stay "a disaster . . . the worst head-of-state visit I have had." The prime minister seemed indifferent to Kennedy, refusing to engage the president in a substantial discussion on global affairs. Kennedy apparently relived the dinner experience he had had with Nehru in New Delhi in 1951. Presidential advisers thought Nehru listless and speculated that Nehru, nearing age seventy-two, lacked the vitality to be head of state. Scholars have suggested that Nehru found the young president aggressive, inexperienced, and not properly deferential to a beloved world leader.[35] Nehru did perk up in the presence of Jacqueline Kennedy. The next year the president's wife traveled to India and had a grand time with the prime minister. Nehru hung a photograph in his residence of the two of them strolling arm in arm through gardens.

Differing conceptions of international affairs rather than health or personality issues probably best explain the lack of communication between Kennedy and Nehru. Nehru continued to critique the Cold War. He criticized the U.S. military buildup in the midst of the Berlin crisis. He advised President Johnson that there was not a military solution to problems in Laos and Vietnam. He ignored a suggestion by Chester Bowles in August 1961 that India should join with Japan and Pakistan to balance the power of China. Despite perceiving China in "an arrogant mood," Nehru told Bowles that the United States might improve relations with China by selling it wheat. India also supported China's admission to the United Nations.[36] In his conversation with President Kennedy, Nehru observed, "The worst of the cold war is that it makes everyone rigid in mind and spirit." He feared that the resumption of nuclear testing could "land the world in a nuclear war." Nehru also reiterated that difficulties in Laos and Vietnam arose because of "the failure to live up to these commitments" made during the Geneva Conference of 1954.[37]

Prime Minister Nehru could irritate any world leader because he presented India as a paragon of virtue, eschewing force and violence in the international arena. In fact, Nehru pursued domestic and international policies suitable for India that had little to do with the Cold War. At home, Nehru emphasized economic development and maintaining peace between the majority Hindu population and India's sizeable Muslim minority. He accepted economic assistance from all sides. The Soviets agreed in 1964, for example, to help finance the Bokaro steel mill. India saw its main foreign policy interests in regional terms, protecting its borders, holding on to Kashmir, and guarding against Pakistani aggression. India implicitly accepted that other nations had regional concerns, even spheres of influence. India had not objected to the Soviet invasion of Hungary. But Nehru also said little about the U.S. invasion of Cuba at the Bay of Pigs and evinced slight interest in the plight of Cheddi Jagan and the Indo-Guyanese in British Guiana who were undergoing the loss of their political rights at the hands of the Kennedy White House.

Jacqueline Bouvier Kennedy is in New Delhi, India, with Prime Minister Jawaharlal Nehru in 1962. In the background are Indira Gandhi, the daughter of Nehru and a future prime minister, and U.S. Ambassador John Kenneth Galbraith. Nehru and President Kennedy did not enjoy each other's company when the prime minister visited Washington in November 1961. The First Lady had a successful visit to India. Jacqueline Kennedy proved to be an effective ambassador for the United States. (John F. Kennedy Presidential Library and Museum, Boston)

India's military seizure of the Portuguese colony of Goa on the western coast of India highlighted India's differences with the United States. When he learned of India's plans to attack Goa in mid-December 1961, Kennedy implored Nehru to reconsider and warned him that the United States would raise the issue at the United Nations. Indeed, UN Ambassador Adlai Stevenson used unusually strong language to denounce the seizure of Goa, suggesting that Indian aggression threatened the very survival of the United Nations. India seemed hypocritical in employing force to resolve a dispute. President Kennedy believed that Nehru should have alerted him to the impending action during their November conversations. More important, Kennedy did not want to anger Portugal, a NATO ally. The United States considered its access to military bases in Portugal's Azores archipelago in the Atlantic Ocean to be critical to U.S. national security. President Kennedy eventually found humor in the flap over Goa. According to India's ambassador to the United States, Kennedy remarked that India "spent the last 15 years preaching morality to us, and then you go ahead and act the way any normal country would behave." The president added, "People are saying that the preacher has been caught coming out of the brothel. And they are clapping. And Mr. Ambassador, I want to tell you, I am clapping too."[38]

In President Kennedy's world, a "normal country" would fear international communism. But his experience with South Asian nations would teach him that India and Pakistan regarded the Kashmir issue as "more important that the struggle against the Communists."[39] The Kennedy administration wanted to preserve its military alliance with Pakistan and access to the communications base at Peshawar. U-2 spy flights operated from Peshawar. President Ayub Khan felt threatened by the economic aid being showered on India and argued that the United States should support its Cold War friend by backing Pakistan's claim to Kashmir. Prime Minister Nehru, however, rejected the idea of the United States mediating the dispute. When Kennedy raised the issue during Nehru's state visit, the prime minister came alive and described Kashmir's history in great detail. India had won a righteous war against Pakistan in 1947–1948. India's position "was that no settlement is possible except on the basis of the situation as it now exists—with minor modifications."[40] In 1962 the United States supported a UN Security Council resolution calling for a plebiscite in Kashmir, but the Soviet Union vetoed the resolution for India. In 1965 India and Pakistan would again go to war over Kashmir, and tension and violence would persist into the twenty-first century. Both countries would develop nuclear weapons. In October 2008, for the first time, the two sides permitted limited trade and travel across the de facto border dividing the Indian and Pakistani parts of Kashmir.[41] The Kashmir issue thwarted the U.S. desire to draw India and Pakistan together to counter the power of China and the Soviet Union. When in 1962 the Kennedy administration delivered twelve F-104 fighter jets to Pakistan, India responded by negotiating for MiG fighter aircraft from the Soviet Union.

SINO-INDIAN WAR

The Kennedy administration interpreted the outbreak of the Sino-Indian border war in October 1962 as a "golden opportunity" to break the logjam over Kashmir and draw India closer to the United States. Prime Minister Nehru panicked as Chinese forces mauled Indian troops in the Himalayan region. Nehru publicly confessed to Indians, "We were getting out of touch with reality in the modern world and we were living in an artificial atmosphere of our own creation." As the military situation worsened, Nehru became anxious that China might bomb population centers or annex part of India.[42] On November 19, he startled Washington by describing the military situation as "really desperate." He asked for twelve squadrons of supersonic, all-weather fighter jets, radar communications equipment, and two B-47 bomber squadrons. India did not have the pilots trained to fly the airplanes. Nehru wanted U.S. pilots to patrol Indian skies to protect Indian cities from Chinese air attacks.[43] In effect, nonaligned India was asking the United States to go to war against China to protect India.

President Kennedy agreed to help India. On October 28, just as the Cuban missile crisis was winding down, he wrote a personal letter to Nehru, telling the prime minister, "I want to give you support as well as sympathy."[44] The United States shipped automatic weapons, long-range mortars, and communication equipment to India. The administration denounced China for "outright military aggression," although the administration thought that Indian troops fired first in early October. After receiving Nehru's frantic November 19 letter, Kennedy dispatched Assistant Secretary of State Averell Harriman to New Delhi to assess India's security needs. Nehru's letter had stunned the administration. Secretary of State Rusk, responding on November 20 with the approval of the president, noted that India now wanted not only a military alliance with the United States but also "a complete commitment by us to a fighting war." Rusk thought India should first enlist the support of the international community. The United States had no desire for war with China because it could lead to another confrontation with the Soviet Union. Rusk archly observed that Nehru's request meant India would hereafter have to forgo the "pretense of non-alignment."[45] Even as Rusk was composing his letter, China declared victory on November 20, ending the war. China's goals had been limited to establishing boundaries as China defined them. Nehru and his country calmed down.

Although the crisis ended abruptly, the administration still tried to redefine its relationship with India, while simultaneously maintaining its alliance with Pakistan. The administration would send appropriate military assistance to India. It would mollify Pakistan by bringing India to the bargaining table. It would also warn Pakistan not to ally with Communist nations. From November 1962 to November 1963, however, the administration encountered frustration rather than success with its South Asian policy. Harriman captured the dilemma when he reported to Kennedy on his mission to India and then Pakistan. Pakistan wanted a Kashmir settlement "on acceptable terms." But, when it came to Kashmir, what was acceptable to Pakistan was unacceptable to India. Responding to U.S. pressure, India agreed to ministerial-level talks on Kashmir. But five rounds of talks ended fruitlessly in May 1963. Pakistan outraged India and angered the United States when it struck a border agreement with China. The administration debated with itself how much military assistance it should grant to India, realizing that any significant aid would outrage Pakistan. Nonetheless, President Kennedy always kept Cold War issues uppermost in his mind. In late April 1963 he told the NSC, "It is hard to see how we can stop the Chinese Communists without India."[46] By mid-November 1963 President Kennedy had not made a decision, although he was mulling over a proposal to grant India over $314 million in military aid over five years. Ambassador Bowles, who met with the president on November 13, thought Kennedy was "favorably impressed" with the proposal.[47]

What course President Kennedy would have followed in South Asia during a second presidential term cannot be determined. He would have encountered new challenges. Prime Minister Nehru died in office in May 1964. In 1965 warfare again broke out between Pakistan and India over border issues. Both nations criticized U.S. policies in the region. India also condemned the growing U.S. military presence in Vietnam.

President Kennedy earned the gratitude of Prime Minister Nehru and his nation for promoting India's economic development. His administration helped hungry people. Introducing the Cold War concerns of the United States into the bilateral relationship, however, predictably soured relations with India.

CHAPTER 8

MIDDLE EAST AND AFRICA

PRESIDENT JOHN F. KENNEDY had far-reaching foreign policy plans for the Middle East and especially Africa. He believed that his unique understanding of the appeal and power of nationalism would help him win respect and friendship for the United States. Crises over Berlin, Cuba, and Vietnam and other international challenges kept the president from focusing on the Middle East and Africa. The Kennedy administration would also find that regional issues in the Middle East proved resistant to U.S. solutions. President Kennedy and his advisers further decided that conciliating Cold War friends took precedence over the aspirations of African nationalists.

Middle East

John F. Kennedy believed that he could help resolve international and domestic problems in the Middle East and enhance the reputation of the United States in the region. Kennedy had not made the U.S. role in the Middle East a central issue during the 1960 campaign, but he had a remarkably ambitious agenda for the region. He sought to mediate the dangerous Arab-Israeli confrontation, work with Arab nationalists, and promote economic development and modernization throughout the region. Armed with new policies and a sympathetic attitude, Kennedy hoped that he could find a just settlement for the Palestinians and push conservative Arab monarchies toward political and economic liberalization. The fruits of this diplomacy would be security for Israel, moderation in the Arab world, continued Western access to Middle Eastern oil, and the exclusion of

Soviet influence from the region. Like presidents before and after him, Kennedy failed to foster peace and justice in the Middle East. The dilemmas associated with the plight of Palestinians and the bitter rivalries between Arab leaders and nations undermined Kennedy's honest efforts. Kennedy found that the United States had little choice but to side with its traditional friends in the Middle East. Nonetheless, Kennedy made an impact in the Middle East. He established precedents for drawing the United States closer to the state of Israel.

EGYPT

The new Kennedy administration thought the key to expanding U.S. influence in the Middle East would be improving the strained relations with Egypt, the most powerful and populous Arab nation. The charismatic Egyptian leader, Gamal Abdel Nasser (1954–1970), dominated political life in the region. Nasser, a military officer, conspired with other officers and overthrew the Egyptian monarch, King Farouk, in 1952. By 1954 Nasser wrested power from other officers and became Egypt's president and prime minister at the age of thirty-six. Nasser had proved his military courage during the first war with Israel in 1948. Feeling humiliated by his nation's defeat, Nasser preached that Egypt needed a modern state and scientific and technological progress. A fervent, strident nationalist, he wanted to remove the vestiges of British and French imperialism from his country. Nasser also called on Arab people to unite, and in 1958 he merged Egypt with Syria in the United Arab Republic. His direct appeals to impoverished, powerless Arabs frightened conservative Arab monarchs such as King Saud of Saudi Arabia. Israel also dreaded the growing power of Egypt. As Israeli Prime Minister David Ben-Gurion once observed to President Kennedy, "All questions in the Middle East depend upon Nasser."[1]

U.S. relations with Nasser's Egypt had deteriorated badly during the Eisenhower presidency. Nasser wanted funding for the Aswan High Dam, a massive public works project that would reclaim land on the Upper Nile River and bring hydroelectric power to Egypt. Alarmed that Egypt had begun to purchase arms from the Soviet bloc and that the Soviet Union had begun its campaign to gain influence with neutral nations in Asia and the Middle East, the United States tentatively agreed in 1955 to arrange Western financing for the Aswan Dam. But in mid-1956 the Eisenhower administration abruptly informed Egypt that it would not finance the project. Nasser's independent foreign policy infuriated Eisenhower and Secretary of State John Foster Dulles. Nasser continued to receive Soviet arms, and he established relations with the People's Republic of China. Nasser responded to the U.S. insult by nationalizing the Suez Canal Company, an Egyptian company with majority British and French stockholders. The tolls collected on ships passing through Suez would be used to finance Aswan. The United Kingdom and France, in conjunction with Israel, attacked Egypt in October 1956. President Eisenhower denounced the attack and actually helped save Nasser by forcing the British, French, and Israeli forces to withdraw from Egypt. Nonetheless, U.S.-Egyptian relations remained uneven during Eisenhower's second term. Nasser obtained more Soviet arms and a Soviet promise to help finance the Aswan Dam. He also poured scorn on the pro-Western monarchies. At the same time, Nasser, ever the nationalist, told the Soviet Union that he opposed the spread of communism in the Arab world. Nasser further became receptive to President Eisenhower's idea that he put the issue of Israel aside in return for U.S. food aid.

President Kennedy believed that he was uniquely suited to build on Eisenhower's effort to improve relations with Egypt. His 1951 tour of the world had included stops in Iran and Israel. Congressman Kennedy told his Boston constituency, "The true enemy of the Arab world was poverty and want." Kennedy built on his 1957 Senate speech about supporting Algerian independence. The United States needed to embrace nationalism in the Middle East, for it reflected "a positive search for political freedom and self-development." He criticized the decision not to finance the Aswan Dam. The United States should support a multilateral development fund, offer food aid, and develop a program for Arab refugees. What was especially required "was active political leadership to break the paralysis of purpose."[2] As he had regarding relations with India, Latin America, and other areas of the world, Kennedy pledged to act differently than Eisenhower. He promised to be a strong, active leader who understood that nationalism and economic development would undermine the appeal of communism.

President Kennedy and President Nasser started off well together. Perhaps they perceived a natural affinity. Both leaders were young, dynamic, and commanded international attention. They exchanged cordial letters. Kennedy emphasized to Nasser his respect for the religious and cultural heritage of Muslim people. Kennedy backed his kind words by appointing John S. Badeau to be his ambassador the United Arab Republic. Badeau, an Arabic speaker, had previously served as the president of the American University in Cairo and prophesied that a modernized Egypt could transform the Middle East. Kennedy also asked Congress for funds to help Egypt preserve ancient temples and monuments in the Nile Valley that might be inundated as a result of the construction of the Aswan Dam. President Nasser responded with messages to Kennedy that the State Department characterized as "extraordinarily warm in tone, mild in language, forthcoming, and hopeful for the relations of the two countries in the future."[3]

The Kennedy administration perceived the Middle East in regional rather than global terms. It did not view the region solely through the prism of the Cold War. It acted differently toward Egypt than it did, for example, toward British Guiana or Vietnam. Intelligence analysts and diplomats accepted the fervor of Nasser's nationalism. As a mid-1961 National Intelligence Estimate put it, Nasser pursued "positive neutralism." He rejected the idea of either becoming dependent or alienated from the West or the Soviet bloc. Arab nationalists were prepared "to respond vigorously to Soviet attacks." The government-controlled press denounced both Moscow and Washington.[4] Ambassador Chester Bowles, who went on a fact-finding mission to Cairo in February 1962, interpreted Nasser and his coterie as "pragmatists searching for techniques that will enable them to expand their economy rapidly and to maintain their political grip." Nasser assured Bowles that communism as a political or economic system was "unworkable" in the Middle East. U.S. officials understood that the Arabs' major concern was Israel, not the Cold War. The United Arab Republic considered Israel the "clear and present danger."[5]

The Kennedy administration decided to seek, in the words of an NSC official, "a limited accommodation" with Nasser. The United States had provided Egypt with wheat under Public Law 480, the "Food for Peace" program, on an annual basis. Egypt asked for a multiyear aid program. Nasser's ambassador to the United States, Mustapha Kamel, suggested that the Egyptian request represented a significant turning point in bilateral relations "since the fiasco of the Aswan Dam." Ambassador Kamel predicted that the United States would strengthen its position with the Middle East's most influential nation and thereby help prevent the penetration of communism in the region. After extensive internal debate, the administration responded positively to the aid request. President Kennedy asked his foreign policy team, "What would the US get out of [an] approach to Nasser?" U.S. officials believed that aid would act as a "restraining influence" on Nasser. The Egyptian might focus on his nation's "colossal" problems and stop meddling in the internal affairs of the Arab allies of the United States. U.S. economic assistance would also help keep President Nasser "out of Khrushchev's clutches."[6] In 1962 President Kennedy authorized a three-year, $500 million Public Law 480 package for Egypt. The State Department judged Nasser's subsequent letter of gratitude "practically unique" in the history of U.S.–United Arab Republic relations. U.S. officials thought that Nasser would now keep his dispute with Israel "in the refrigerator" and avoid provocative actions in the Middle East.[7] By mid-1962 the Kennedy administration appeared to have achieved a significant diplomatic triumph.

The Kennedy administration held that economic development could also work wonders in the conservative nations of the region. President Kennedy repeatedly warned the advisers of King Idris of Libya that Libya needed to transform its oil money into "the achievement of progress and prosperity" for the king's subjects. The widespread graft, corruption, and squandering of petrodollars would foster radicalism in Libya. Kennedy also urged the U.S. client, Shah Mohammed Reza Pahlavi of Iran, to modernize his country and avoid excessive military expenditures. Kennedy doubted that complacent Middle Eastern monarchs, the friends of the United States, could survive unless they addressed the twentieth-century desires of people for respect, dignity, and a modern economic life. Speaking of the Saudi kingdom, Kennedy complained to an aide, "Our clients were the ones who somehow represented yesterday rather than tomorrow."[8]

The conservative monarchs ruled over nations rich in oil resources. But economic imperatives did not primarily motivate Kennedy to call for change and development in the Middle East. U.S. oil companies had profitable investments and business in the Middle East. And European allies of the United States depended on Middle Eastern oil. But the world was awash in oil in the early 1960s. The price of oil was barely above $2.00 a barrel at the time. U.S. citizens paid at the pump as little as 19 cents for a gallon of gasoline. The United States was still a net exporter of petroleum products. What oil the United States imported came from Venezuela, a reliable U.S. ally. President Kennedy judged economic and social development as being the key to realizing political order and stability in the Middle East and avoiding communism and extreme nationalism.

The Kennedy administration's approach to the Middle East fell into disarray during the fall of 1962. President Nasser proved unwilling and perhaps incapable of assuming "a key role in bringing the Middle East peacefully into our modern world." Nasser had suffered a blow to his prestige in the Arab world when Syria seceded from the United Arab Republic after a right-wing coup in Damascus in September 1961. He saw an opportunity to restore his standing in the pan-Arab movement when pro-Nasser officers led by Col. Abdullah Sallal in Yemen overthrew the monarchy and appealed to Nasser for military help to secure their revolution. In October 1962 Nasser rushed troops, tanks, and jet fighters to Yemen, an impoverished country at the mouth of the Red Sea. Yemen's neighbor, Saudi Arabia, fearing that Nasser-style nationalism would spread to the kingdom, began to supply royalist guerrillas in Yemen. King Hussein of Jordan, a traditional friend of the United States, backed the Saudi effort. The Egyptians eventually had 70,000 troops in Yemen. Egyptian bombers attacked royalist fighter camps in Saudi Arabia. The war in Yemen dragged on for five years.[9]

Nasser's intervention in Yemen forced the United States to make unhappy choices. The administration saw great benefits in its relationship with Nasser. The Egyptian seemed less dependent on the Soviet Union, and he kept his pledge not to agitate the Palestinian refugee issue. As President Kennedy noted to the NSC, "the balance of power would swing against us," if the United States did not maintain its relationship with leading neutralists like Nasser. Kennedy decided in mid-November 1962 to recognize the new Yemeni government led by Colonel Sallal, while he simultaneously called on all sides to withdraw troops and cease meddling in Yemen. Kennedy conceded his plan was "full of hopes" rather than substance. The administration discussed inviting Nasser for his first-ever state visit to Washington.[10] Judging that their national survival depended on restoring the royalists in Yemen, however, the Saudis resisted U.S. pleas to stop opposing the new Yemeni government. The Saudis considered themselves reliable friends of the United States and the guarantors of substantial U.S. investments in the kingdom.

President Kennedy also found that he could not persuade Nasser to end the war. He wrote several letters to Nasser, pointing out his "personal role" in the issue.[11] Beyond Saudi Arabia and Jordan, the United Kingdom and Israel were criticizing Kennedy for recognizing the new Yemeni government and supporting Nasser. Congress, responding to both domestic and international criticism of U.S. policy, was moving toward eliminating U.S. food aid to Egypt. By the fall of 1963 the president seemed to have grown completely exasperated with President Nasser. In previous months, he had ordered a small contingent of U.S. fighters to Saudi Arabia to serve as a symbolic deterrent against Nasser. Kennedy's foreign-policy success and failure almost always revolved around Cold War issues. In the case of Nasser and the United Arab Republic, a policy that Kennedy had considered far-sighted, generous, and within U.S. national interest had become hostage to rivalries within the Arab world. President Lyndon Johnson considered Nasser to be duplicitous and abandoned the U.S. attempt to conciliate the Egyptian.

Israel

In the midst of the imbroglio over Yemen, Simon Peres, the future prime minister of Israel, pointedly remarked to State Department officers, "Rightly or wrongly, there is a general impression in the area that the United States thinks Nasser holds the key to [the] future and prefers him to truer friends."[12] Israel obviously considered itself that "truer friend." Although it had not been a foreign policy objective of John Kennedy to bind the United States to Israel, the president's decisions had the effect of forging an alliance between the two nations.

The United States had been directly involved with Israel from its birth as a modern state. The desire among Jews around the world for a Jewish state in the traditional homeland in the Middle East had taken on urgency after the near annihilation of European Jewry by Adolf Hitler and the Nazis. In mid-May 1948 President Harry S. Truman rejected the advice of Defense Department and State Department officials, including Secretary of State George Marshall, and extended diplomatic recognition to Israel, hours after it declared its independence. Truman's advisers believed that recognition would alienate Arab nations and jeopardize Western access to oil resources. They also doubted whether Israel could survive the expected onslaught from the Arab world. President

Truman acted because he sympathized with the plight of Jewish refugees and he saw domestic political gains in recognition. Israel not only survived the war of 1948–1949 but actually extended its boundaries. The effect of the war was to leave up to 750,000 Palestinian Arabs as refugees.

The Eisenhower administration maintained correct but not warm relations with Israel. It wanted to conciliate Arab nations in order to contain the Soviet Union and safeguard trade and investments in oil. It supplied Israel with economic aid of about $150 million a year but not arms. President Eisenhower denied Israeli requests for antiaircraft missiles but authorized the sale of a sophisticated radar system to Israel in 1960. Israel obtained its arms primarily from France. The arms race was accelerating in the 1950s, with Egypt obtaining arms from the Soviet Union. President Eisenhower was outraged when Israel joined in the attack on the Suez Canal in 1956. Eisenhower also worried that the nuclear reactor Israel was building at Dimona in the Negev Desert would be used to develop weapons-grade plutonium for atomic bombs. He passed those suspicions on to President-elect Kennedy at their meeting on January 19, 1961.

John Kennedy knew something about Israel and had a good standing with Jewish voters in the United States. His 1951 tour of the world had included a stop in Israel and dinner with Prime Minister David Ben-Gurion, a founding father of the state of Israel. Congressman Kennedy left Israel impressed with the élan of Israelis and their dedication to the new state. During his 1952 senatorial campaign, Kennedy courted Jewish voters, assuring them he did not share the anti-Semitic sentiments his father had expressed in the 1930s. During the presidential campaign, Kennedy gave speeches to Jewish organizations, asserting that friendship with Israel was not a partisan issue but "a national commitment." Kennedy's appeal to Jewish voters was practical politics. Jewish voters had been voting overwhelmingly for the Democratic Party since the era of Franklin Roosevelt. Kennedy also appealed to citizens of Irish, Italian, and Polish ancestry. Although a friend of Israel, Kennedy expressed sympathy for Palestinian Arabs. In 1959 he told a Jewish organization that the refugee issue "has lain like a naked sword between Israel and the Arab states." Kennedy pledged to work on the issue, if elected president.[13]

President Kennedy's meeting on May 30, 1961, at the Waldorf Astoria Hotel in New York City with Prime Minister Ben-Gurion centered on key U.S.-

Israeli issues. The president immediately pressed Ben-Gurion on the purposes of the Dimona reactor. The Israeli leader assured Kennedy that the reactor would generate electricity for peaceful purposes, although he hedged his response with the observation that Israel might one day need a plant to process plutonium to protect itself from Arab aggression. Ben-Gurion renewed his request for high performance Hawk antiaircraft (surface-to-air) missiles to protect Israel from bombers supplied to Egypt by the Soviet Union. Kennedy responded that he did not want to escalate the arms race in the Middle East by introducing missiles into the region. He predicted that Arab nations might then want ground-to-ground missiles. Ben-Gurion also implicitly asked for U.S. security guarantees, noting, "We are the only remnants of a people that have been fighting for survival for the past 4,000 years. If Nasser defeats us, we are destroyed." Ben-Gurion further reminded Kennedy that Israel supported U.S. Cold War positions. For his part, Kennedy noted that he wanted to be helpful in the Middle East by improving relations with President Nasser and addressing the refugee issue. Ben-Gurion thought that Nasser was intent on destroying Israel and that "the Arabs do not value human life." He added that Arab nations cared little about Palestinian refugees as people; they used the refugee issue as a weapon against Israel.[14] Developments over the next thirty months demonstrated that Prime Minister Ben-Gurion would achieve Israeli objectives, whereas President Kennedy ended up siding with Israel more than he had anticipated.

By the summer of 1962 the Kennedy administration had decided to sell the Hawk missiles to Israel on favorable terms. The Israelis persistently lobbied the administration, emphasizing the dangers that their country faced. Both State and Defense officials gradually reasoned that the Hawks were "defensive" weapons and would not upset the balance of power in the region. They also thought President Nasser would remain calm about the sale because the United States provided aid to him. Indeed, Nasser did not object vociferously to the U.S. decision. Although President Kennedy and Secretary of State Rusk seemed to have believed that they had made a decision with limited consequences, the Israeli leaders celebrated, believing that they had transformed U.S. policy. In November 1963 the Israelis submitted requests for "offensive" weapons such as tanks. They would find that President Johnson would readily accede to the requests, approving the sale of 210 U.S. tanks in 1965 and 48 Skyhawk bombers in 1966.[15]

The Kennedy administration had faint hopes that the sale of Hawks would help persuade Israel to address the Palestinian refugee issue. In August 1961 Kennedy and Secretary Rusk persuaded the United Nations to appoint Joseph E. Johnson of the Carnegie Endowment for International Peace to address the refugee issue. Kennedy's action showed both his humanitarian side and his understanding that resolving the Palestinian refugee issue was essential for peace in the Middle East. Johnson's plan, which he had developed after several visits to the Middle East, called for refugees to be secretly polled on whether they wanted to return to Israel or be settled in Arab lands. Johnson expected that most refugees would not choose to be repatriated to Israel. Johnson envisioned the United States contributing up to $700 million over ten years to cover the cost of repatriation and resettlement. But neither Israeli leaders nor President Nasser displayed any flexibility or goodwill. Ben-Gurion feared that Israel would be overwhelmed by repatriated Palestinians who hated Israel. Nasser wanted all Palestinians to have the right of return to Israel. Faced with such fears and narrow-mindedness, President Kennedy gave up on the Johnson plan by the end of 1962.[16]

President Nasser's intransigence both on the refugee issue and the crisis over Yemen also seems to have contributed to Kennedy's decision to give Israel what it wanted most desperately—a U.S. pledge to guarantee its survival. In 1963 Ben-Gurion peppered Kennedy with letters, warning that Arab nations contemplated the annihilation of Israel. Ben-Gurion suggested that U.S. economic aid to Arab nations left them in a stronger position to attack Israel. The prime minister called for a public declaration, perhaps a joint U.S.-Soviet declaration, guaranteeing the territorial integrity of Middle Eastern nations. President Kennedy responded coolly to these heated messages, noting to Ben-Gurion that the United States monitored the region and that he did not believe the balance of power had shifted against Israel. He assured Ben-Gurion that the United States was a "particular friend" of Israel. Kennedy observed that what especially worried him was the not the present situation but the introduction of "advanced offensive systems" into the region.[17] Kennedy constantly worried about nuclear proliferation and the introduction of nuclear weapons into the Middle East. He unsuccessfully attempted to persuade Egypt and Israel to renounce the acquisition of nuclear weapons.

The failure to establish the Middle East as a nuclear-free zone seems to have prompted the president to take an additional step to relieve Israeli fears. On October 2, 1963, Kennedy wrote to Levi Eshkol, Israel's new prime minister. He pointed out to the prime minister that the mighty U.S. Sixth Fleet patrolled the nearby Mediterranean Sea, proving "we can back up our assurances." Kennedy still saw no wisdom in providing an explicit security guarantee to Israel. A public declaration might drive the Arab nations into the hands of the Soviet Union. He noted, however, "There is no doubt in Arab minds as to how we would respond to an unprovoked aggression by them." Kennedy concluded that he knew that Prime Minister Eshkol needed "no reassurance as to the constant and special United States concern for the security and independence of Israel."[18]

Kennedy perhaps believed that his extraordinary letter of U.S. support to Eshkol would assist him in stopping Israel from developing atomic weapons. Ben-Gurion had lied to the president about Israeli intentions during their meeting at the Waldorf Astoria Hotel. Israeli leaders believed an atomic bomb was vital to Israel's security. Kennedy learned that the Israelis were tightly controlling U.S. and international scientists who inspected the Dimona reactor. The intelligence community also informed him that Egypt had not started a nuclear weapons development program. The president sent tough messages to Ben-Gurion in 1962–1963 about the issue. In late December 1962 he met Golda Meir, the formidable foreign minister of Israel, at the vacation spot of Palm Beach, Florida. He warned Meir that the "special relationship" between the two countries was "a two-way street." Israel's security depended on how it treated both its Arab neighbors and the United States. He bluntly told her, "We are opposed to nuclear proliferation." Meir was less than forthright in her responses to the president.[19] In July 1963 Kennedy congratulated Eshkol on his new position and immediately reminded him that he had written to his predecessor that "this Government's commitment to and support of Israel could be seriously jeopardized" if Israel withheld information on the Dimona plant. In August, Prime Minister Eshkol promised to open the Dimona plant to comprehensive inspections.[20] Kennedy did not live long enough to find out whether Israel would fulfill that pledge.

Given the intensity of his views on the issue of nuclear proliferation and his recent achievement of a great diplomatic triumph with the Limited Test Ban Treaty with the Soviet Union, President Kennedy probably would have insisted on meaningful inspections of the Dimona nuclear reactor. As the president saw it, he had given his word to protect Israel in his October 2 letter to Prime Minister Eshkol. He had gone farther than Presidents Truman or Eisenhower in tying the United States to Israel's security. President Johnson did not, however, share Kennedy's worries about the regional and global consequences of an Israel armed with atomic weapons. Sham inspections of Dimona continued. By the time of the Six-Day War of 1967, the Dimona plant had produced material for a nuclear arsenal.

President John F. Kennedy worked hard to bring peace, economic development, and stability to the Middle East. But by November 1963 he had little to show for his honest and farsighted efforts. U.S relations with President Nasser and other Arab nationalists remained difficult. Conservative monarchies resisted Kennedy's calls for political liberalization and socioeconomic development. The Palestinian refugee issue remained unresolved and dangerous. Despite the president's misgivings, the United States had entered the business of arming Israel. Israel was developing a nuclear weapon. If he had lived, Kennedy might have taken some comfort in knowing that his presidential successors also saw their good efforts stymied by the passions and realities that characterize life in the Middle East.

Africa

Observers of international affairs would have confidently predicted in January 1961 that the new presidential administration would make Africa a centerpiece of its foreign policies. Africa seemed to be the most vibrant area in the world. Between 1957 and 1963, thirty-five new nations had joined the United Nations. Thirty of those nations came from the great continent of Africa. Senator Kennedy pointed to the significance of this development throughout the 1960 presidential campaign. He mentioned developments in Africa 479 times, and he gave thirteen major speeches about the region. By comparison, he barely mentioned Vietnam in the campaign. Kennedy's campaign rhetoric on Africa did not, however, match his presidential record. Although Kennedy devoted presidential time to African affairs, he did not change the basic U.S. approach to the region. Kennedy administration policies on Africa will be examined by first noting the relationship of Africa to the U.S. civil rights movement and then by surveying the administration's policies toward Algeria, Angola, and South Africa. Kennedy administration officials recognized that African leaders wanted the new president to focus on "the three 'A's' of Africa: Algeria, Angola, and Apartheid."[21] To be sure, Kennedy also devoted energy trying to resolve the political chaos in the former Belgium colony of the Congo and on developing an economic aid program for Ghana.[22]

CIVIL RIGHTS AND AFRICA

Entering the presidential campaign against Vice President Richard M. Nixon as a distinct underdog, Senator Kennedy and his campaign advisers knew that they had to prove many things to U.S. voters. Kennedy needed to show independent voters that he could match the vice president in his knowledge of international affairs. As a Democrat, Kennedy also needed to secure votes from two irreconcilable parts of his party's base—white voters in the South and African-American voters. The issue of U.S. policies toward Africa provided Senator Kennedy with an opportunity to address his campaign needs.

Richard Nixon had gained extensive experience in international affairs during his eight years serving as vice president, and he considered himself prescient on the emerging role of Africa in global affairs. He had represented the United States at the 1957 independence ceremony of Ghana, the first African nation to emerge from colonialism. He had also taken a fact-finding tour of the continent and warned President Eisenhower that the newly emergent nations of Africa "could well prove to be the decisive factor in the conflict between forces of freedom and international communism."[23] Nixon was handicapped, however, by his administration's uncertain stance toward decolonization. Both President Eisenhower and Secretary of State Dulles favored the end of colonialism, but they always listened to the concerns of European allies, the colonial masters of Africa. After the election in December 1960, at the behest of the United Kingdom, the administration abstained on a UN resolution calling for the rapid end of colonialism. The resolution passed 89-0, with the United States and the European colonialists abstaining on the vote.

With seventeen African nations gaining their independence in 1960 alone, Senator Kennedy seized on the African issue to demonstrate that his knowledge of international affairs matched Nixon's and that his understanding of nationalism would prove effective in winning the allegiance of the new African nations. Kennedy made a winning gesture when his family's foundation provided $100,000 to pay the airfare of 280 African students who had been accepted for study at American universities. The Eisenhower administration had initially been unwilling to help the students. Focusing on Africa also appealed to conservative, anti-Communist southern voters who worried about winning the Cold War. These southern voters also wanted to maintain segregation and deny African Americans the right to vote. Senator Kennedy raised the issue of Africa far more often than that of civil rights during the 1960 campaign. He carried many of the states of the Old Confederacy in the 1960 election.

Kennedy also desperately wanted African-American votes. Since 1936 African Americans had been voting reliably for the Democratic Party and its philosophy of social welfare. But during the 1950s African Americans began to question their party's tepid response to the emerging civil rights movement in the aftermath of the Supreme Court's *Brown vs. Board of Education* (1954) ruling, which declared segregation unconstitutional. In the 1956 election, Adlai Stevenson did not garner as high a percentage of African-American voters as he had in 1952. Both Dr. Martin Luther King Jr. and his father voted for Eisenhower in 1956. Talking about Africa helped Kennedy generate enthusiasm in the black community. Senator Kennedy made another important gesture when he telephoned Coretta Scott King to express his concern about her husband, after Dr. King was arrested and sentenced to four months of hard labor for trying to integrate a restaurant in Atlanta, Georgia. Robert Kennedy subsequently persuaded the sentencing judge to release Dr. King. Candidate Nixon did not react to Dr. King's arrest. Kennedy won over 75 percent of the African-American vote in northern urban areas, helping him carry states such as Illinois and Michigan.[24]

President Kennedy continued to tie Africa and civil rights together. He appointed G. Mennen Williams, the former governor of Michigan, to be his assistant secretary of state for African Affairs. Williams had gained a national reputation as a champion of civil rights. Williams immediately made his presence felt when, during his initial tour of Africa, he replied to a question about U.S. foreign policy in Africa by noting, "What we want for Africans is what Africans want for themselves." His reply indicated that the United States opposed colonialism and would no longer be bound by ties to Western allies when it came to Africa. President Kennedy publicly backed Williams. In response to a question of whether "Africa was for Africans," he quipped, "I don't know who else Africa would be for."[25] The president also made efforts to send African-American diplomats to African capitals and around the world. During the presidential campaign, Kennedy lamented that only twenty-six African Americans served in the 6,000-person Foreign Service. Secretary of State Rusk carried out Kennedy's goal of diversifying the Foreign Service. Rusk labeled racism at home "the biggest single burden that we carry on our backs in foreign relations."[26]

President Kennedy hosted a parade of U.S. civil rights and African leaders at the White House. Twenty-eight African leaders visited with the president. Like Latin American officials, Africans left the Oval Office appreciative of Kennedy's characteristic graciousness and amazed at the depth of his knowledge about their respective countries. The president stunned Kenyan Tom Mboya when he began to discuss labor issues in Nairobi. The president may have hosted as many black people, foreign and domestic, as all of his presidential predecessors combined. Although he did not visit Africa, the president dispatched the vice president and three members of his family on goodwill tours of the continent. Kennedy also became agitated when African diplomats encountered discrimination in states like Maryland and Virginia and directed aides to pressure restaurateurs to serve all customers.[27] Africans and African Americans perhaps most appreciated President Kennedy's embrace, however belated, of the civil rights movement and his moving speech of June 11, 1963, calling for legislation to end segregation in U.S. life. Kennedy tied equal justice for African Americans directly to international affairs, noting, "We preach freedom around the world, and we mean it . . . but are we to say to the world, and much more importantly, to each other, that this is a land of the free except for the Negroes?"[28] Although President Kennedy approached the issue of civil rights cautiously, his actions and gestures toward Africans demonstrated that he believed in racial equality both at home and abroad. Civil rights activist James Meredith was arguably correct when he remarked that in personal terms John Kennedy was the first U.S. president who was not a racist.[29]

Algeria and Angola

Although committed to racial justice, President Kennedy was also a Cold Warrior and one who prided himself at looking at issues dispassionately. His initial

President Kennedy greets President Kwame Nkrumah of Ghana on March 8, 1961. Ghana became the first African nation to gain its independence in the postwar world. President Kennedy hoped to signal his interest in Africa by hosting a leading African official early in his term. The president thereafter would host twenty-seven African leaders during his brief presidency. (John F. Kennedy Presidential Library and Museum, Boston)

enthusiasm for bold moves in Africa waned quickly. African issues were complex, and the United States had limited interests in the region. In 1960 U.S. exports and imports from Africa amounted to less than 4 percent of U.S. trade, and U.S. direct investments were similarly minuscule. Except for South Africa, African countries did not ship vital strategic minerals to the United States. In a 1963 review of "the strategic importance of Africa," Department of Defense officials concluded that "Africa is not an area of primary strategic importance to US, and we therefore have a strong interest in restricting our involvement" there.[30] President Kennedy did not completely accept such recommendations. As he did in other developing areas of the world, he tried to help generate economic growth in Africa. Africa received a substantial number of the 7,000 Peace Corps volunteers that the Kennedy administration dispatched abroad. Ethiopia, for example, accepted 275 volunteers, with many of them working as schoolteachers. The president also persuaded the U.S. Congress to allocate almost $500 million in economic aid for Africa, an amount that more than doubled the Eisenhower administration's foreign-aid budget for Africa. Kennedy did not, however, propose something akin to the Alliance for Progress with Latin America for the African continent.[31]

In relations with individual countries, President Kennedy acted in a cautious, traditional fashion. Senator Kennedy first gained favorable attention with Africans with his famous 1957 speech on Algeria, calling for independence for the French colony. The speech served as a rebuke both to European colonialists and the Eisenhower and Truman administrations for deferring to European interests. Secretary of State Dulles and former Secretary of State Dean Acheson both resented the speech. As president, Kennedy pursued policies toward Algeria that resembled the approaches of Acheson and Dulles. Between 1958 and 1960, the Eisenhower administration continued to follow France's lead in North Africa, as it tried to suppress the rebellion in Algeria. The old but difficult U.S. friend, Charles de Gaulle, returned to power in 1958. The Eisenhower administration continued to supply weapons to the French army and, at the behest of President de Gaulle, declined to talk directly with the Algerian National Liberation Front (FLN) or its political representatives. Senator Kennedy did not speak about Algeria again until 1959 and then modified his call for "independence" into "self-determination." He did not raise the Algerian issue during the presidential campaign. As president, Kennedy took the position that President de Gaulle would eventually find a way to overcome militant French colonialists and grant independence to Algeria. In any case, he needed the French leader's support during the Berlin crisis. As Kennedy told presidential aide Arthur Schlesinger, "our sympathy is with the anti-colonial nations," but it would be in the best U.S. interest to "sit this one out." The Kennedy administration also would not talk directly with the FLN and even worried that the Algerian freedom fighters were drawing too close to Communists. President de Gaulle ended the Algerian war and granted the colony its independence. On June 3, 1962, the United States recognized the new nation of Algeria.[32]

Placing European interests over anticolonial sentiments also characterized the Kennedy administration's policies toward Portugal and its African colonies.

The right-wing authoritarian António de Oliveira Salazar (1932–1968) controlled political life in one of Europe's poorest countries. Salazar denied that Portugal had colonies in places such as Angola, Mozambique, and Goa, arguing that they were politically integrated into Portugal. India had tired of this charade and invaded Goa in late 1961. To U.S. officials, Salazar seemed to be living in a different historical era. In 1963 President Kennedy dispatched Undersecretary of State George Ball to Lisbon to reason with Salazar. Ball wrote back to the president that it had been wrong to think that a dictator ruled Portugal. Instead, Portugal was "ruled by a triumvirate consisting of Vasco da Gama, Prince Henry the Navigator, and Salazar."[33] Salazar seemed delusional, as he boasted that Angola enjoyed peace and prosperity. Less than 1 percent of the colonial population attended school. Angolan feedom fighters began attacking Portuguese colonial authorities and institutions in 1961.

The Kennedy administration initially won plaudits from African nations by taking a hard line on Portuguese colonialism. In March 1961 it supported a UN resolution calling on Portugal to end colonialism and to cease violence against Angolans seeking independence. The administration also sent supplies and money to an Angolan independence group led by Holden Roberto. The administration feared the Marxist proclivities of other Angolan liberation movements. But the administration soon rethought its position. Dean Acheson denounced the administration for "misguided idealism," in opposing a NATO ally. The administration also understood that Salazar held a trump card—the lease to the air base in the Azores. Salazar could terminate the lease at the end of 1962. U.S. military officials wanted continued access to the base in order to airlift equipment and men to Europe if war broke out over Berlin. U.S. policy became confused and contradictory. Portuguese forces used U.S.-supplied bombs and napalm to attack Angolans, even as the the United States provided medicine and food to Angolan refugees across the border in the Congo. U.S. diplomats also broached the idea of a substantial economic aid package for both Portugal and Angola, if Portugal would establish a process leading to Angolan self-determination. The rigid Salazar rejected the idea of forfeiting the colonial empire, labeling his Angolan opponents as "Communists." Salazar further feared that Portugal would lose access to cheap colonial labor and materials and that 500,000 Portuguese nationals living in Africa would flee to the impoverished mother country.[34]

President Kennedy decided not to fight the Portuguese dictator on behalf of Africa. In mid-1963 the United States abstained on a UN resolution calling for the end of Portuguese colonialism and a ban on supplying military weapons to Portugal. Kennedy suggested to aides, "We should so far as possible, sit back and let others take the lead." The United States would offer "no specific solutions." President Kennedy had higher priorities than Angola. Wanting ratification of a test ban treaty, Kennedy did not want to anger political conservatives in the United States by denouncing the anti-Communist Prime Minister Salazar. The president also reminded aides, "It is of the utmost importance to avoid a risk of losing the Azores." The president's decision to oppose mandatory sanctions against Portugal disappointed administration officials such as UN Ambassador Adlai Stevenson and Assistant Secretary Williams. They continued to believe that Senator Kennedy had been correct when he argued that the United States needed to align itself with the forces of nationalism in the world and the "tidal wave" of history in Africa. In his last conversation on Angola on November 7, 1963, the president told the Portuguese foreign minister that the United States disagreed with Portugal's position but that the U.S.-Portuguese relationship would survive and that the United States would work to keep UN resolutions "as restrained as possible."[35]

Stevenson, Williams, and African leaders proved prescient about the long-term implications of a decision to "sit back" on the Angolan issue. The liberation wars against Portugal lasted until 1975, when Angola finally gained its independence. Angola became a major Cold War battleground in the 1970s, with the introduction of Cuban troops. Civil war raged in the country after independence and lasted until the early twenty-first century. Perhaps 1.5 million Angolans perished during these wars.

SOUTH AFRICA

South Africa presented a unique problem for the United States. Unlike Algeria and Angola, South Africa had not been a European colonial possession in the first half of the twentieth century. From the 1600s on, significant numbers of Dutch and then British settlers had been in the region that would become South Africa. The Europeans pushed aside the black African population, gaining control of the region's fertile land and valuable natural resources. As a result of the Boer War (1899–1902), the United Kingdom consolidated control of the region, and in 1910 it established the Union of South Africa as a self-governing dominion within the British Empire. South Africa fought on the side of the Allies during World Wars I and II and became a Cold War ally of the United States in the postwar period. South African troops participated in the Berlin airlift and the U.S.-led coalition in the Korean War. South Africans also developed what appeared to be the leading economy on the continent of Africa, although black Africans did not share in that prosperity.

African leaders judged South Africa a "colonial" society not only because black South Africans suffered economic discrimination but also because the majority black population exercised no political rights. The initial constitution of the union gave almost total power to whites. The fortunes of black South Africans sank further when the National Party gained power in 1948. The National Party represented the descendants of Dutch settlers known as Afrikaners. The National Party, especially under Prime Minister Hendrik Verwoerd (1958–1966), transformed the nation into an authoritarian police state, imposing the death penalty on those who tried to overthrow white-minority rule. The National Party also began to implement the policy of *apartheid*, the Afrikaner word for "separateness." The authorities in Pretoria, the capital, intended to force all black South Africans into "Homelands" on about 13 percent of the land. The remaining 87 percent of the land, the best land, would be reserved for whites. In 1960 South Africa had a population of over 16 million, with whites making up about 19 percent of the population. Black South Africans represented 68 percent of the population, with people of mixed ancestry and Asian background representing the rest of the population. Black South Africans who peacefully protested the apartheid system met brutal repression. On March 21, 1960, South African police fired into a crowd, murdering 69 and injuring another 180 unarmed protestors in what became known as the Sharpeville Massacre. Amid international criticism of apartheid, the defiant Afrikaners voted to declare themselves a republic and withdrew from the British Commonwealth in October 1961.

Both the Truman and Eisenhower administrations acquiesced in the denial of the basic human rights of South Africans. Grateful for South Africa's support in Korea, the Truman administration abstained on UN resolutions opposing apartheid, reasoning that apartheid was a domestic, not an international, issue.

The Eisenhower administration developed military and scientific ties with the racist regime in Pretoria. The U.S. Navy participated in joint naval exercises with the South African Navy in 1959. U.S. military planners considered access to South African ports vital for projecting power in both the Indian and South Atlantic oceans. In 1960 the administration struck an agreement to build three missile-tracking stations in South Africa. The Eisenhower administration expressed dismay over the Sharpeville Massacre, recalled the U.S. ambassador from Pretoria, and supported a UN resolution deploring the behavior of the South African government. But commercial relations between the two countries continued. In 1960 the United States exported $277 million to South Africa and imported $108 million. U.S. direct investments totaled $286 million. By global standards the U.S. trade and investment with South Africa was modest, but it was the largest with any African nation. South Africa played a key role in international commerce because its mines produced gold, diamonds, manganese, platinum, and chrome.[36]

President Kennedy did not talk directly to South Africans. As a signal of his distaste for apartheid, the president refused to invite Prime Minister Verwoerd to the White House. Secretary Rusk spent many lengthy sessions with South African officials and passed on his observations and recommendations to the president. Kennedy supported Rusk's approach and that of his ambassador, Joseph Satterthwaite, in Pretoria. Satterthwaite had previously served as Eisenhower's assistant secretary for African Affairs. Both Rusk and Satterthwaite opposed imposing economic sanctions or diplomatic isolation on South Africa. The Department of Defense and the Joint Chiefs of Staff supported Rusk's position. Kennedy rejected the views of UN Ambassador Stevenson and Assistant Secretary Williams, who argued for pressure on South Africa.

The Kennedy administration changed the style but not the substance of U.S. policy toward South Africa. The State Department shocked South African whites when in August 1961 it informed the South African government that the United States found itself "unable to accept a governmental policy which compels and perpetuates a system which denies fundamental human rights to [the] vast majority of [the] country's population only because of [the] color of their skin." The United States did not accept the proposition that South Africa's racial system was exclusively a domestic matter. As the State Department put it, apartheid "not only does violence to [the] human rights provision of the UN Charter but tends to weaken [the] position of [the] West in its efforts to resist Communist influence and penetration in newly emerged Afro-Asian nations." The South African government's reaction to the U.S. denunciation of apartheid was "adverse in the extreme."[37] Over the next two years, South African officials repeatedly tried to justify their racism, variously arguing that they were Europeans not Africans, that they were preserving Western identity, or that they were the only reliable Cold Warriors on the continent. The South African ambassador to the United States even offered that the United States should treat South Africa like Israel for both were "little nation[s] that needed similar support for survival." The Kennedy administration rejected this sophistry. Undersecretary of State Chester Bowles labeled South Africa "the most unpopular nation outside the Communist world."[38] The State Department further iritated the South African government when it instructed Ambassador Satterthwaite to violate apartheid rules by inviting blacks and racially mixed people to the U.S. embassy and consulates in South Africa. The South African government refused to attend the integrated Independence Day celebration hosted by Ambassador Satterthwaite on July 4, 1963.

The stinging verbal attack on apartheid did not preface a change in policy. The Kennedy administration maintained the Eisenhower administration's policy of cooperation with white South Africa. Joint naval exercises continued. The United States renewed the leases on the missile-tracking stations. The administration acquiesced in South African requests for loans from financial agencies such as the International Monetary Fund. U.S. trade and investment with South Africa flourished. In late 1963 the administration agreed to support a UN resolution imposing an arms embargo on South Africa, but it qualifed the resolution with exceptions for spare parts and weapons needed for South Africa's external defense. In late 1963 President Kennedy authorized the sale of spare parts for C-130 transport planes and also approved opening negotiations for the sale of three submarines to South Africa. Perceiving South Africa as a vital part of the U.S. strategy to contain the Soviet Union and communism provided the rationale for working with the South African government.[39] The perception of South Africa's critical role in U.S. national security did not, however, match the facts. At the behest of critics within the administration, including Undersecretary

Bowles, who challenged cooperation with South Africa, Jerome Wiesner, the scientific adviser to the president, studied the missile-tracking site issue. Dr. Wiesner concluded that "the loss of this site would be painful, but not fatal" to national security.[40] Other studies demonstrated that the United States did not depend on South Africa's raw materials.

President Kennedy and his secretary of state opposed economic and military sanctions on South Africa. Responding to requests from Assistant Secretary Williams for new measures against South Africa, Rusk explained to his State Department colleagues his philosophy of international relations. The problem was how the United States related to nations whose internal arrangments are "repugnant to us." He noted that the United States conducted relations with unsavory regimes in both the Communist and non-Communist worlds. Conceding that apartheid represented "a case of unusual difficulty," Rusk asserted that he would not put apartheid "ahead of the violations of human rights within the communist bloc or certain countries governed on an authoritarian basis with which we have correct and sometimes even friendly relations." U.S. officials could not assume the role of "self-elected gendarmes," with responsibility for correcting the political and social problems of other states.[41] Rusk might have been more candid if he admitted the inconsistences in the administration's approach to nasty regimes. In his memorandum, he cited Haiti as a country where "obnoxious practices" existed. In fact, the Kennedy administration tried to overthrow the vicious, racist regime of François "Papa Doc" Duvalier (1957–1971).[42] In any case, President Kennedy thoroughly agreed with Rusk's position, opposing both a trade embargo and mandatory sanctions against South Africa.

The Kennedy administration essentially adopted a position toward South Africa that would be dubbed "constructive engagement" and pursued during the 1980s by the Ronald Reagan administration. The Kennedy administration thought it could encourage moderate, evolutionary change in South Africa if it maintained lines of communication with Pretoria. Secretary Rusk and Ambassador Satterthwaite bent over backward trying to appear reasonable to South African white leaders. U.S. officials assured white South Africans that the United States was not calling for the immediate implementation of democracy and "one man, one vote." Rusk suggested to the South African ambassador that a policy of accommodation would help the white minority survive "in a sea of blacks." The secretary of state even discussed partioning the entire southern region of Africa into two areas—one for blacks and one for whites.[43] The administration could not, however, demonstrate how talking to South African whites improved the lives of the black majority. The Verwoerd regime dismissed U.S. requests for moderation in racial relations. It responded that only apartheid could guarantee the survival of whites in South Africa. Constructive engagement proved fruitless both in the 1960s and 1980s. South Africa would not begin to dismantle the apartheid system until 1990, when it faced severe political and economic sanctions that had been imposed on the country by the United States.

The Kennedy administration not only failed to change the apartheid system but also hurt the fortunes of the black majority. The administration declined to cultivate South Africans who opposed apartheid. The African National Congress (ANC) was the leading political organization attacking racial discrimination and apartheid. Chief Albert John Luthuli (1898–1967), a veteran leader of the ANC, was awarded the Nobel Prize for Peace in 1960 for his efforts to combat racial discrimination. President Kennedy initially declined to send a message of congratulations to be read at the awards ceremony in Oslo, Norway. After a personal letter from Assistant Secretary Williams, Kennedy agreed to send a message. But his letter of congratulations did not mention South Africa or apartheid.[44] After the Sharpeville Massacre, the South African authorities outlawed the ANC. Banned from conducting open and peaceful demonstrations, the ANC went underground and turned to sabotage and armed resistance. The Kennedy administration declined to support the ANC because it had resorted to armed struggle and because it consorted with members of South Africa's banned Communist Party. The administration told itself that it did not "assume a stance against revolution." But a special CIA report of May 10, 1963, on "Subversive Movements in South Africa" used the words ANC and "terrorism" together. The report alleged that ANC members who joined the armed struggle, known as *Umkhonto we Sizwe*, or "Spear of the Nation," were either Communists or Communist sympathizers.[45] In the previous year, CIA agents reportedly alerted South African authorities to the location of a leader of *Umkhonto we Sizwe*, the lawyer and prominent ANC official, Nelson Rolihlahla Mandela (1918–).[46] The South African authorities arrested Mandela on August 5, 1962, and sentenced him to life imprisonment for sabotage.

Over the next twenty-eight years, Nelson Mandela bore his imprisonment with dignity. He became the world's most famous political prisoner. The South African government released him in 1990, as the apartheid system collapsed under the weight of international sanctions. His release from prison was broadcast globally. Mandela became South Africa's first democratically elected president (1994–1999). He tried to conciliate all racial groups in South Africa. Awarded the Nobel Prize for Peace in 1993, Nelson Mandela became one of the most admired political leaders in modern history. That the Kennedy administration may have aided in the arrest of Mandela serves as an ironic but telling commentary on President Kennedy's foreign policies in Africa. Kennedy and his advisers celebrated nationalism and denounced racism. But their fervor in waging Cold War often overwhelmed their good judgment in analyzing the politics of Algeria, Angola, South Africa, and other countries on the great continent.

CHAPTER 9

JOHN F. KENNEDY: THE FUTURE VERSUS THE PAST

INTERPRETERS OF PRESIDENT JOHN F. KENNEDY'S performance as world leader inevitably grapple with the issue of what policies Kennedy would have pursued if he had enjoyed a full eight years as president of the United States. Implicit in biographer Robert Dallek's choice of the book title *An Unfinished Life* is the suggestion that Kennedy would have done great and good things from November 22, 1963, to January 19, 1969. Robert A. Divine, the distinguished professor emeritus of U.S. foreign relations at the University of Texas at Austin, first set the tone of the scholarly speculation about a second Kennedy presidential term. In his seminal essay, "The Education of John F. Kennedy" (1974), Divine theorized that, in the last year of his life, President Kennedy was beginning to display a mature concern about the ultimate issues of war and peace in the nuclear age. Divine conceded that Kennedy had been impetuous and confrontational, as evidenced in the Bay of Pigs invasion, the Berlin showdown, and the missile crisis. But Divine saw the Cuban missile crisis as representing a sobering turning point in the president's intellectual journey. Having looked into the fires of nuclear inferno, the president became determined to work to reduce international tensions. Kennedy had learned the hard lesson in the school of international relations that the United States could not resolve foreign policy dilemmas by flaunting U.S. power. Divine pointed to the president's magnificent speech at American University in June 1963 and his subsequent negotiation of the Limited Test Ban Treaty as signs of a leader now prepared "to put his hard-won education to work."[1]

Kennedy emerged from the Cuban missile crisis in a powerful political position. His job approval ratings soared to 75 percent in December 1962 and stayed at a high level through 1963. The president and his advisers helped generate popular enthusiasm by providing insider accounts of the crisis to friendly journalists. They emphasized that the president had acted boldly and decisively, minimizing the confusion and mistakes that had actually dominated the crisis. President Kennedy had emerged triumphant, the "Alpha Male" of the universe. Indeed, Kennedy, referring to Soviet Premier Nikita Khrushchev, had boasted, "I cut his balls off."[2] Operating from a position of strength, Kennedy took up the cause championed by President Dwight Eisenhower of a nuclear test ban. He corresponded with Chairman Khrushchev and used Norman Cousins, a renowned literary figure and independent peace activist, as an intermediary between himself and the Soviet leader. Both leaders understood that the world would welcome a test ban. The resumption of open-air nuclear testing in 1961 meant that the United States and the Soviet Union were again poisoning the atmosphere with radioactive fallout. Since the first open-air test at Alamogordo, New Mexico, in July 1945, the two superpowers had conducted more than 400 nuclear tests in the atmosphere. Babies and children drank milk laced with radioactive contaminants.

President Kennedy achieved true eloquence on June 10, 1963, when he delivered the commencement address at American University in Washington, D.C. According to speechwriter Theodore Sorensen, the president wanted "the usual threats of destruction, boasts of nuclear stockpiles, and lectures on Soviet treachery" left out of this speech.[3] Kennedy told the university graduates that the United States wanted a "genuine peace" and "not a Pax Americana enforced on the world by American weapons of war." He noted that U.S. and Soviet citizens abhorred war, adding that no nation had suffered more than the Soviet Union during World War II. At least twenty million Soviet citizens had perished, and Nazi Germany had turned one-third of Soviet territory into a wasteland, "a loss equivalent to the devastation of this country east of Chicago." In reviewing history, Kennedy made points to the U.S. public that had been made to him two years previously by Khrushchev at the Vienna meeting. The president called on his fellow Americans to reexamine their attitude toward the Soviet Union.

Mutual fear fed Cold War appetites, with both sides "caught in a vicious and dangerous cycle in which suspicion on one side breeds suspicion on the other, and new weapons beget counterweapons." Kennedy conceded that fundamental differences over politics and economics separated the two societies, but he observed that their common humanity also linked them. Kennedy reminded, "We all inhabit this small planet. We all breathe the same air. We all cherish our children's future. And we are all mortal." Calling for a "fresh start," Kennedy pledged, at the end of his address, that the United States would not test nuclear weapons in the atmosphere "so long as other states do not do so."[4]

Kennedy's elegant, lyrical address and generous pledge helped produce substantive results. Chairman Khrushchev responded positively, calling it "the best speech by any President since [Franklin] Roosevelt." Despite his blustering belligerence, Khrushchev considered himself a man of peace. Beyond meeting with Norman Cousins, he corresponded with the pontiff in Vatican City, the saintly Pope John XXIII (1958–1963). Pope John's final papal encyclical was *Pacem in Terris* (*Peace on Earth*). Khrushchev wanted to achieve in 1963 what he thought was possible in 1960 before the U-2 incident—a meaningful arms agreement with the United States. He confidentially told Soviet officials that a test ban agreement "could lead to a real turning point, and the end of the cold war."[5] Khrushchev also needed a big achievement because his position had weakened both internationally and domestically. President Kennedy had exposed Soviet military weakness during the missile crisis. The Chinese insulted him endlessly, and Khrushchev had found himself caught in the middle of the war between India and China. The economic aid offensive in Asia, Africa, and the Middle East that Khrushchev had launched in the 1950s had not produced striking diplomatic gains for the Soviet Union. At home, Khrushchev's agricultural schemes had proved disastrous. His Soviet colleagues would subsequently seize on his weaknesses and remove Khrushchev from power in October 1964.

Using as his emissary the veteran diplomat Averell Harriman, Kennedy struck a deal with Khrushchev in July 1963 to ban the testing of nuclear weapons in the atmosphere. Kennedy then gave an effective televised address, urging the U.S. Senate to ratify the treaty. Republican senators and U.S. military officers had questioned whether the Soviets could be trusted to abide by any treaty. By

September 1963, 81 percent of the U.S. public supported the treaty, and the Senate ratified the treaty by an overwhelming vote of 80-19.

President Kennedy's creation, the Test Ban Treaty, remains in effect in the twenty-first century. Since 1963 neither the United States nor the Soviet Union (Russia since 1991) has exploded a nuclear weapon in the atmosphere. The atmospheric test ban has helped preserve the environment and the health of global citizens. The treaty also set a precedent for future Soviet-American arms control treaties such as the Nuclear Non-Proliferation Treaty (1969) and SALT I (1972), which prohibited either side from building an antiballistic missile system. The Kennedy administration took a step toward stabilizing the forbidding nuclear arms race. The president had exercised leadership.

The atmospheric test ban treaty did not, however, usher in an era of good sense when it came to nuclear weapons. President Kennedy did not achieve a comprehensive test ban treaty, which would have prohibited the underground testing of nuclear weapons. (President Kennedy's Cold War and post–Cold War successors have also not secured Senate ratification of such a treaty.) In the early 1960s the Joint Chiefs of Staff opposed a comprehensive treaty, and the Soviets showed little interest. Khrushchev opposed the onsite inspections thought necessary to ensure compliance with a comprehensive test ban. The Soviet leader alleged that the CIA would use onsite inspections as a way to spy on his country. Between 1963 and 1990 the two superpowers conducted nearly 1,100 underground nuclear tests. The development of nuclear weapons continued apace and arguably accelerated because the public took little notice of underground tests. The Kennedy administration's test ban initiative also took place simultaneously with its massive buildup of nuclear delivery vehicles such as ICBMs and Polaris submarines. The Kennedy-era buildup stimulated the Soviet arms buildup of the late 1960s under the direction of Khrushchev's successor, Leonid Brezhnev. Professor Divine conceded that the huge nuclear buildup of the 1960s became "Kennedy's grimmest legacy."[6] Former Secretary of Defense Robert McNamara regretfully agreed with that assessment.

Whether the atmospheric test ban treaty heralded a new approach by President Kennedy toward the Soviet Union and Cold War remains a matter of conjecture, not scholarly certainty. Kennedy made other conciliatory gestures toward the Soviets in the later half of 1963. A "hot line" between Washington

President Kennedy gives the commencement address at American University on June 10, 1963. In this speech, the president called for peace between the United States and the Soviet Union and pledged to stop testing nuclear weapons in the atmosphere. The president's conciliatory gestures led to the negotiation of a limited test ban treaty. The next day, the eloquent president made another momentous address on national television, calling for the passage of a civil rights act. Many scholars consider these two speeches the best of the Kennedy presidency. They speculate that the president was moving in a new direction, both internationally and domestically.
(John F. Kennedy Presidential Library and Museum, Boston)

and Moscow was set up to give the leaders the ability to speak directly during a crisis. Kennedy agreed to sell wheat to the always-hungry Soviet Union, and he proposed in a speech at the United Nations that the two nations cooperate in space exploration and "keep weapons of mass destruction out of outer space."[7] Kennedy also gave another gracious address about peace in the nuclear age when he spoke at the Mormon Tabernacle in Salt Lake City on September 26, 1963. The test ban treaty was "one chance to end the radiation and the possibilities of burning." The president assured the Mormons he would use diplomacy to avoid a nuclear holocaust and the massacre of "300 million men and women in 24 hours." In delivering this impressive address, Kennedy may have wanted to make amends for the aggressive speech he gave in the Utah capital during the 1960 campaign, when he had depicted the Cold War as a struggle for supremacy between God and America versus Satan and the Soviet Union. He now asserted that the United States could not pursue a "black or white, all or nothing policy" and that he favored a world safe for the "forces of diversity."[8]

President Kennedy had not, however, abandoned his confrontational public approach toward the Soviet Union. His triumphal appearance and speech in Berlin came less than three weeks after his American University address. The hideous nature of the Berlin Wall may have imposed on the president a sense that he had a moral duty to make a strong statement. But Kennedy attacked communism and Fidel Castro in Miami on November 18, in his last speech on inter-American affairs. And in the address he intended to deliver at the Trade Mart in Dallas on November 22, Kennedy would have boasted in great detail about the prowess of U.S. nuclear and conventional forces.[9] The speech seemed designed to overawe the president's right-wing critics, including the extremist publishers and editors of the *Dallas Morning News*. But a Soviet leader or citizen could have been justifiably alarmed by the speech. Reviewing these speeches and the internal debates within official circles in both Moscow and Washington, Melvyn P. Leffler, a careful, insightful scholar of Cold War history, concluded that the future of détente, a relaxation of tensions, was "unclear." Kennedy wavered between working to make the world safe for diversity and "winning" the Cold War by defeating communism throughout the world. As Professor Leffler noted, President Kennedy eloquently championed peace, but he was a "conflicted" champion.[10]

Predictions of great Kennedy deeds in other areas of the world seem dubious. Robert Dallek opined, "A second Kennedy term might have brought a resolution to unproductive tensions with Castro and foreclosed more than forty years of Cuban-American antagonism."[11] Dallek based his prediction on the administration's tentative discussions with Cuban diplomats in late 1963 and the president's use of a French journalist as an emissary to Fidel Castro. But the Kennedy administration wanted Castro to renounce communism. The Kennedy brothers continued to wage war against Castro's Cuba. In June and November 1963 the president met with CIA officers and approved specific sabotage and terrorist missions against Cuba. On November 18 he made a threatening speech against Cuba and pronounced his "Kennedy Doctrine," vowing to prevent another Communist regime in the Western Hemisphere. Kennedy was upholding his vow, authorizing destabilization campaigns against President João Goulart of Brazil and Prime Minister Cheddi Jagan of British Guiana. On November 22 a CIA agent met with a Cuban in Paris and passed him an instrument for assassinating Castro. The Cuban had previously been assured that the CIA operated with the approval of Robert Kennedy. Former CIA agents have alleged that the president's November 18 speech was linked to the assassination plot. These machinations appalled President Lyndon Johnson, who shut down the war against Castro's Cuba.

The evidence is mixed on what policies President Kennedy might have implemented in Asia in 1964 and thereafter. Given his cautious approach in the midst of the Bay of Pigs, Berlin, and Cuban missile crises, it is probably reasonable to conclude that Kennedy would have discarded his own outlandish idea to bomb China's nuclear-processing facilities. The president would have learned to live with a People's Republic of China that had atomic bombs. Kennedy's demonstrated desire to avoid full-scale warfare strengthens the arguments of scholars who believe that he would not have sent 500,000 troops to Vietnam. Kennedy also had repeatedly expressed misgivings, both publicly and privately, about the U.S. mission in Vietnam. Dallek foresaw "a carefully managed stand-down from the sort of involvement that occurred under LBJ."[12] Scholars agree that Kennedy's two decisions—to accept the Taylor-Rostow recommendation in 1961 to expand U.S. troop strength and to accede in 1963 to the overthrow of President Ngo Dinh Diem—deepened U.S. involvement in Vietnam and raised the international stakes for the United States. U.S. prestige and credibility had become tied to the war in Vietnam. President Kennedy had established himself as a strong foreign policy leader. But to believe that Kennedy would have withdrawn from Vietnam is to accept what historian Gary Hess has dubbed "Kennedy exceptionalism."[13] The president would have paid a heavy political price for reversing course in Southeast Asia and accepting the near inevitable—a unified, Communist Vietnam. Ho Chi Minh and his North Vietnamese supporters probably would have accepted a temporary neutralization of South Vietnam in order to avoid war with the United States. The Vietnamese Communists believed, however, that it was their "sacred mission" to unify the country and carry out a Communist revolution. They further held that they had been denied the fruits of their victory at the end of World War II and in the aftermath of the Geneva Accords of 1954. The critical issue would have been whether President Kennedy could persuade both himself and the U.S. polity that a Communist Vietnam could pursue nationalistic foreign policy goals and develop a normal relationship with the United States.

Historians are more comfortable debating the meaning and implications of past events rather than trying to predict the unknowable future. James N. Giglio argues that a U.S. president should be judged on whether he fulfilled his promises and improved the quality of life in the country.[14] Kennedy, an activist foreign policy president, rejuvenated life in the United States and enhanced the global prestige of the United States with the space program and the Peace Corps. President Kennedy also rapidly expanded U.S. nuclear and conventional forces. Kennedy's triumph in the missile crisis and passage of the atmospheric test ban treaty made him the undisputed leader of the world. Kennedy's economic policies generated economic growth, and in mid-1963 he finally embraced the civil rights movement and put the full weight of the presidency behind legislation to strike down discrimination and segregation in U.S. life. President Kennedy had "the country moving again" and restored U.S. supremacy in the world.

President Kennedy also merits great credit for rejecting the concept of thermonuclear war. He stood down advisers, such as Dean Acheson, Paul Nitze, and Gen. Curtis LeMay, who advocated risky courses during the Berlin and Cuban crises. If a nuclear exchange had broken out, the consequences would still be with the world in the twenty-first century. As Robert Dallek noted, Kennedy had provided "an imperishable example of how one man prevented a catastrophe that may yet afflict the world."[15] The presidential leadership that Kennedy displayed during momentous crises must be balanced, however, by hard questioning of why the president found himself in these superpower showdowns. The president's overblown rhetoric, nuclear arms buildup, and reckless behavior toward Castro's Cuba helped precipitate these confrontations. Fortunately for the United States and the world, Nikita Khrushchev shared the president's dread of war and negotiated with Kennedy. The two leaders found acceptable resolutions to the crises.

Scholars can also ask whether President Kennedy and his foreign policy team left the world in a more peaceful state than they had found in January 1961. U.S. economic aid improved the quality of life in India, and the administration made an honest, albeit unsuccessful, effort to improve relations with Egypt. Armed with his test ban treaty, Kennedy also seemed prepared in late 1963 to challenge Israel's drive to acquire nuclear weapons. The goals of the Alliance for Progress, "the Marshall Plan for Latin America," proved too ambitious, although the administration helped democratic countries such as Venezuela and Costa Rica. The administration also made a series of symbolic gestures to new African nations to demonstrate U.S. sympathy for their political and economic aspirations. The president and his advisers disdained racism and displayed comfort working with people from all regions of the world. The president further professed a political philosophy that the U.S. government had a duty to help poor and oppressed people, both at home and abroad.

President Kennedy both eased and exacerbated global tensions. In Asia, the administration avoided one pitfall by declining to intervene militarily in Laos. But Kennedy perpetuated conflict with the People's Republic of China and refused to make conciliatory gestures such as offering food aid to the world's most populous nation. Like President Eisenhower, Kennedy declined to support Taiwan's mad schemes to invade China. Kennedy went farther than Eisenhower, however, in tying the United States to Generalissimo Jiang Jieshi by secretly pledging to veto China's admission to the United Nations. Kennedy surprisingly indulged in "yellow peril" discourses that dehumanized the Chinese leaders in Beijing. Leaving aside what Kennedy might have done in a second term, he bequeathed a terrible legacy in Vietnam to President Johnson. Between 1961 and 1963, the United States deepened its involvement in South Vietnam as disorder and warfare spread throughout the country. Kennedy and his advisers bear responsibility for the disastrous U.S. intervention in Vietnam and the "wasting" of millions of American and Asian lives.

The president undermined his admirable intentions in Latin America by destabilizing constitutional regimes because they did not share his analysis of the dangers of communism. In demanding that the United Kingdom postpone British Guiana's independence, Kennedy asserted that an independent Guyana under the leadership of the self-proclaimed Marxist Cheddi Jagan would jeopardize Kennedy's reelection bid in 1964. The CIA intervention in British Guiana aggravated racial tensions between Guyanese of African and Indian heritages. The small South American country still suffers from the implications of the racial violence that erupted in the 1960s. The U.S. intervention in Brazil against President João Goulart led to a military dictatorship that lasted for more than two decades in the region's largest and most influential country. The covert intervention in Brazil helped precipitate a "domino effect" in the cone of South America, with generals assuming power in Argentina, Chile, and Uruguay in the 1960s and 1970s. Ghastly, unspeakable political violence characterized the region, as the South American generals and their minions hunted down alleged "Communists." Perhaps 30,000 Argentines perished in the nation's "dirty war" (*la guerra sucia*).

The attacks on Jagan and Goulart, the rejection of the African National Congress, the drive to enlist India in the Cold War, and the denial of the legitimacy of the Viet Cong and North Vietnamese point to the Kennedy administration's inability to separate nationalism from communism. Senator Kennedy first came to international attention with his attack on French colonialism in Algeria. He ridiculed President Eisenhower and Secretary of State John Foster Dulles for failing to support nationalist movements and leaders. As president, he promised change, and Kennedy worked hard to direct U.S. economic aid to new and poor nations. But like his predecessors and successors in the Oval Office, he grew suspicious of political and economic radicals, fearing they would enlist in Khrushchev's "wars of national liberation." As Divine, Dallek, and others have suggested, President Kennedy may have been in the process of rethinking his approach to the Cold War. But continuity rather than change characterized the Kennedy administration's foreign policies toward nations in Asia, Africa, Latin America, and the Middle East. President Eisenhower destabilized governments in Iran (1953) and Guatemala (1954), President Johnson invaded the Dominican Republic (1965), and President Richard M. Nixon undermined the Chilean government of Salvador Allende (1970–1973). President Gerald R. Ford and Secretary of State Henry Kissinger argued that U.S. security depended on keeping radicals out of power in Angola, and President Ronald Reagan implied that the Sandinistas in tiny Nicaragua might invade Texas. President Kennedy's policies and his 163 covert interventions around the world reflected this same fear of a global Communist conspiracy. As the perceptive historian Anna Kasten Nelson sees it, President Kennedy "was just another in a long line of cold warriors."[16]

During his brief time in office, President John F. Kennedy became a world leader. He faced momentous international crises, and he made decisions that had lasting implications for both U.S. and global citizens. The Kennedy presidency will always merit study and debate.

Appendix of Documents

1. John F. Kennedy's Inaugural Address, January 20, 1961

President Kennedy set the tone for his administration in his famous inaugural address. He emphasized the U.S. role in the world, as befitted a president who wanted to be a foreign policy president. Perceiving the world as a perilous place, the president called for duty, sacrifice, and service from U.S. citizens.

Source: *Public Papers of the Presidents of the United States: John F. Kennedy, 1961* (Washington, DC: Government Printing Office, 1962), 1–3.

We observe today not a victory of party but a celebration of freedom—symbolizing an end as well as a beginning—signifying renewal as well as change. For I have sworn before you and Almighty God the same solemn oath our forebears prescribed nearly a century and three quarters ago.

The world is very different now. For man holds in his mortal hands the power to abolish all forms of human poverty and all forms of human life. And yet the same revolutionary beliefs for which our forebears fought are still at issue around the globe—the belief that the rights of man come not from the generosity of the state but from the hand of God.

We dare not forget today that we are the heirs of that first revolution. Let the word go forth from this time and place, to friend and foe alike, that the torch has been passed to a new generation of Americans—born in this century, tempered by war, disciplined by a hard and bitter peace, proud of our ancient heritage—and unwilling to witness or permit the slow undoing of those human rights to which this nation has always been committed, and to which we are committed today at home and around the world.

Let every nation know, whether it wishes us well or ill, that we shall pay any price, bear any burden, meet any hardship, support any friend, oppose any foe to assure the survival and the success of liberty.

This much we pledge—and more.

To those old allies whose cultural and spiritual origins we share, we pledge the loyalty of faithful friends. United, there is little we cannot do in a host of cooperative ventures. Divided, there is little we can do—for we dare not meet a powerful challenge at odds and split asunder.

To those new states whom we welcome to the ranks of the free, we pledge our word that one form of colonial control shall not have passed away merely to be replaced by a far more iron tyranny. We shall not always expect to find them supporting our view. But we shall always hope to find them strongly supporting their own freedom—and to remember that, in the past, those who foolishly sought power by riding the back of the tiger ended up inside.

To those peoples in the huts and villages of half the globe struggling to break the bonds of mass misery, we pledge our best efforts to help them help themselves, for whatever period is required—not because the communists may be doing it, not because we seek their votes, but because it is right. If a free society cannot help the many who are poor, it cannot save the few who are rich.

To our sister republics south of our border, we offer a special pledge—to convert our good words into good deeds—in a new alliance for progress—to assist free men and free governments in casting off the chains of poverty. But this peaceful revolution of hope cannot become the prey of hostile powers. Let all our neighbors know that we shall join with them to oppose aggression or subversion anywhere in the Americas. And let every other power know that this Hemisphere intends to remain the master of its own house.

To that world assembly of sovereign states, the United Nations, our last best hope in an age where the instruments of war have far outpaced the instruments of peace, we renew our pledge of support—to prevent it from becoming merely a forum for invective—to strengthen its shield of the new and the weak—and to enlarge the area in which its writ may run.

Finally, to those nations who would make themselves our adversary, we offer not a pledge but a request: that both sides begin anew the quest for peace, before the dark powers of destruction unleashed by science engulf all humanity in planned or accidental self-destruction.

We dare not tempt them with weakness. For only when our arms are sufficient beyond doubt can we be certain beyond doubt that they will never be employed.

But neither can two great and powerful groups of nations take comfort from our present course—both sides overburdened by the cost of modern weapons, both rightly alarmed by the steady spread of the deadly atom, yet both racing to alter that uncertain balance of terror that stays the hand of mankind's final war.

So let us begin anew—remembering on both sides that civility is not a sign of weakness, and sincerity is always subject to proof. Let us never negotiate out of fear. But let us never fear to negotiate.

Let both sides explore what problems unite us instead of belaboring those problems which divide us.

Let both sides, for the first time, formulate serious and precise proposals for the inspection and control of arms—and bring the absolute power to destroy other nations under the absolute control of all nations.

Let both sides seek to invoke the wonders of science instead of its terrors. Together let us explore the stars, conquer the deserts, eradicate disease, tap the ocean depths and encourage the arts and commerce.

Let both sides unite to heed in all corners of the earth the command of Isaiah—to "undo the heavy burdens . . . [and] let the oppressed go free."

And if a beach-head of cooperation may push back the jungle of suspicion, let both sides join in creating a new endeavor, not a new balance of power, but a new world of law, where the strong are just and the weak secure and the peace preserved.

All this will not be finished in the first one hundred days. Nor will it be finished in the first one thousand days, nor in the life of this Administration, nor even perhaps in our lifetime on this planet. But let us begin.

In your hands, my fellow citizens, more than mine, will rest the final success or failure of our course. Since this country was founded, each generation of Americans has been summoned to give testimony to its national loyalty. The graves of young Americans who answered the call to service surround the globe.

Now the trumpet summons us again—not as a call to bear arms, though arms we need—not as a call to battle, though embattled we are—but a call to bear the burden of a long twilight struggle, year in and year out, "rejoicing in hope, patient in tribulation"—a struggle against the common enemies of man: tyranny, poverty, disease and war itself.

Can we forge against these enemies a grand and global alliance, North and South, East and West, that can assure a more fruitful life for all mankind? Will you join in that historic effort?

In the long history of the world, only a few generations have been granted the role of defending freedom in its hour of maximum danger. I do not shrink from this responsibility—I welcome it. I do not believe that any of us would exchange places with any other people or any other generation. The energy, the faith, the devotion which we bring to this endeavor will light our country and all who serve it—and the glow from that fire can truly light the world.

And so, my fellow Americans: ask not what your country can do for you—ask what you can do for your country.

My fellow citizens of the world: ask not what America will do for you, but what together we can do for the freedom of man.

Finally, whether you are citizens of America or citizens of the world, ask of us here the same high standards of strength and sacrifice which we ask of you. With a good conscience our only sure reward, with history the final judge of our deeds, let us go forth to lead the land we love, asking His blessing and His help, but knowing that here on earth God's work must truly be our own.

Berlin Crisis

2. President Kennedy and Chairman Khrushchev Debate the Fate of Berlin at the Vienna Summit, June 4, 1961

In this brutally frank meeting between the two leaders, Khrushchev talks of war, if the United States does not relinquish its treaty rights and access to the city of Berlin. President Kennedy believed that Khrushchev had successfully bullied him at Vienna. The transcript of this conversation reveals, however, that Kennedy conveyed U.S. resolve to the Soviet leader.

Source: Excerpted from *Foreign Relations of the United States, 1961–1963*, vol. 5: *Soviet Union* (Washington, DC: Government Printing Office, 1998), 229–31.

Vienna, June 4, 1961, 3:15 p.m.
SUBJECT
Vienna Meeting between the President and Chairman Khrushchev
PARTICIPANTS
The President and Chairman Khrushchev [with interpreters]

After lunch, the President said he wanted to have a few words with the Chairman in private.

The President opened the conversation by saying that he recognized the importance of Berlin and that he hoped that in the interests of the relations between our two countries, which he wanted to improve, Mr. Khrushchev would not present him with a situation so deeply involving our national interest. Of course, he recognized that the decision on East Germany, as far as the USSR was concerned, was with the Chairman. The President continued by saying that evolution is taking place in many areas of the world and no one can predict which course it would take. Therefore, it is most important that decisions be carefully considered. Obviously the Chairman will make his judgment in the light of what he understands to be the best interests of his country. However, the President said, he did want to stress the difference between a peace treaty and the rights of access to Berlin. He reiterated his hope that the relations between the two countries would develop in a way that would avoid direct contact or confrontation between them.

Mr. Khrushchev said he appreciated the frankness of the President's remarks but said that if the President insisted on US rights after the signing of a peace treaty and that if the borders of the GDR [East Germany]—land, air, or sea borders—were violated, they would be defended. The US position is not based on juridical grounds. The US wants to humiliate the USSR and this cannot be accepted. He said that he would not shirk his responsibility and would take any action that he is duty bound to take as Prime Minister. He would be glad if the US were to agree to an interim agreement on Germany and Berlin with a time limit so that the prestige and the interests of the two countries would not be involved or prejudiced. However, he said, he must warn the President that if he envisages any action that might bring about unhappy consequences, force would be met by force. The US should prepare itself for that and the Soviet Union will do the same.

The President inquired whether under an interim arrangement forces in Berlin would remain and access would be free. Mr. Khrushchev replied that would be so for six months. In reply to the President's query whether the forces would then have to be withdrawn, the Chairman replied in the affirmative.

The President then said that either Mr. Khrushchev did not believe that the US was serious or the situation in that area was so unsatisfactory to the Soviet Union that it had to take this drastic action. The President referred to his forthcoming meeting with Macmillan and said the latter would ask what had happened. The President said that he would have to say that he had gained the impression that the USSR was presenting him with the alternative of accepting the Soviet act on Berlin or having a face to face confrontation. He had come here to prevent a confrontation between our two countries and he regretted to leave Vienna with this impression.

Mr. Khrushchev replied that in order to save prestige we could agree that token contingents of troops, including Soviet troops, could be maintained in West Berlin. However, this would be not on the basis of some occupation rights, but on the basis of an agreement registered with the UN. Of course, access would be subject to GDR's control because this is its prerogative. Mr. Khrushchev continued by saying that he wanted peace and that if the US wanted war, that was its problem. It is not the USSR that threatens with war, it is the US.

The President stressed that it was the Chairman, not he, who wanted to force a change.

Mr. Khrushchev replied that a peace treaty would not involve any change in boundaries. In any event, the USSR will have no choice other than to accept the challenge; it must respond and it will respond. The calamities of a war will be shared equally. War will take place only if the US imposes it on the USSR. It is up to the US to decide whether there will be war or peace. This, he said, can be told to Macmillan, De Gaulle and Adenauer. The decision to sign a peace treaty is firm and irrevocable and the Soviet Union will sign it in December if the US refuses an interim agreement.

The President concluded the conversation by observing that it would be a cold winter.

3. President Kennedy Urges Citizens to Prepare for Nuclear War, July 25, 1961

In his report to the nation after his meeting with Khrushchev in Vienna, President Kennedy made a dramatic address on radio and television, calling for an immediate buildup in U.S. conventional forces to counter the Soviet threat to Berlin. The president also raised the possibility of nuclear war and called for increased expenditures on civil defense.

Source: Excerpted from *Public Papers of the Presidents of the United States: John F. Kennedy, 1961* (Washington, DC: Government Printing Office, 1962), 533–40.

We have another sober responsibility. To recognize the possibilities of nuclear war in the missile age, without our citizens knowing what they should do and where they should go if bombs begin to fall. In May, I pledged a new start on Civil Defense. Last week, I assigned, on the recommendation of the Civil Defense Director, basic responsibility for this program to the Secretary of Defense, to make certain it is administered and coordinated with our continental defense efforts at the highest civilian level. Tomorrow, I am requesting of the Congress new funds for the following immediate objectives: to identify and mark space in existing structures—public and private—that could be used for fall-out shelters in case of attack; to stock those shelters with food, water, first-aid kits and other minimum essentials for survival; to increase their capacity; to improve our air-raid warning and fall-out detection systems, including a new household warning system which is now under development; and to take other measures that will be effective at an early date to save millions of lives if needed.

In the event of an attack, the lives of those families which are not hit in a nuclear blast and fire can still be saved—if they can be warned to take shelter and if that shelter is available. We owe that kind of insurance to our families—and to our country. In contrast to our friends in Europe, the need for this kind of protection is new to our shores. But the time to start is now. In the coming months, I hope to let every citizen know what steps he can take without delay to protect his family in case of attack. I know that you will want to do no less.

◆ ◆ ◆

The addition of $207 million in Civil Defense appropriations brings our total new defense budget requests to $3.454 billion, and a total of $47.5 billion for the year. This is an increase in the defense budget of $6 billion since January, and has resulted in official estimates of a budget deficit of over $5 billion. The Secretary of the Treasury and other economic advisers assure me, however, that our economy has the capacity to bear this new request.

4. PRESIDENT KENNEDY EXERTS COMMAND OVER U.S. NUCLEAR FORCES, OCTOBER 20, 1961

Scholars have praised President Kennedy for rejecting advice to use nuclear weapons during the Berlin and Cuban crises. In this precisely worded letter to Gen. Lauris Norstad, the commander of U.S. forces in Europe, the president makes clear that General Norstad is to base his defense of Berlin on nonnuclear forces and to avoid "going off half-cocked."

Source: Excerpted from *Foreign Relations of the United States, 1961–1963*, vol. 14: *Berlin Crisis, 1961–1962* (Washington, DC: Government Printing Office, 1993), 520–21.

Washington, October 20, 1961

DEAR GENERAL NORSTAD: Since your visit here I have given further thought to the two principal subjects of our discussion in relation to the Berlin situation, namely, contingency planning and the preparatory build-up in NATO military strength.

◆ ◆ ◆

Two aspects of my present thinking about Berlin planning and preparation deserve especial emphasis.

First: What I want is a sequence of graduated responses to Soviet/GDR [East German] actions in denial of our rights of access. The purpose is to maintain our rights and preserve our alliance. The responses after Phase I should begin with the non-military and move to the military. We cannot plan in advance the exact time each response should be initiated; for one reason, because we cannot now predict the date of Soviet/GDR action, for another because we cannot foresee the duration or the consequences of each response. But there are some principles applicable to this matter of timing. The earlier responses should be thoroughly prepared in advance and the purpose should be to initiate them and keep them going long enough so that the next response may, if necessary, come in when needed. This requires vigor in preparation, readiness for action, and caution against going off half-cocked.

Second: At this juncture I place as much importance on developing our capacity and readiness to fight with significant non-nuclear forces as on measures designed primarily to make our nuclear deterrent more credible. In saying this I am not in any sense depreciating the need for realization by the U.S.S.R. of the tremendous power of our nuclear forces and our will to use them, if necessary, in support of our objectives. Indeed, I think the two aspects are interrelated. It seems evident to me that our nuclear deterrent will not be credible to the Soviets unless they are convinced of NATO's readiness to become engaged on a lesser level of violence and are thereby made to realize the great risks of escalation to nuclear war. I will be interested to hear of any suggestion from you as to how we might intensify that realization.

When contingency plans have been completed and received through established channels, the Joint Chiefs of Staff will review them with me and my other advisors.

Sincerely,
John F. Kennedy

Cuban Crises

5. President-elect Kennedy Receives Advice from President Eisenhower on Cuba, January 19, 1961

President Kennedy received strong advice from various quarters, including the CIA, to launch the Bay of Pigs invasion. President Eisenhower made it clear to the incoming president that he should continue the Eisenhower administration's plans to overthrow Fidel Castro.

Source: Excerpted from *Foreign Relations of the United States, 1961–1963*, vol. 10: *Cuba, 1961–1962* (Washington, DC: Government Printing Office, 1997), 44.

On January 19, 1961, President Eisenhower and President-elect Kennedy met at the White House, together with their principal advisers, to discuss various foreign policy concerns. According to a memorandum prepared by Clark Clifford, who was helping to organize the transition for Kennedy, Eisenhower brought up the issue of Cuba briefly, in a discussion devoted to the problem of Laos:

"President Eisenhower said with reference to guerrilla forces which are opposed to Castro that it was the policy of this government to help such forces to the utmost. At the present time, we are helping train anti-Castro forces in Guatemala. It was his recommendation that this effort be continued and accelerated."

Robert McNamara also prepared a memorandum for the President-elect in which he summarized the discussion at the meeting. His summary of the discussion on Cuba reads as follows:

"President Eisenhower stated in the long run the United States cannot allow the Castro Government to continue to exist in Cuba."

6. Attorney General Robert Kennedy Is Briefed on CIA Contacts with Organized Crime in Plots against Fidel Castro, May 14, 1962

What knowledge President Kennedy had of the many U.S. plots to assassinate Fidel Castro cannot be determined. The president's closest adviser, his brother, received a briefing about the CIA's contacts with figures—John Rosselli and Sam Giancana—in organized crime. The CIA supplied the criminals with lethal pills. Organized criminals made three efforts to assassinate Castro between early 1961 and mid-1962.

Source: Excerpted from *Foreign Relations of the United States, 1961–1963*, vol. 10: *Cuba, 1961–1962* (Washington, DC: Government Printing Office, 1997), 807–9.

Washington, May 14, 1962.

1. This memorandum for the record is prepared at the request of the Attorney General of the United States following a complete oral briefing of him relative to a sensitive CIA operation conducted during the period approximately August 1960 to May 1961. In August 1960 the undersigned was approached by Mr. Richard Bissell, then Deputy Director for Plans of CIA, to explore the

possibility of mounting this sensitive operation against Fidel Castro. It was thought that certain gambling interests which had formerly been active in Cuba might be willing and able to assist and further, might have both intelligence assets in Cuba and communications between Miami, Florida and Cuba. Accordingly, Mr. Robert Maheu, a private investigator of the firm of Maheu and King, was approached by the undersigned and asked to establish contact with a member or members of the gambling syndicate to explore their capabilities. Mr. Maheu was known to have accounts with several prominent business men and organizations in the United States. Maheu was to make his approach to the syndicate as appearing to represent big business organizations which wished to protect their interests in Cuba. Mr. Maheu accordingly met and established contact with one John Rosselli of Los Angeles. Mr. Rosselli showed interest in the possibility and indicated he had some contacts in Miami that he might use. Maheu reported that John Rosselli said he was not interested in any remuneration but would seek to establish capabilities in Cuba to perform the desired project. Towards the end of September Mr. Maheu and Mr. Rosselli proceeded to Miami where, as reported, Maheu was introduced to Sam Giancana of Chicago. Sam Giancana arranged for Maheu and Rosselli to meet with a "courier" who was going back and forth to Havana. From information received back by the courier the proposed operation appeared to be feasible and it was decided to obtain an official Agency approval in this regard. A figure of one hundred fifty thousand dollars was set by the Agency as a payment to be made on completion of the operation and to be paid only to the principal or principals who would conduct the operation in Cuba. Maheu reported that Rosselli and Giancana emphatically stated that they wished no part of any payment. The undersigned then briefed the proper senior officials of this Agency on the proposal. Knowledge of this project during its life was kept to a total of six persons and never became a part of the project current at the time for the invasion of Cuba and there were no memoranda on the project nor were there other written documents or agreements. The project was duly orally approved by the said senior officials of the Agency.

◆ ◆ ◆

3. During the period from September on through April efforts were continued by Rosselli and Maheu to proceed with the operation. The first principal in Cuba withdrew and another principal was selected as has been

briefed to The Attorney General. Ten thousand dollars was passed for expenses to the second principal. He was further furnished with approximately one thousand dollars worth of communications equipment to establish communications between his headquarters in Miami and assets in Cuba. No monies were ever paid to Rosselli and Giancana. Maheu was paid part of his expense money during the periods that he was in Miami. After the failure of the invasion of Cuba word was sent through Maheu to Rosselli to call off the operation and Rosselli was told to tell his principal that the proposal to pay one hundred fifty thousand dollars for completion of the operation had been definitely withdrawn.

◆ ◆ ◆

5. I have no proof but it is my conclusion that Rosselli and Giancana guessed or assumed that CIA was behind the project. I never met either of them.

Sheffield Edwards [Director of CIA Security]

7. President Kennedy Explains His Decision Not to Launch an Air Strike against Cuba, October 22, 1962

President Kennedy has received high praise from scholars and citizens for staying steady and calm during the Cuban missile crisis. An example of the president's leadership was his rejection of advice from the Joint Chiefs and some aides to launch an air strike against Cuba. An air strike would have accelerated the crisis and perhaps led to a catastrophic nuclear war.

Source: Excerpted from *Foreign Relations of the United States, 1961–1963,* vol. 13: *Cuban Missile Crisis and Aftermath* (Washington, DC: Government Printing Office, 1996), 156.

Portion of the NSC Meeting Minutes, Monday, October 22, 1962

The President discussed the reasons why he had decided against an air strike now. First, there was no certainty that an air strike would destroy all missiles now in Cuba. We would be able to get a large percentage of these missiles, but could not get them all.

In addition we would not know if any of these missiles were operationally ready with their nuclear warheads and we were not certain that our intelligence had discovered all the missiles in Cuba. Therefore, in attacking the ones we had located, we could not be certain that others unknown to us would not be launched against the United States. The President said an air strike would involve an action comparable to the Japanese attack on Pearl Harbor. Finally, an air strike would increase the danger of a worldwide nuclear war.

The President said he had given up the thought of making an air strike only yesterday morning. In summary, he said an air strike had all the disadvantages of Pearl Harbor. It would not insure the destruction of every strategic missile in Cuba, and would end up eventually in our having to invade.

Mr. Bundy added that we should not discuss the fact that we were not able to destroy all the missiles by means of an air strike because at some later time we might wish to make such an attack.

8. Higher Authority (President Kennedy) Approves a Sabotage Program against Cuba, June 19, 1963

This document demonstrates that President Kennedy continued a hostile policy toward Cuba, in the aftermath of the missile crisis. The term "Higher Authority" is used to provide the president with "plausible deniability." The president did not want to be identified as approving violent attacks against Cuba.

Source: Excerpted from *Foreign Relations of the United States, 1961–1963*, vol. 13: *Cuban Missile Crisis and Aftermath* (Washington, DC: Government Printing Office, 1996), 837–38.

Washington, June 19, 1963

SUBJECT

Meeting at the White House concerning Proposed Covert Policy and Integrated Program of Action towards Cuba

PRESENT

Higher Authority

Secretary McNamara

Under Secretary Harriman

Mr. McCone

Mr. McGeorge Bundy

Mr. Thomas Parrott
Mr. Desmond FitzGerald
Air Force Vice Chief of Staff, General W. F. McKee

1. The program as recommended by the Standing Group of the NSC was presented briefly to Higher Authority who showed a particular interest in proposed external sabotage operations. He was shown charts indicating typical targets for this program and a discussion of the advantages and disadvantages ensued. It was well recognized that there would be failures and a considerable noise level. [*two lines of source text not declassified*] Mr. Bundy described the integrated nature of the program presented and made the point that, having made the decision to go ahead, we be prepared to take the consequences of flaps and criticisms for a sufficient period to give the program a real chance. Mr. Harriman stated that the program would be "reviewed weekly" by the Special Group. (It is believed that an arrangement can be made with Mr. Bundy for less detailed control by the Special Group than was indicated by Mr. Harriman.)

2. Higher Authority asked how soon we could get into action with the external sabotage program and was told that we should be able to conduct our first operation in the dark-of-the-moon period in July, although he was informed that we would prefer to start the program with some caution, selecting softer targets to begin with. Higher Authority said this was a matter for our judgment. Although at one stage in the discussion Higher Authority said that we should move ahead with the program "this summer," it is believed that Mr. Bundy will be able to convince him that this is not a sufficiently long trial period to demonstrate what the program can do.*

Desmond FitzGerald
Chief, Special Affairs Staff [CIA]

* [CIA Director John] McCone added an addendum to this memorandum stating that he emphasized to the President "the importance and necessity for continuous operations," and he also pointed out that the activities "would create quite a high noise level." McCone also stated that the noise level "must be absorbed and not create a change in policy." He concluded that "no single event would be conclusive."

Latin America

9. President Kennedy Debates the Issue of Communist Influence in Latin America with the President of Mexico, June 29, 1962

In this conversation with President Adolfo López Mateos of Mexico, President Kennedy expresses his concerns about Communist influence in Latin America. Kennedy often let his fears about communism overwhelm his commitment to the Alliance for Progress. President López Mateos seemingly had more faith in the Alliance than did the president.

Source: Excerpted from *Foreign Relations of the United States, 1961–1963*, vol. 12: *American Republics* (Washington, DC: Government Printing Office, 1996), 312–14.

Mexico City, June 29, 1962, 4:45 p.m.

President Kennedy, following up on President Lopez Mateos' appraisal of Castro's chances for survival, then asked what President Lopez Mateos thought could be done to prevent the spread of Soviet power and doctrine via Cuba to other American Republics. President Kennedy mentioned his concern with Soviet activities in countries like Venezuela, Colombia, Guatemala and Ecuador. Guerrilla activities in Colombia and the recent revolts in Venezuela were specifically mentioned.

President Lopez Mateos repeated the familiar Mexican thesis: The important thing is to create better economic and social conditions and especially to provide jobs. When the people were better off, he thought it would not be easy for the Communists to lead them astray. He stressed his opinion that the Alliance for Progress is the best way to combat Communism.

President Kennedy replied that he did not underestimate the importance of economic growth and social progress; nor was he suggesting that Communism was an immediate danger in the United States or Mexico. But he pointed out it would take a decade to achieve the objectives of the Alliance for Progress even under the best of conditions. In the meantime, the question was: What did Mexico think should be done to prevent the spread of Communism in other American Republics? President Kennedy pointed out that, as Cuba shows, once a Communist regime has fastened itself on a country, it is most difficult for the people to rid themselves of it.

◆ ◆ ◆

President Kennedy returned again and again to his question of what President Lopez Mateos thought was the best way to deal with the obvious danger of an expansion of Communist influence in Latin America. President Lopez Mateos each time repeated his view that rapid economic development and social progress was the answer. In the end he said he would give the matter more thought.

Vietnam

10. President Kennedy Expresses Reservations about Expanding the U.S. Role in South Vietnam, November 15, 1961

As these notes from a National Security Council meeting demonstrate, President Kennedy had many questions in 1961 about whether the United States could succeed in South Vietnam. The president was meeting in the aftermath of the recommendations of the Taylor-Rostow report to increase the U.S. military presence in South Vietnam substantially. Some advisers spoke of sending 200,000 U.S. troops to the area. The president subsequently authorized a significant expansion of U.S. military advisers and aid to South Vietnam.

Source: Excerpted from *Foreign Relations of the United States, 1961–1963*, vol. 1: *Vietnam, 1961* (Washington, DC: Government Printing Office, 1988), 607–10.

Notes from NSC Meeting, November 15, 1963, 10:00 a.m.

Mr. Rusk explained the draft of Memorandum on South Viet Nam. He added the hope that, in spite of the magnitude of the proposal, any U.S. actions would not be hampered by lack of funds nor failure to pursue the program vigorously. The President expressed the fear of becoming involved simultaneously on two fronts on opposite sides of the world. He questioned the wisdom of involvement in Viet Nam since the basis thereof is not completely clear. By comparison he noted that Korea was a case of clear aggression which was opposed by the United States and other members of the U.N. The conflict in Viet Nam is more obscure and less flagrant. The President then expressed his strong feeling that in such a situation the United States needs even more the support of allies in such an endeavor as Viet Nam in order to avoid sharp domestic partisan criticism as well as strong objections from other nations of the world. The President said that he could even make a rather strong case against intervening in an area 10,000 miles away against 16,000 guerrillas with a native army of 200,000 where millions have been spent for years with no success. The President repeated his apprehension concerning support, adding that none could be expected from the French, and Mr. Rusk interrupted to say that the British were tending more and more to take the French point of view. The President compared the obscurity of the issues in Viet Nam to the clarity of the positions in Berlin, the contrast of which could even make leading Democrats wary of proposed activities in the Far East.

Mr. Rusk suggested that firmness in Viet Nam in the manner and form of that in Berlin might achieve desired results in Viet Nam without resort to combat. The President disagreed with the suggestion on the basis that the issue was clearly defined in Berlin and opposing forces identified whereas in Viet Nam the issue is vague and action is by guerrillas, sometimes in a phantom-like fashion. Mr. McNamara expressed an opinion that action would become clear if U.S. forces were involved since this power would be applied against sources of Viet Cong power including those in North Viet Nam. The President observed that it was not clear to him just where these U.S. forces would base their operations other than from aircraft carriers which seemed to him to be quite vulnerable. General Lemnitzer confirmed that carriers would be involved to a considerable degree and stated that Taiwan and the Philippines would also become principal bases of action.

11. The Kennedy Administration Initiates the Process of Overthrowing President Ngo Dinh Diem of South Vietnam, August 24, 1963

President Kennedy approved this memorandum, which gave wide latitude to his representatives in Saigon to support the overthrow of President Diem. This came after Diem's brother, Ngo Dinh Nhu, carried out his attacks on Buddhists. Kennedy later wished he had consulted more advisers before signing off on the memorandum. Nonetheless, he never repudiated the policy.

Source: Excerpted from *Foreign Relations of the United States, 1961–1963*, vol. 3: *Vietnam, 1963* (Washington, DC: Government Printing Office, 1991), 628–29.

Telegram from State Department to Embassy in Vietnam

Washington, August 24, 1963—9:36 p.m.

Eyes only for Ambassador [Henry Cabot] Lodge.

It is now clear that whether military proposed martial law or whether [Ngo Dinh] Nhu tricked them into it, Nhu took advantage of its imposition to smash pagodas with police and Tung's Special Forces loyal to him, thus placing onus on military in eyes of world and Vietnamese people. Also clear that Nhu has maneuvered himself into commanding position.

US Government cannot tolerate situation in which power lies in Nhu's hands. Diem must be given chance to rid himself of Nhu and his coterie and replace them with best military and political personalities available.

If, in spite of all of your efforts, Diem remains obdurate and refuses, then we must face the possibility that Diem himself cannot be preserved.

We now believe immediate action must be taken to prevent Nhu from consolidating his position further. Therefore, unless you in consultation with [Gen. Paul] Harkins perceive overriding objections you are authorized to proceed along following lines:

(1) First, we must press on appropriate levels of GVN [South Vietnam] following line:

> (a) USG [U.S. government] cannot accept actions against Buddhists taken by Nhu and his collaborators under cover martial law.
>
> (b) Prompt dramatic actions [to] redress situation must be taken, including repeal of decree 10, release of arrested monks, nuns, etc.

(2) We must at same time also tell key military leaders that US would find it impossible to continue support GVN militarily and economically unless above steps are taken immediately which we recognize requires removal of the Nhus from the scene. We wish give Diem reasonable opportunity to remove Nhus, but if he remains obdurate, then we are prepared to accept the obvious implication that we can no longer support Diem. You may also tell appropriate military commanders we will give them direct support in any interim period of breakdown central government mechanism.

(3) We recognize the necessity of removing taint on military for pagoda raids and placing blame squarely on Nhu. You are authorized to have such statements made in Saigon as you consider desirable to achieve this objective. We are prepared to take same line here and to have Voice of America make statement along lines contained in next numbered telegram whenever you give the word, preferably as soon as possible.

Concurrently with above, Ambassador and country team should urgently examine all possible alternative leadership and make detailed plans as to how we might bring about Diem's replacement if this should become necessary.

Assume you will consult with General Harkins re any precautions necessary [to] protect American personnel during crisis period.

You will understand that we cannot from Washington give you detailed instructions as to how this operation should proceed, but you will also know we will back you to the hilt on actions you take to achieve our objectives.

Needless to say we have held knowledge of this telegram to minimum essential people and assume you will take similar precautions to prevent premature leaks.

[Undersecretary of State George] **Ball**

12. President Kennedy Offers Conflicting Views on the U.S. Role in South Vietnam, September 2 and 9, 1963

Scholars who debate what course President Kennedy would have followed in South Vietnam from 1964 on can find the president saying different things at different times. Excerpted below are two interviews the president gave to newscasters Walter Cronkite, Chet Huntley, and David Brinkley in September 1963.

Source: Excerpted from *Public Papers of the Presidents of the United States: John F. Kennedy, 1963* (Washington, DC: Government Printing Office, 1964), 651–52, 658–59.

MR. CRONKITE: Mr. President, the only hot war we've got running at the moment is of course the one in Viet-Nam, and we have our difficulties there, quite obviously.

THE PRESIDENT: I don't think that unless a greater effort is made by the Government to win popular support that the war can be won out there. In the final analysis, it is their war. They are the ones who have to win it or lose it. We can help them, we can give them equipment, we can send our men out there as advisers, but they have to win it, the people of Viet-Nam, against the Communists.

We are prepared to continue to assist them, but I don't think that the war can be won unless the people support the effort and, in my opinion, in the last 2 months, the government has gotten out of touch with the people.

The repression's against the Buddhists, we felt, were very unwise. Now all we can do is to make it very dear that we don't think this is the way to win. It is my hope that this will become increasingly obvious to the government, that they will take steps to try to bring back popular support for this very essential struggle.

◆ ◆ ◆

MR. HUNTLEY: Are we likely to reduce our aid to South Viet-Nam now?

THE PRESIDENT: I don't think we think that would be helpful at this time. If you reduce your aid, it is possible you could have some effect upon the government structure there. On the other hand, you might have a situation which could bring about a collapse. Strongly in our mind is what happened in the case of China at the end of World War II, where China was lost, a weak government became increasingly unable to control events. We don't want that.

MR. BRINKLEY: Mr. President, have you had any reason to doubt this so-called "domino theory," that if South Viet-Nam falls, the rest of southeast Asia will go behind it?

THE PRESIDENT: No, I believe it. I believe it. I think that the struggle is close enough. China is so large, looms so high just beyond the frontiers, that if South Viet-Nam went, it would not only give them an improved geographical position for a guerrilla assault on Malaya, but would also give the impression that the wave of the future in southeast Asia was China and the Communists. So I believe it.

Asian Issues

13. President Kennedy Promises to Protect Taiwan's Seat on the Security Council at the United Nations, October 16, 1961

President Kennedy maintained U.S. ties to Taiwan and refused to recognize the People's Republic of China. In this message he gave a secret and extraordinary pledge to veto China's admission to the United Nations. Kennedy administration officials would deny for decades that such a pledge had been offered.

Source: Excerpted from *Foreign Relations of the United States, 1961–1963*, vol. 22: *Northeast Asia* (Washington, DC: Government Printing Office, 1996), 160.

Washington, October 16, 1961, 9:09 p.m.
Telegram from the Department of State to the Embassy in the Republic of China

Following instruction is from the President:

At earliest opportunity you should seek meeting with President Chiang [Jiang Jieshi] and inform him orally of this private assurance from me. "I wish to assure you that if at any time a US veto is necessary and will be effective in preventing Chinese Communist entry into the UN, the US will use that veto." You should tell him that this assurance is given privately because of the unfavorable impact that public disclosure would have on our common position at the UN. This is my policy, and President Chiang is entitled to know it, but any public use of this assurance would force a diplomatic denial here.

You should also inform President Chiang that I now plan to make a strong public statement of support for GRC in UN in following terms Wednesday, Oct. 18. "The US has always considered the Government of the Republic of China the only rightful government representing China and has always given full support to the position and to all the rights of that government in the UN. Therefore, the US firmly opposes the entry of the Chinese Communists into the UN or into any of the components of the UN."

14. President Kennedy Seeks Soviet Cooperation to Prevent China from Developing Nuclear Weapons, July 15, 1963

President Kennedy repeatedly expressed alarm over the prospect of the People's Republic of China developing a nuclear weapon. In the summation below, the president asked his arms control negotiator, Averell Harriman, to sound out Nikita Khrushchev in Moscow about a joint Soviet-American position against China. As the editorial note indicates, Khrushchev evinced little interest in Kennedy's proposal.

Source: Excerpted from *Foreign Relations of the United States, 1961–1963*, vol. 22: *Northeast Asia* (Washington, DC: Government Printing Office, 1996), 370–71.

A July 15 [1963] message from Kennedy to Harriman, sent in telegram 191 to Moscow of that date, reads in part as follows:

"I remain convinced that Chinese problem is more serious than Khrushchev comments in first meeting suggest, and believe you should press question in private meeting with him. I agree that large stockpiles are characteristic of US and USSR only, but consider that relatively small forces in hands of people like ChiComs could be very dangerous to us all. Further believe even limited test ban can and should be means to limit diffusion.

"You should try to elicit Khrushchev's view of means of limiting or preventing Chinese nuclear development and his willingness either to take Soviet action or to accept US action aimed in this direction."

A memorandum from John J. de Martino of the Department of State Executive Secretariat to Executive Secretary Benjamin H. Read, dated October 2, 1964, reads as follows:

"A search of our records of the Test Ban Treaty negotiations in Moscow fails to reveal any Harriman proposal for a joint US-USSR effort to slow down Red China's nuclear weapons development. On the other hand the question of Chinese nuclear capacities came up in various Harriman/Khrushchev conversations. Harriman probed USSR knowledge of Chinese capacities and its attitude toward them. He expressed our concern regarding this matter and said he hoped that the problem would be solved by eventual Chinese adherence to the Treaty or by disarmament. Khrushchev was obviously unwilling to talk at much length on the question and he tried to give the impression of not being greatly concerned.

"One of the reasons that the Chinese issue was raised with Khrushchev was Harriman's theory that Khrushchev's interest in a test ban treaty flowed from his desire to isolate Red China in the international communist movement. Aside from this Harriman was also under instructions to express the President's great concern over Chinese development of nuclear weapons."

Final Statements

15. PRESIDENT KENNEDY'S COMMENCEMENT ADDRESS AT AMERICAN UNIVERSITY, JUNE 10, 1963

Many scholars believe that President Kennedy's commencement address at American University represents the president's finest hour. In the speech, he said conciliatory things about the Soviet Union and announced that the United States would stop testing nuclear weapons in the atmosphere. The president's gesture led to the successful negotiation of a treaty that ended atmospheric testing. Some scholars believe that the address signaled that President Kennedy intended to devote the rest of his presidency toward working for peace with the Soviet Union.

Source: Excerpted from *Public Papers of the Presidents of the United States: John F. Kennedy, 1963* (Washington, DC: Government Printing Office, 1964), 459–64.

I have, therefore, chosen this time and this place to discuss a topic on which ignorance too often abounds and the truth is too rarely perceived—yet it is the most important topic on earth: world peace.

What kind of peace do I mean? What kind of peace do we seek? Not a Pax Americana enforced on the world by American weapons of war. Not the peace of the grave or the security of the slave. I am talking about genuine peace, the kind of peace that makes life on earth worth living, the kind that enables men and nations to grow and to hope and to build a better life for their children—not merely peace for Americans but peace for all men and women—not merely peace in our time but peace for all time.

I speak of peace because of the new face of war. Total war makes no sense in an age when great powers can maintain large and relatively invulnerable nuclear forces and refuse to surrender without resort to those forces. It makes no sense in an age when a single nuclear weapon contains almost ten times the explosive force delivered by all of the allied air forces in the Second World War. It makes no sense in an age when the deadly poisons produced by a nuclear exchange would be carried by wind and water and soil and seed to the far corners of the globe and to generations yet unborn.

◆ ◆ ◆

No government or social system is so evil that its people must be considered as lacking in virtue. As Americans, we find communism profoundly repugnant as a negation of personal freedom and dignity. But we can still hail the Russian people for their many achievements—in science and space, in economic and industrial growth, in culture and in acts of courage.

Among the many traits the peoples of our two countries have in common, none is stronger than our mutual abhorrence of war. Almost unique, among the major world powers, we have never been at war with each other. And no nation in the history of battle ever suffered more than the Soviet Union suffered in the course of the Second World War. At least 20 million lost their lives. Countless millions of homes and farms were burned or sacked. A third of the nation's territory, including nearly two thirds of its industrial base, was turned into a wasteland—a loss equivalent to the devastation of this country east of Chicago.

Today, should total war ever break out again—no matter how—our two countries would become the primary targets. It is an ironic but accurate fact that the two strongest powers are the two in the most danger of devastation. All we have built, all we have worked for, would be destroyed in the first 24 hours. And even in the cold war, which brings burdens and dangers to so many countries, including this Nation's closest allies—our two countries bear the heaviest burdens. For we are both devoting massive sums of money to weapons that could be better devoted to combating ignorance, poverty, and disease. We are both caught up in a vicious and dangerous cycle in which suspicion on one side breeds suspicion on the other, and new weapons beget counter-weapons.

In short, both the United States and its allies, and the Soviet Union and its allies, have a mutually deep interest in a just and genuine peace and in halting the arms race. Agreements to this end are in the interests of the Soviet Union as well as ours—and even the most hostile nations can be relied upon to accept and keep those treaty obligations, and only those treaty obligations, which are in their own interest.

So, let us not be blind to our differences—but let us also direct attention to our common interests and to the means by which those differences can be resolved. And if we cannot end now our differences, at least we can help make the world safe for diversity. For, in the final analysis, our most basic common link is that we all inhabit this small planet. We all breathe the same air. We all cherish our children's future. And we are all mortal.

16. President Kennedy Ties Civil Rights Legislation to International Affairs, June 11, 1963

A day after his American University address, President Kennedy spoke eloquently to the nation about the need for civil rights legislation to end segregation in the South and protect the rights of African Americans. In the portions excerpted below, the president notes that simple justice for black people in the United States had implications for the U.S. standing in the world.

Source: Excerpted from *Public Papers of the Presidents of the United States: John F. Kennedy, 1963* (Washington, DC: Government Printing Office, 1964), 468–70.

Today we are committed to a worldwide struggle to promote and protect the rights of all who wish to be free. And when Americans are sent to Viet-Nam or West Berlin, we do not ask for whites only. It ought to be possible, therefore, for American students of any color to attend any public institution they select without having to be backed up by troops.

We preach freedom around the world, and we mean it, and we cherish our freedom here at home, but are we to say to the world, and much more importantly, to each other, that this is a land of the free except for the Negroes; that we have no second-class citizens except Negroes; that we have no class or cast system, no ghettoes, no master race except with respect to Negroes?

17. President Kennedy's Undelivered Remarks at the Trade Mart in Dallas, November 22, 1963

President Kennedy was assassinated before he delivered this address. The tone of this speech contrasts sharply with his American University commencement address in June. The president celebrated U.S. military strength, took a hard line against international communism, and spoke of the U.S. commitment in South Vietnam.

Source: Excerpted from *Public Papers of the Presidents of the United States: John F. Kennedy, 1963* (Washington, DC: Government Printing Office, 1964), 890–94.

I want to discuss with you today the status of our strength and our security because this question clearly calls for the most responsible qualities of leadership and the most enlightened products of scholarship. For this Nation's strength and security are not easily or cheaply obtained, nor are they quickly and simply explained. There are many kinds of strength and no one kind will suffice. Overwhelming nuclear strength cannot stop a guerrilla war. Formal pacts of alliance cannot stop internal subversion. Displays of material wealth cannot stop the disillusionment of diplomats subjected to discrimination.

Above all, words alone are not enough. The United States is a peaceful nation. And where our strength and determination are clear, our words need merely to convey conviction, not belligerence. If we are strong, our strength will speak for itself. If we are weak, words will be of no help.

I realize that this Nation often tends to identify turning-points in world affairs with the major addresses which preceded them. But it was not the Monroe Doctrine that kept all Europe away from this hemisphere—it was the strength of the British fleet and the width of the Atlantic Ocean. It was not General Marshall's speech at Harvard which kept communism out of Western Europe—it was the strength and stability made possible by our military and economic assistance.

In this administration also it has been necessary at times to issue specific warnings—warnings that we could not stand by and watch the Communists conquer Laos by force, or intervene in the Congo, or swallow West Berlin, or maintain offensive missiles on Cuba. But while our goals were at least temporarily obtained in these and other instances, our successful defense of freedom was due not to the words we used, but to the strength we stood ready to use on behalf of the principles we stand ready to defend.

This strength is composed of many different elements, ranging from the most massive deterrents to the most subtle influences. And all types of strength are needed—no one kind could do the job alone. Let us take a moment, therefore, to review this Nation's progress in each major area of strength.

First, as Secretary McNamara made clear in his address last Monday, the strategic nuclear power of the United States has been greatly modernized and expanded in the last 1,000 days by the rapid production and deployment of the most modern missile systems, that any and all potential aggressors are clearly confronted now with the impossibility of strategic victory—and the certainty of total destruction—if by reckless attack they should ever force upon us the necessity of a strategic reply.

In less than 3 years, we have increased by 50 percent the number of Polaris submarines scheduled to be in force by the next fiscal year, increased by more than 70 percent our total Polaris purchase program, increased by more than 75 percent our Minuteman purchase program, increased by 50 percent the portion of our strategic bombers on 15-minute alert, and increased by 100 percent the total number of nuclear weapons available in our strategic alert forces. Our security is further enhanced by the steps we have taken regarding these weapons to improve the speed and certainty of their response, their readiness at all times to respond, their ability to survive an attack, and their ability to be carefully controlled and directed through secure command operations.

But the lessons of the last decade have taught us that freedom cannot be defended by strategic nuclear power alone. We have, therefore, in the last 3 years accelerated the development and deployment of tactical nuclear weapons, and increased by 60 percent the tactical nuclear forces deployed in Western Europe.

Nor can Europe or any other continent rely on nuclear forces alone, whether they are strategic or tactical. We have radically improved the readiness of our conventional forces—increased by 45 percent the number of combat-ready Army divisions, increased by 100 percent the procurement of modern Army weapons and equipment, increased by 100 percent our ship construction, conversion, and modernization program, increased by 100 percent our procurement of tactical aircraft, increased by 30 percent the number of tactical air squadrons, and increased the strength of the Marines. As last month's "Operation Big Lift"—which originated here in Texas—showed so clearly, this Nation is prepared as never before to move substantial numbers of men in surprisingly little time to advanced positions anywhere in the world. We have increased by 175 percent the procurement of airlift aircraft, and we have already achieved a 75 percent increase in our existing strategic airlift capability. Finally, moving beyond the traditional roles of our military forces, we have achieved an increase of nearly 600 percent in our special forces—those forces that are prepared to work with our allies and friends against the guerrillas, saboteurs, insurgents and assassins who threaten freedom in a less direct but equally dangerous manner.

But American military might should not and need not stand alone against the ambitions of international communism. Our security and strength, in the last analysis, directly depend on the security and strength of others, and that is why our military and economic assistance plays such a key role in enabling those who live on the periphery of the Communist world to maintain their independence of choice. Our assistance to these nations can be painful, risky and costly, as is true in Southeast Asia today. But we dare not weary of the task. For our assistance makes possible the stationing of 3.5 million allied troops along the Communist frontier at one-tenth the cost of maintaining a comparable number of American soldiers. A successful Communist breakthrough in these areas, necessitating direct United States intervention, would cost us several times as much as our entire foreign aid program, and might cost us heavily in American lives as well.

About 70 percent of our military assistance goes to nine key countries located on or near the borders of the Communist bloc—nine countries confronted directly or indirectly with the threat of Communist aggression—Viet-Nam, Free China, Korea, India, Pakistan, Thailand, Greece, Turkey, and Iran. No one of these countries possesses on its own the resources to maintain the forces which our own Chiefs of Staff think needed in the common interest. Reducing our efforts to train, equip, and assist their armies can only encourage Communist penetration and require in time the increased overseas deployment of American combat forces. And reducing the economic help needed to bolster these nations that undertake to help defend freedom can have the same disastrous result. In short, the $50 billion we spend each year on our own defense could well be ineffective without the $4 billion required for military and economic assistance.

Our foreign aid program is not growing in size. It is, on the contrary, smaller now than in previous years. It has had its weaknesses, but we have undertaken to correct them. And the proper way of treating weaknesses is to replace them with strength, not to increase those weaknesses by emasculating essential programs. Dollar for dollar, in or out of government, there is no better form of investment in our national security than our much-abused foreign aid program. We cannot afford to lose it. We can afford to maintain it. We can surely afford, for example, to do as much for our 19 needy neighbors of Latin America as the Communist bloc is sending to the island of Cuba alone.

Notes

Some ideas in this book found expression earlier in Stephen G. Rabe, *The Road to OPEC: United States Relations with Venezuela, 1919–1976* (Austin: University of Texas Press, 1982), 139–67; Stephen G. Rabe, *Eisenhower and Latin America: The Foreign Policy of Anticommunism* (Chapel Hill: University of North Carolina Press, 1988); Stephen G. Rabe, *The Most Dangerous Area in the World: John F. Kennedy Confronts Communist Revolution in Latin America* (Chapel Hill: University of North Carolina Press, 1999); James F. Giglio and Stephen G. Rabe, *Debating the Kennedy Presidency* (Lanham, MD: Rowman & Littlefield, 2003); and Stephen G. Rabe, *U.S. Intervention in British Guiana: A Cold War Story* (Chapel Hill: University of North Carolina Press, 2005). This study offers a fresh interpretation of President Kennedy's global policies.

Chapter 1: John F. Kennedy in History

1. Anna Kasten Nelson, "President Kennedy's National Security Policy: A Reconsideration," *Reviews in American History* 19 (March 1991): 1–14.
2. Arthur M. Schlesinger Jr., *A Thousand Days: John F. Kennedy in the White House* (Boston: Houghton Mifflin, 1965), 1030–31.
3. Roger Hilsman, *To Move a Nation: The Politics of Foreign Policy in the Kennedy Administration* (Garden City, NY: Doubleday, 1967), 582; Theodore Sorensen, *Kennedy* (New York: Harper & Row, 1965), 5–7.
4. "Week in Review," *New York Times*, August 18, 1996, 2; "Washington, Lincoln Most Popular Presidents: Nixon, Bush Least Popular," July 4, 2007, Rasmussen Reports (rasmussenreports.com).
5. Kennedy quoted in Robert Dallek, *An Unfinished Life: John F. Kennedy, 1917–1963* (Boston: Little, Brown, 2003), 299.
6. Alan Brinkley, *Liberalism and Its Discontents* (Cambridge, MA: Harvard University Press, 1998), 210–21.
7. Philip Caputo, *A Rumor of War* (New York: Ballantine Books, 1978), xii–xv.
8. Robert K. Murray and Tim H. Blessing, "The Presidential Performance Study:

A Progress Report," *Journal of American History* 70 (December 1983): 535–55; Arthur M. Schlesinger Jr., "The Ultimate Approval Rating," *New York Times Magazine*, December 15, 1996, 46–51; for C-Span surveys, see www.c-span.org/presidentialsurvey; "Survey on the American Presidency," *Chicago Sun Times*, October 1, 2000.

9. James N.Giglio, *The Presidency of John F. Kennedy*, 2nd ed., revised (Lawrence: University Press of Kansas, 2006), 303–9.
10. Dallek, *Unfinished Life*, 574, 707–15.
11. Thomas G. Paterson, ed., *Kennedy's Quest for Victory: American Foreign Policy, 1961–1963* (New York: Oxford University Press, 1989); Diane B. Kunz, ed., *The Diplomacy of the Crucial Decade: American Foreign Relations during the 1960s* (New York: Columbia University Press, 1994); Mark J. White, ed., *Kennedy: The New Frontier Revisited* (New York: New York University Press, 1998).
12. Burton I. Kaufman, "John F. Kennedy as World Leader," *Diplomatic History* 17 (Summer 1993): 447–69.

Chapter 2: Background, Beliefs, People

1. A copy and analysis of NSC 68/2 can be found in Ernest R. May, ed., *American Cold War Strategy: Interpreting NSC 68* (Boston: Bedford Books, 1993).
2. Christopher A. Preble, *John F. Kennedy and the Missile Gap* (Dekalb: University of Northern Illinois Press, 2004), 57–64.
3. John F. Kennedy, *The Strategy of Peace*, ed. Allan Nevins (New York: Harper & Bros., 1960), 66–80; W. W. Rostow, *Eisenhower, Kennedy, and Foreign Aid* (Austin: University of Texas Press, 1985), 3–12, 57–72.
4. Rabe, *Most Dangerous Area*, 16–18, 100–101.
5. Mary L. Dudziak, *Cold War Civil Rights: Race and the Image of American Democracy* (Princeton: Princeton University Press, 2000), 152–202.
6. John F. Kennedy, "A Democrat Looks at Foreign Policy," *Foreign Affairs* 36 (October 1957): 44–59.
7. Mark Haefele, "John F. Kennedy, USIA, and World Public Opinion," *Diplomatic History* 25 (Winter 2001): 68–69.
8. Kennedy quoted in Richard J. Walton, *Cold War and Counterrevolution: The Foreign Policy of John F. Kennedy* (New York: Viking Press, 1972), 9, 36–38. See also Kent M. Beck, "Necessary Lies, Hidden Truths: Cuba in the 1960 Campaign," *Diplomatic History* 8 (Winter 1984): 37–59.
9. Preble, *John F. Kennedy and the Missile Gap*, 95–146.
10. Anna Kasten Nelson, "The 'Top of the Policy Hill': President Eisenhower and the National Security Council," *Diplomatic History* 7 (Fall 1983): 307–26.
11. Dallek, *Unfinished Life*, 307–15.
12. David Halberstam, *The Best and the Brightest* (New York: Random House, 1972).
13. David Kaiser, "Men and Policies, 1961–1969," in Kunz, ed., *Diplomacy of the Crucial Decade*, 11–41; Giglio, *Presidency of John F. Kennedy*, 19–23.

Chapter 3: Soviet Union

1. Annual Message to Congress on State of the Union, January 30, 1961, *Public Papers of the Presidents: John F. Kennedy, 1961* (Washington, DC: Government Printing Office, 1962), 19–28 (hereafter *PPP: JFK*, with year).
2. Nelson, "President Kennedy's National Security Policy," 1–14; Ronald E. Powaski, *March to Armageddon: The United States and the Nuclear Arms Race, 1939 to the Present* (New York: Oxford University Press, 1987), 93–112.
3. Rabe, *Most Dangerous Area*, 125–47.
4. Robert R. Bowie and Richard H. Immerman, *Waging Peace: How Eisenhower Shaped an Enduring Cold War Strategy* (New York: Oxford University Press, 1998), 149–241.
5. Robert Divine, *Blowing on the Wind: The Nuclear Test Ban Debate, 1954–1960* (New York: Oxford University Press, 1978); Benjamin P. Greene, *Eisenhower, Science Advice, and the Nuclear Test-Ban Debate, 1945–1963* (Stanford: Stanford University Press, 2007), 134–232.
6. David Alan Rosenberg, "A Smoking Radiating Ruin at the End of Two Hours: Documents of American Plans for Nuclear War with the Soviet Union, 1954–1955," *International Security* 6 (Winter 1981–82): 3–38; H. W. Brands, "The Age of Vulnerability: Eisenhower and the National Insecurity State," *American Historical Review* 94 (October 1989): 963–89.
7. Alexsandr Fursenko and Timothy Naftali, *Khrushchev's Cold War: The Inside Story of an American Adversary* (New York: W. W. Norton, 2006), 370–71; Dallek, *Unfinished Life*, 336–48; Haefele, "John F. Kennedy, USIA, and World Public Opinion," 63–84.
8. Gilpatric speech discussed in Michael Beschloss, *The Crisis Years: Kennedy and Khrushchev* (New York: Edward Burlingame Books, 1991), 329–31. See also Secretary of State Dean Rusk's comments on speech in *Department of State Bulletin* (hereafter *DSB*) 45 (November 13, 1961), 801–3.
9. Robert S. McNamara, *In Retrospect: The Tragedy and Lessons of Vietnam* (New York: Times Books, 1995), 337–46.
10. Address to the Nation, July 25, 1961, *PPP: JFK, 1961*, 533–40.
11. Jokes quoted in Dallek, *Unfinished Life*, 391.
12. Ibid., 343–47; David C. Coleman, "The Missiles of November, December, January, February . . . The Problem of Acceptable Risk in the Cuban Missile Crisis Settlement," *Journal of Cold War Studies* 9 (Summer 2007): 46.
13. Dealey quoted in Dallek, *Unfinished Life*, 433.
14. Speech to American Society of Newspaper Editors, April 20, 1961, *PPP: JFK, 1961*, 304–6; transcript of interview with Adzhubei, November 25, 1961, ibid., 741–52.
15. William Taubman, *Khrushchev: The Man and His Era* (New York: W. W. Norton, 2003), 45–324; Melvyn P. Leffler, *For the Soul of Mankind: The United States, the Soviet Union, and the Cold War* (New York: Hill and Wang, 2007), 157–58.

16. Ibid., 166–70, 193–94; Taubman, *Khrushchev*, 270–75, 371–75, 481–82.
17. Fursenko and Naftali, *Khrushchev's Cold War*, 540–45.
18. Ibid., 336; Dallek, *Unfinished Life*, 410; Taubman, *Khrushchev*, 657.
19. Fursenko and Naftali, *Khrushchev's Cold War*, 354–55; Dallek, *Unfinished Life*, 347.
20. Harriman quoted in Dallek, *Unfinished Life*, 402.
21. Fursenko and Naftali, *Khrushchev's Cold War*, 355–59.
22. Memorandums of conversations between Kennedy and Khrushchev, June 3–4, 1961, U.S. Department of State, *Foreign Relations of the United States, 1961–1963* (hereafter *FRUS*), vol. 5: *Soviet Union* (Washington, DC: Government Printing Office, 1993), 172–228.
23. Dallek, *Unfinished Life*, 406–15; Fursenko and Naftali, *Khrushchev's Cold War*, 367.
24. Memorandum of conversation between Kennedy and Khrushchev, June 4, 1961, *FRUS, 1961–1963*, vol. 5: *Soviet Union*, 229–31.
25. Fursenko and Naftali, *Khrushchev's Cold War*, 355–59; Dallek, *Unfinished Life*, 414.
26. Taubman, *Khrushchev*, 178; Leffler, *For the Soul of Mankind*, 163, 194–95; Fursenko and Naftali, *Khrushchev's Cold War*, 359–66.
27. Good analyses of the Berlin crisis can be found in Beschloss, *Crisis Years*, 211–90; Georg Schild, "The Berlin Crisis," in White, ed., *Kennedy*, 91–131; and Lawrence Freedman, *Kennedy's Wars: Berlin, Cuba, Laos, and Vietnam* (New York: Oxford University Press, 2000), 45–120.
28. Acheson quoted in record of meeting of the Interdepartmental Coordinating Group on Berlin Contingency Planning, June 16, 1961, *FRUS, 1961–1963*, vol. 14: *Berlin, 1961–1962*, 119; and report by Dean Acheson, June 28, 1961, ibid., 141. Nitze and others quoted in minutes of meeting on Berlin buildup and contingency planning, October 10, 1961, ibid., 487–89; Kennedy to General Norstad, October 20, 1961, ibid., 520–21.
29. Address to the Nation, July 25, 1961, *PPP: JFK, 1961*, 533–40; Dallek, *Unfinished Life*, 418–25.
30. Vladislav M. Zubok, "Khrushchev and the Berlin Crisis, 1958–1962," Working Paper No. 6, May 1993, Cold War International History Project, Woodrow Wilson International Center for Scholars, Washington, DC, 18; Fursenko and Naftali, *Khrushchev's Cold War*, 377.
31. Fulbright and Kennedy quoted in Dallek, *Unfinished Life*, 425.
32. Fursenko and Naftali, *Khrushchev's Cold War*, 377–85; Giglio, *Presidency of John F. Kennedy*, 85–86; Dallek, *Unfinished Life*, 426.
33. Address to the General Assembly of the United Nations, September 25, 1961, *PPP: JFK, 1961*, 618–26.
34. Raymond L. Garthoff, "Berlin, 1961: The Record Corrected," *Foreign Policy* 84 (Fall 1991): 142–56.
35. For a history see Frederick Taylor, *The Berlin Wall: A World Divided* (New York: HarperCollins, 2007).

36. Brandt cited in Kennedy's "Remarks in the Rudolph Wilde Platz," Berlin, June 26, 1963, *PPP: JFK, 1963*, 524–25.
37. Ibid.

Chapter 4: Cuba

1. Louis A. Pérez Jr., *Cuba under the Platt Amendment, 1902–1934* (Pittsburgh: University of Pittsburgh Press, 1986), 333–40; Thomas G. Paterson, *Contesting Castro: The United States and the Cuban Revolution* (New York: Oxford University Press, 1994), 15–65; Ramón Eduardo Ruiz, *Cuba: The Making of a Revolution* (New York: W. W. Norton, 1970), 133–40.
2. Richard E. Welch Jr., *Response to Revolution: The United States and the Cuban Revolution, 1959–1961* (Chapel Hill: University of North Carolina Press, 1985), 3–26.
3. Rabe, *Eisenhower and Latin America*, 117–33, 162–73. The official quoted is Col. J. C. King, chief of the CIA's Western Hemisphere Division.
4. CIA memorandum, "Johnny Rosselli," not dated, 12–16; and Howard J. Osborn, Director of Security, to Director of CIA, "Johnny Rosselli," November 19, 1970, 44–48, both in CIA "Family Jewels" Project on Freedom of Information Act (FOIA), http://www.foia.cia.gov.
5. Eisenhower quoted in Rabe, *Eisenhower and Latin America*, 170–71.
6. Kennedy quoted in Dallek, *Unfinished Life*, 363. A reliable study of the invasion is Peter Wyden, *The Bay of Pigs: The Untold Story* (New York: Simon & Schuster, 1979).
7. CIA papers on Cuba prepared by Richard Bissell, February 17, 1961, March 11, 1961, and March 15, 1961, all in *FRUS, 1961–1963*, vol. 10: *Cuba, 1961–1962*, 102–9, 137–42, 145–48.
8. Joint Chiefs to Secretary of Defense McNamara, February 3, 1961, ibid., 67–78.
9. Acheson quoted in Giglio, *Presidency of John F. Kennedy*, 56.
10. Schlesinger to president, April 5 and April 10, 1961, *FRUS, 1961–1963*, vol. 10: *Cuba, 1961–1962*, 186–89, 196–203.
11. Memorandum prepared in CIA to Gen. Maxwell D. Taylor on report of Col. Hawkins prepared on April 13 and April 26, 1961, ibid., 221–22.
12. Dallek, *Unfinished Life*, 362.
13. Peter Kornbluh, ed., *Bay of Pigs Declassified: The Secret CIA Report on the Invasion of Cuba* (New York: Free Press, 1998), 10–12.
14. Actions and Notes of 483rd meeting of NSC, May 5, 1961, *FRUS, 1961–1963*, vol. 10: *Cuba, 1961–1962*, 476–83; Burke's memorandum for the record, May 5, 1961, ibid., 484.
15. Don Bohning, *The Castro Obsession: U.S. Covert Operations against Cuba, 1959–1965* (Washington, DC: Potomac Books, 2006), 79–85.
16. Robert Kennedy quoted in memorandum from Richard Helms of CIA to Director John McCone, January 19, 1962, *FRUS, 1961–1963*, vol. 10: *Cuba, 1961–1962*, 719–20.

17. Interagency Task Force on Cuba paper for NSC, May 4, 1961, ibid., 459–75.
18. Rabe, *Most Dangerous Area*, 32.
19. Editorial note on Robert Kennedy's handwritten notes, November 7, 1961, *FRUS, 1961–1963*, vol. 10: *Cuba, 1961–1962*, 666.
20. Memorandum from Sherman Kent, Chairman of the Board of National Estimates, to CIA Director Dulles, November 3, 1961, ibid., 668–72; "The Cuba Project," program review by Lansdale, January 18, 1962, ibid., 710–18.
21. Anna Kasten Nelson, "Operation Northwoods and the Covert War against Cuba, 1961–1963," *Cuban Studies* 32 (2002): 145–54. For Kennedy's scheme to attack Guantánamo, see memorandum of discussion in Secretary of State Rusk's office, August 21, 1962, *FRUS, 1961–1963*, vol. 10: *Cuba, 1961–1962*, 947–49.
22. Memorandum for record for Robert Kennedy on CIA briefing, May 14, 1962, ibid., 807–9. For an investigation of U.S. efforts to assassinate Castro, Rafael Trujillo of the Dominican Republic, and others, see U.S. Senate, Select Committee to Study Governmental Operations with Respect to Intelligence Activities, *Alleged Assassination Plots Involving Foreign Leaders*, 94th Cong., 1st sess. (Washington, DC: Government Printing Office, 1975).
23. Memorandum for record prepared by Thomas A. Parrott, assistant to Gen. Maxwell Taylor, on president's interest in Castro's removal, October 5, 1961, *FRUS, 1961–1963*, vol. 10: *Cuba, 1961–1962*, 659–60; Arthur M. Schlesinger Jr., *Robert Kennedy and His Times* (Boston: Houghton Mifflin, 1978), 498; Helms quoted in Tim Weiner, *Legacy of Ashes: The History of the CIA* (New York: Doubleday, 2007), 187.
24. Seymour M. Hersh, *The Dark Side of Camelot* (Boston: Little, Brown, 1997), 268–93.
25. Don Munton and David Welch, *The Cuban Missile Crisis: A Concise History* (New York: Oxford University Press, 2007), 1.
26. Kennedy and Gromyko quoted in ibid., 28, 43–44; Special National Intelligence Estimate, "The Threat to US Security Interests in the Caribbean," January 17, 1962, *FRUS, 1961–1963*, vol 10: *Cuba, 1961–1962*, 706–9.
27. Kennedy quoted in Ernest R. May and Philip D. Zelikow, eds., *The Kennedy Tapes: Inside the White House during the Cuban Missile Crisis* (Cambridge, MA: Belknap Press of Harvard University Press, 1997), 107.
28. Memorandum by Lansdale for Special Group (Augmented), May 31, 1962, *FRUS, 1961–1963*, vol. 10: *Cuba, 1961–1962*, 824; McNamara quoted in Giglio, *Presidency of John F. Kennedy*, 205; Thomas G. Paterson, "Defense-of-Cuba Theme and the Missile Crisis," *Diplomatic History* 14 (Spring 1990): 249–56.
29. Dominic Tierney, "'Pearl Harbor in Reverse': Moral Analogies in the Cuban Missile Crisis," *Journal of Cold War Studies* 9 (Summer 2007): 66
30. Two excellent studies of the missile crisis are Munton and Welch, *Cuban Missile Crisis*; and Alexandr Fursenko and Timothy Naftali, *"One Hell of a Gamble": Khrushchev, Castro, and Kennedy, 1958–1964* (New York: W. W. Norton, 1997).

31. On Kennedy-Gromyko meeting of October 18, 1962, see *FRUS, 1961–1963*, vol. 11: *Cuban Missile Crisis and Aftermath*, 110–14; Kennedy quoted in May and Zelikow, *Kennedy Tapes*, 169.
32. Minutes of 505th meeting of NSC, October 20, 1962, *FRUS, 1961–1963*, vol. 11: *Cuban Missile Crisis and Aftermath*, 134.
33. Munton and Welch, *Cuban Missile Crisis*, 71, 98–99.
34. Ibid., 77, 81; Coleman, "Missiles of November," 29–30.
35. LeMay quoted in May and Zelikow, *Kennedy Tapes*, 178.
36. Kennedy quoted in Coleman, "Missiles of November," 46; Khrushchev letter to Kennedy, October 26, 1962, *FRUS, 1961–1963*, vol. 11: *Cuban Missile Crisis and Aftermath*, 235–241.
37. Stephen G. Rabe, "After the Missiles of October: John F. Kennedy and Cuba, November 1962 to November 1963," *Presidential Studies Quarterly* 30 (December 2000): 714–26.
38. President Kennedy to Secretary of Defense McNamara, April 29, 1963, *FRUS, 1961–1963*, vol. 11: *Cuban Missile Crisis and Aftermath*, 791.
39. Memorandum from Special Assistant Joseph Califano to Secretary of the Army Cyrus Vance on presidential decisions on Cuba, April 9, 1963, ibid., 754–55. On Cuban-Soviet relations see James G. Blight and Philip Brenner, *Sad and Luminous Days: Cuba's Struggle with the Superpowers after the Missile Crisis* (Lanham, MD: Rowman & Littlefield, 2007), 73–119.
40. Memorandum for record of White House meeting on Cuba, June 19, 1963, *FRUS, 1961–1963*, vol. 11: *Cuban Missile Crisis and Aftermath*, 837–38; CIA memorandum of record of meeting of November 12, 1963, to review Cuban program, *FRUS, 1961–1963*, Microfiche Supplement, vols. 10–12, 718.
41. Memorandum of conversation between Ambassador Llewellyn Thompson and Soviet Ambassador Anatoly Dobrynin with Kennedy's oral statement attached, September 13, 1963, *FRUS, 1961–1963*, vol. 11: *Cuban Missile Crisis and Aftermath*, 866–68.
42. Piero Gleijeses, *Conflicting Missions: Havana, Washington, and Africa, 1959–1976* (Chapel Hill: University of North Carolina Press, 2002), 12–29, 374–79.
43. Rabe, "After the Missiles of October," 722–23. See also Gleijeses, *Conflicting Missions*, 23.
44. Weiner, *Legacy of Ashes*, 207–9.
45. Kennedy speech in *DSB* 49 (December 9, 1963), 900–904; Hersh, *Dark Side of Camelot*, 440. Hersh's assertion about the intention of Kennedy's speech is supported by documentary record in memorandum of meeting with President Johnson, December 19,1963, *FRUS, 1961–1963*, vol. 11: *Cuban Missile Crisis and Aftermath*, 904–9.
46. Dallek, *Unfinished Life*, 709.
47. Rabe, "After the Missiles of October," 723–24.
48. Memorandum of meeting with President Johnson, December 19, 1963, *FRUS, 1961–1963*, vol. 11: *Cuban Missile Crisis and Aftermath*, 904–9.

49. Bohning, *Castro Obsession*, 214–54.
50. Johnson quoted in editorial note on meeting between Johnson and CIA Director John McCone, December 27, 1963, *FRUS, 1961–1963*, vol. 11: *Cuban Missile Crisis and Aftermath*, 911; and in Bohning, *Castro Obsession*, 177.
51. Telephone conversation between Johnson and Assistant Secretary of State Thomas Mann, June 11, 1964, *FRUS, 1964–1968*, vol. 32: *Dominican Republic; Cuba; Haiti; Guyana*, 658–60; Mann to Secretary of State Rusk, July 14, 1964, ibid., 734–36.

Chapter 5: Latin America

1. Kennedy quoted in Richard N. Goodwin, *Remembering America: A Voice from the Sixties* (Boston: Little, Brown, 1988), 148.
2. *DSB* 44 (April 3, 1961), 471–74.
3. Ibid.
4. Memorandum of conversation between Kennedy and Prime Minister Harold Macmillan, June 30, 1963, *FRUS, 1961–1963*, vol. 12: *American Republics*, 607–9.
5. Rabe, *Most Dangerous Area*, 22–23.
6. Kennedy quoted in Goodwin, *Remembering America*, 147.
7. Lincoln Gordon, "US–Brazilian Reprise," *Journal of Inter-American Studies and World Affairs* 32 (Summer 1990): 168.
8. Kennedy quoted in Report on Berlin Crisis, July 25, 1961, *PPP: JFK, 1961*, 441–45; Rusk quoted in Rabe, *Most Dangerous Area*, 21.
9. Memorandum of conversation between Rusk and Argentine diplomats, 18 January 1962, *FRUS, 1961–1963*, vol. 12: *American Republics*, 292–94.
10. Kennedy quoted in Rabe, *Most Dangerous Area*, 19–20.
11. Schlesinger, *A Thousand Days*, 773.
12. Michael E. Latham, *Modernization as Ideology: American Social Science and "Nation Building" in the Kennedy Era* (Chapel Hill: University of North Carolina Press, 2000), 1–108; Jeffrey F. Taffet, *Foreign Aid as Foreign Policy: The Alliance for Progress in Latin America* (New York: Routledge, 2007).
13. Rabe, *Most Dangerous Area*, 17–18.
14. Kennedy speech in Miami, November 18, 1963, *DSB* 49 (December 9, 1963), 900–904.
15. Rabe, *Most Dangerous Area*, 148–72.
16. Ibid., 162–64.
17. Ibid., 164–67.
18. Weiner, *Legacy of Ashes*, 180.
19. Schlesinger, *A Thousand Days*, 769
20. Rabe, *Most Dangerous Area*, 34–48.
21. Rabe, *Road to OPEC*, 139–67.
22. Ibid., 142–52.
23. Stephen G. Rabe, "The Caribbean Triangle: Betancourt, Castro, and Trujillo and United States Foreign Policy, 1958–1963," in *Empire and Revolution: The*

United States and the Third World since 1945, ed. Peter L. Hahn and Mary Ann Heiss (Columbus: Ohio State University Press, 2001), 48–70.

24. State Department paper, "Guidelines of U.S. Policy and Operations, Brazil," February 7, 1963, *FRUS, 1961–1963*, vol. 12: *American Republics*, 488–90; Kennedy conversation with Brazilian Foreign Minister, March 13, 1963, ibid., 500–503.
25. Ambassador Lincoln Gordon to State Department on conversation with President Goulart, October 21, 1961, ibid., 448–50.
26. Cabot quoted in Rabe, *Most Dangerous Area*, 65.
27. Memorandum of conversation between Kennedy and Brazilian Finance Minister, May 15, 1961, *FRUS, 1961–1963*, vol. 12: *American Republics*, 435–36.
28. Ambassador Gordon's views in W. Michael Weis, *Cold Warriors and Coups d'Etat: Brazilian American Relations, 1945–1964* (Albuquerque: University of New Mexico Press, 1993), 149–66.
29. Memorandum of conversation between Kennedy and Kubitschek, December 13, 1962, *FRUS, 1961–1963*, vol. 12: *American Republics*, 117–25; Rabe, *Most Dangerous Area*, 67–68.
30. Jan Knippers Black, *United States Penetration of Brazil* (Philadelphia: University of Pennsylvania Press), 1977; Ruth Leacock, *Requiem for Revolution: The United States and Brazil, 1961–1969* (Kent, OH: Kent State University Press, 1990); Phyllis R. Parker, *Brazil and the Quiet Intervention, 1964* (Austin: University of Texas Press, 1979); Weis, *Cold Warriors and Coups d'Etat*.
31. Walter quoted in Parker, *Quiet Intervention*, 62–63.
32. Rabe, *Most Dangerous Area*, 70.
33. State Department to Embassy in Brazil, December 25,1968, *FRUS, 1964–1968*, vol. 31: *South and Central America; Mexico*, 534–37.

Chapter 6: Vietnam

1. Dallek, *Unfinished Life*, 442–61; David Kaiser, *American Tragedy: Kennedy, Johnson, and the Origins of the Vietnam War* (Cambridge, MA: Belknap Press of Harvard University Press, 2000), 1–9; Giglio, *Presidency of John F. Kennedy*, 268–70; Fredrik Logevall, "Vietnam and the Question of What Might Have Been," in White, ed., *Kennedy: The New Frontier Revisited*, 19–62; Robert D. Schulzinger, *A Time for War: The United States and Vietnam, 1941–1975* (New York, 1997), 122; George C. Herring, *America's Longest War: The United States and Vietnam, 1950–1975*, 4th ed. (New York: McGraw-Hill, 2002), 127–29.
2. Caputo, *A Rumor of War*, xiii–xxi.
3. *New York Times*, September 18, 2007; *Time*, March 12, 2007, 31.
4. A concise biography of Ho Chi Minh is David Halberstam, *Ho* (Lanham, MD: Rowman & Littlefield, 2007).
5. Stanley Karnow, *Vietnam: A History* (New York: Viking, 1983), 135–48.
6. Ho's letter and Moffat's report can be found in U.S. Senate, Committee on Foreign Relations, *The United States and Vietnam, 1944–1947: A Staff Study Based*

on the Pentagon Papers, 92nd Cong., 2nd sess. (Washington, DC: Government Printing Office, 1972), 9–14.

7. Seth Jacobs, *Cold War Mandarin: Ngo Dinh Diem and the Origins of America's War in Vietnam, 1950–1963* (Lanham, MD: Rowman & Littlefield, 2006), 15–33.
8. An excellent study of Eisenhower's Vietnam policy is David L. Anderson, *Trapped by Success: The Eisenhower Administration and Vietnam, 1953–1961* (New York: Columbia University Press, 1991).
9. William Duiker, *Sacred War: Nationalism and Revolution in a Divided Vietnam* (New York: McGraw-Hill, 1994), 116–34.
10. Kennedy quoted in Dallek, *Unfinished Life*, 167; Giglio, *Presidency of John F. Kennedy*, 255–56.
11. NSAM 52, May 11, 1961, *FRUS, 1961–1963*, vol 1: *Vietnam, 1961*, 132–34.
12. Kennedy quoted in Dallek, *Unfinished Life*, 677.
13. Johnson and journalist quoted in Jacobs, *Cold War Mandarin*, 124, 129; Kennedy quoted in Giglio, *Presidency of John F. Kennedy*, 264.
14. Taylor to president, November 3, 1961, *FRUS, 1961–1963*, vol. 1: *Vietnam, 1961*, 477–532.
15. McNamara to president, November 5, 1961, ibid., 538–40; McNamara to president, November 8, 1961, ibid., 559–61; Taylor quoted in ibid., 477–78.
16. Kennedy quoted in Dallek, *Unfinished Life*, 450; notes on NSC meeting, November 15, 1961, *FRUS, 1961–1963*, vol. 1: *Vietnam, 1961*, 607–10.
17. Lawrence J. Bassett and Stephen R. Pelz, "The Failed Search for Victory: Vietnam and the Politics of War," in Paterson, ed., *Kennedy's Quest for Victory*, 223–52.
18. Dallek, *Unfinished Life*, 453–54; Kaiser, *American Tragedy*, 91–121.
19. Michael Hunt, *Lyndon Johnson's War: America's Cold War Crusade in Vietnam, 1945–1968* (New York: Hill and Wang, 1996), 42–71; Herring, *America's Longest War*, 89–129.
20. George W. Ball, *The Past Has Another Pattern: Memoirs* (New York: W. W. Norton, 1982), 366.
21. Giglio, *Presidency of John F. Kennedy*, 262.
22. Dallek, *Unfinished Life*, 446–47.
23. Ibid., 679; Jacobs, *Cold War Mandarin*, 130.
24. News conference, December 12, 1962, *PPP: JFK, 1962*, 870.
25. Jacobs, *Cold War Mandarin*, 125–27.
26. Ibid, 140–41; Hunt, *Lyndon Johnson's War*, 37–40.
27. Schulzinger, *Time for War*, 127–34, 140.
28. Jacobs, *Cold War Mandarin*, 142–54.
29. Kennedy quoted in ibid., 149.
30. Telegram, State Department to U.S. embassy in Saigon, August 24, 1963, *FRUS, 1961–1963*, vol. 3: *Vietnam, January–August 1963*, 628–29.
31. Lodge quoted in Herring, *America's Longest War*, 116; on Conein, see Weiner, *Legacy of Ashes*, 210–21.

32. Kennedy quoted in Giglio, *Presidency of John F. Kennedy*, 265–66.
33. CIA in Saigon to Agency on meeting with General Minh, October 5, 1963, *FRUS, 1961–1963*, vol. 4: *September to December 1963*, 365–67; McGeorge Bundy to Ambassador Lodge, October 5, 1963, ibid., 379; CIA to Ambassador Lodge, October 9, 1963, ibid., 393; Bundy to Lodge, October 25, 1963, ibid., 437.
34. Jacobs, *Cold War Mandarin*, 173–81.
35. Maxwell Taylor, *Swords and Plowshares* (New York: W. W. Norton, 1972), 301.
36. A transcript of Kennedy's taped recording can be found in Kaiser, *American Tragedy*, 276–77.
37. Philip E. Catton, *Diem's Final Failure: Prelude to America's War in Vietnam* (Lawrence: University Press of Kansas, 2002), 209–11.
38. Gary R. Hess, *Vietnam: Explaining America's Lost War* (Malden, MA: Blackwell Publishing, 2009), 57.
39. Interviews of September 2 and September 9, 1963, *PPP: JFK, 1963*, 651–52, 658–59.
40. Dallek, *Unfinished Life*, 668; Giglio, *Presidency of John F. Kennedy*, 269; Evan Thomas, *Robert F. Kennedy: His Life* (New York: Simon & Schuster, 2000), 311–16.
41. Kennedy quoted in Dallek, *Unfinished Life*, 685–86; undelivered November 22, 1963, speech, *PPP: JFK, 1963*, 890–94.
42. Hess, *Vietnam: Explaining America's Lost War*, 57–62; David L. Anderson, "Reestablishing Credibility: Foreign Relations of the United States and Vietnam, 1961–1964," *Documentary Editing* 15 (September 1993): 53.
43. Herring, *America's Longest War*, 121–22.
44. Duiker, *Sacred War*, 158–64; Jacobs, *Cold War Mandarin*, 165–66.
45. Ball, *Past Has Another Pattern*, 366–67.

Chapter 7: Asia

1. Nancy Bernkopf Tucker, "John Foster Dulles and the Taiwan Roots of the 'Two Chinas' Policy," in *John Foster Dulles and the Diplomacy of the Cold War*, ed. Richard H. Immerman (Princeton: Princeton University Press, 1990), 235–62.
2. Eisenhower quoted in Gordon H. Chang, *Friends and Enemies: The United States, China, and the Soviet Union, 1948–1972* (Stanford: Stanford University Press, 1990), 170–74.
3. Kennedy quoted in ibid., 236; Arthur Waldron, "From Non-Existent to Almost Normal: U.S.–China Relations in the 1960s," in Kunz, ed., *Diplomacy of the Crucial Decade*, 220.
4. Fursenko and Naftali, *Khrushchev's Cold War*, 239–40, 327–28, 526–28.
5. Noam Kochavi, *A Conflict Perpetuated: China Policy during the Kennedy Years* (Westport, CT: Praeger, 2002), 25–44; Waldron, "From Non-Existent to Almost Normal," 223–26.
6. Memorandum of conversation between Kennedy and Prime Minister Macmil-

lan, April 5, 1961, *FRUS, 1961–1963*, vol. 22: *Northeast Asia*, 42–45; Dean Rusk, *As I Saw It, As Told to Richard Rusk* (New York: W. W. Norton, 1990), 282–84.

7. Kochavi, *Conflict Perpetuated*, 78–79; embassy in Poland to State Department on talks with China, March 7, 1961, *FRUS, 1961–1963*, vol. 22: *Northeast Asia*, 25–26.
8. Memorandum of conversation between Kennedy and Holyoake, March 3, 1961, ibid., 20–22; memorandum of conversation between Rusk and Macmillan, June 24, 1961, ibid., 276–77.
9. Kennedy quoted in Kochavi, *Conflict Perpetuated*, 70–74; James Fetzer, "Clinging to Containment: China Policy," in Paterson, ed. *Kennedy's Quest for Victory*, 196; Leffler, *For the Soul of Mankind*, 175.
10. Kennedy's veto pledge in State Department to Embassy in Republic of China, October 16, 1961, *FRUS, 1961–1963*, vol. 22: *Northeast Asia*, 160; Warren I. Cohen, "Kennedy's China," *Diplomatic History* 28 (January 2004): 156, fn. 3.
11. Editorial note on Bowles and wheat issue, February 6, 1961, *FRUS, 1961–1963*, vol. 22: *Northeast Asia*, 185; draft memorandum from Rusk to Kennedy on wheat, April 4, 1962, ibid., 208–10; Harriman to Rusk, April 13, 1962, ibid., 216–17; Fetzer, "Clinging to Containment," 190–93.
12. Special National Intelligence Estimate, "Probable Consequences of Chinese Nationalist Military Operations on the China Mainland," March 28, 1962, *FRUS, 1961–1963*, vol. 22: *Northeast Asia*, 200–201.
13. Draft memorandum of Kennedy to Harriman on meetings with Jiang, March 9, 1962, ibid., 192–93; embassy in Poland to State Department on meeting with Ambassador Wang, June 23, 1962, ibid., 273–75.
14. Embassy in Republic of China to State Department, January 10, 1963, ibid., 337–38; editorial note on CIA operations, September 19, 1963, ibid., 397.
15. Embassy in Poland to State Department on talks with Ambassador Wang, September 20, 1962, ibid., 318–20; Policy Planning Council, "US Policy toward Communist China," November 30, 1962, ibid., 325–32.
16. Kennedy quoted in William Burr and Jeffrey T. Richelson, "Whether to 'Strangle the Baby in the Cradle': The United States and the Chinese Nuclear Program, 1960–64," *International Security* 25 (Winter 2000–2001): 54; Chang, *Friends and Enemies*, 232–37; Kochavi, *Conflict Perpetuated*, 217–20.
17. Burr and Richelson, "Whether to 'Strangle the Baby in the Cradle,'" 57–59, 63.
18. Editorial notes on Kennedy discussions on China and bomb, January 10, 1963, and January 22, 1963, *FRUS, 1961–1963*, vol. 22: *Northeast Asia*, 339–41.
19. Embassy in Poland to State Department on talks with Ambassador Wang, August 7, 1963, ibid., 378–82.
20. Memorandum by CIA Deputy Director of Intelligence Ray Cline, January 14, 1963, ibid., 340.
21. Editorial note on Kennedy's instructions to Harriman, July 15, 1963, ibid., 370–71; Burr and Richelson, "Whether to 'Strangle the Baby in the Cradle,'" 71; Kochavi, *Conflict Perpetuated*, 222–25.

22. Burr and Richelson, "Whether to 'Strangle the Baby in the Cradle,'" 74–75.
23. Memorandum of conversation between Kennedy and Jiang Jingguo, September 11, 1963, *FRUS, 1961–1963*, vol. 22: *Northeast Asia*, 386–92.
24. Highlights from Rusk's Policy Planning meeting, October 15, 1963, ibid., 399–402; Robert W. Komer of NSC to Bundy on Chinese nuclear capabilities, November 5, 1963, ibid., 405–8.
25. News conference, November 14, 1963, *PPP: JFK, 1961*, 845–46.
26. Hilsman speech in *DSB* 50 (January 6, 1964), 11–17; Hilsman, *To Move a Nation*, 350–57; Hilsman to Stevenson, December 19, 1963, *FRUS, 1961–1963*, vol. 22: *Northeast Asia*, 411–12.
27. H. W. Brands, *India and the United States: The Cold Peace* (Boston: Twayne Publishers, 1990), 90–96; Andrew J. Rotter, *Comrades at Odds: The United States and India, 1947–1964* (Ithaca, NY: Cornell University Press, 2000), 277–78.
28. Dallek, *Unfinished Life*, 165; Kennedy, "A Democrat Looks at Foreign Policy," 59; Rostow, *Eisenhower, Kennedy, and Foreign Aid*, 3–12; Kennedy's presidential campaign statement in Kochavi, *Conflict Perpetuated*, 146.
29. Nehru to Kennedy, May 13, 1961, *FRUS, 1961–1963*, vol. 19: *Southeast Asia*, 39–40.
30. Walter K. Andersen, "U.S.–Indian Relations, 1961–1963: Good Intentions and Uncertain Results," in *The Hope and the Reality: U.S.–Indian Relations from Roosevelt to Reagan*, ed. Harold A. Gould and Sumit Ganguly (Boulder, CO: Westview Press, 1992), 73; Dennis Merrill, *Bread and the Ballot: The United States and India's Economic Development, 1947–1963* (Chapel Hill: University of North Carolina Press, 1990), 175–78; Gary Hess, "Accommodation amid Discord: The United States, India, and the Third World," *Diplomatic History* 16 (Winter 1992): 19–20.
31. Hess, "Accommodation amid Discord," 11; Merrill, *Bread and Ballot*, 171–79, 198–99.
32. Kennedy quoted in Dennis Kux, *India and the United States: Estranged Democracies, 1941–1991* (Washington, DC: National Defense University Press, 1992), 189.
33. Bowles quoted in Merrill, *Bread and the Ballot*, 201; Hess, "Accommodation amid Discord," 19.
34. Johnson quoted in Robert J. McMahon, *The Cold War on the Periphery: The United States, India, and Pakistan* (New York: Columbia University Press, 1994), 277; memorandum of conversation between Johnson and Nehru, May 18, 1961, *FRUS, 1961–1963*, vol. 19: *Southeast Asia*, 39–40.
35. Kux, *India and the United States*, 193–96; John Kenneth Galbraith, *Ambassador's Journal: A Personal Account of the Kennedy Years* (Boston: Houghton Mifflin, 1969), 245–53; Rotter, *Comrades at Odds*, 276–80.
36. Memorandum of conversation between Johnson and Nehru, May 18, 1961,

FRUS, 1961–1963, vol. 19: *Southeast Asia*, 39–40; memorandum of conversation between Bowles and Nehru, August 8–9, 1961, ibid., 80–86.

37. Memorandum of conversation between Kennedy and Nehru, November 7, 1961, ibid., 128–35.
38. Kennedy quoted in Kux, *India and the United States*, 197–98.
39. Sorensen, *Kennedy*, 664.
40. Memorandum of conversation between Kennedy and Nehru, November 7, 1961, *FRUS, 1961–1963*, vol. 19: *Southeast Asia*, 128–35.
41. *New York Times*, October 22, 2008, A10.
42. Nehru quoted in Kux, *India and the United States*, 204; Galbraith, *Ambassador's Journal*, 428–97.
43. Text of Nehru's message in Embassy in India to State Department, November 19, 1962, *FRUS, 1961–1963*, vol. 19: *Southeast Asia*, 397. See also McMahon, *Cold War on the Periphery*, 286–92.
44. Kennedy letter in State Department to Embassy in India, October 28, 1962, *FRUS, 1961–1963*, vol. 19: *Southeast Asia*, 360.
45. Rusk to Embassy in India, November 20, 1962, ibid., 402.
46. McMahon, *Cold War on the Periphery*, 293–304; Kennedy quoted in Kochavi, *Conflict Perpetuated*, 151.
47. Memorandum from Robert W. Komer of NSC to Bundy, November 14, 1963, *FRUS, 1961–1963*, vol. 19: *Southeast Asia*, 690.

Chapter 8: Middle East and Africa

1. Memorandum of conversation between Kennedy and Ben-Gurion, May 30, 1961, *FRUS, 1961–1963*, vol. 17: *Near East, 1961–1962*, 139.
2. Kennedy, "A Democrat Looks at Foreign Policy," 44, 50–51.
3. State Department to Embassy in Cairo with Kennedy letter to Nasser, May 11, 1961, *FRUS, 1961–1963*, vol. 17: *Near East, 1961–1962*, 110–13; Nasser's reply to Kennedy with State Department comment, August 30, 1961, ibid., 242–43.
4. National Intelligence Estimate on Nasser and Future of Arab Nationalism, June 27, 1961, ibid., 164–66.
5. Bowles to Kennedy in Embassy in Ethiopia to State Department, February 21, 1962, *FRUS, 1961–1963*, vol. 17: *Near East, 1961–1962*, 481–89.
6. Memorandum by Robert Komer of NSC to Walt Rostow, June 30, 1961, ibid., 173; memorandum of conversation between Ambassador Kamel and Phillips Talbot of State Department, December 1, 1961, ibid., 354–55; Rusk to Kennedy on Action Program for United Arab Republic, January 10, 1962, ibid., 384–89; Komer to Kennedy, January 23, 1962, ibid., 438–39.
7. Nasser to Kennedy in State Department to NSC, June 25, 1962, ibid., 755–56.
8. Kennedy quoted in Douglas Little, "The New Frontier on the Nile: JFK, Nasser, and Arab Nationalism," *Journal of American History* 75 (September 1988): 520. See also James Goode, "Reforming Iran during the Kennedy Years," *Diplomatic History* 15 (Winter 1991): 13–29; Douglas Little, *American Orientalism: The*

United States and the Middle East since 1945 (Chapel Hill: University of North Carolina Press, 2002), 210–11.

9. Little, "New Frontier on the Nile," 501–27.
10. Kennedy to Prime Minister Macmillan, November 15, 1962, *FRUS, 1961–1963*, vol. 18: *Near East, 1962–1963*, 223–24, fn. 1; Rusk to Kennedy on Nasser visit, December 17, 1962, ibid., 267–68.
11. State Department to Embassy in Cairo containing Kennedy message to Nasser, October 19, 1963, ibid., 752.
12. Peres quoted in Little, "New Frontier on the Nile," 523.
13. Warren Bass, *Support Any Friend: Kennedy's Middle East and the Making of the U.S.-Israel Alliance* (New York: Oxford University Press, 2003), 51–54; Dallek, *Unfinished Life*, 165, 175.
14. Memorandum of conversation between Kennedy and Ben-Gurion, May 30, 1961, *FRUS, 1961–1963*, vol. 17: *Near East, 1961–1962*, 134–41.
15. Douglas Little, "A Fool's Errand: America and the Middle East, 1961–1969," in Kunz, ed., *Diplomacy of the Crucial Decade*, 288–98.
16. Little, *American Orientalism*, 276–78.
17. Kennedy to Ben-Gurion, May 4, 1963, *FRUS, 1961–1963*, vol. 18: *Near East, 1962–1963*, 511–14.
18. Kennedy to Eshkol, ibid., 720–22.
19. Kennedy quoted in Bass, *Support Any Friend*, 206–7.
20. Ibid., 186–238.
21. Address by Assistant Secretary of State for African Affairs, G. Mennen Williams, before Overseas Press Club, October 31, 1961, *DSB* 45 (November 27, 1961), 885–88.
22. Accounts of the Congo crisis can be found in Madeleine G. Kalb, *The Congo Cables: The Cold War in Africa—From Eisenhower to Kennedy* (New York: Macmillan, 1982); Richard D. Mahoney, *JFK: Ordeal in Africa* (New York: Oxford University Press, 1983).
23. Nixon quoted in James H. Meriwether, "'Worth a Lot of Negro Votes': Black Voters, Africa, and the 1960 Campaign," *Journal of American History* 95 (December 2008): 743.
24. Gary A. Donaldson, *The First Modern Campaign: Kennedy, Nixon, and the Election of 1960* (Lanham, MD: Rowman & Littlefield, 2007), 156.
25. Robert Kinlock Massie, *Loosing the Bonds: The United States and South Africa in the Apartheid Years* (New York: Nan A. Talese, 1997), 115.
26. Rusk quoted in Thomas Borstelmann, "'Hedging Our Bets and Buying Time': John Kennedy and Racial Revolutions in the American South and Southern Africa," *Diplomatic History* 24 (Summer 2000): 440.
27. Thomas J. Noer, "New Frontiers and Old Priorities in Africa," in Paterson, ed., *Kennedy's Quest for Victory*, 260; Massie, *Loosing the Bonds*, 120–22.
28. "Radio and Television Report to the American People on Civil Rights," June 11, 1963, *PPP: JFK, 1963*, 468–70.

29. James Meredith's remark in Borstelmann, "'Hedging Our Bets and Buying Time,'" 437.
30. Defense department officials quoted in ibid., 450.
31. Gary May, "Passing the Torch and Lighting Fires: The Peace Corps," in Paterson, ed., *Kennedy's Quest for Victory*, 300; Gerald E. Thomas, "The Black Revolt: The United States and Africa in the 1960s," in Kunz, ed., *Diplomacy of the Crucial Decade*, 325–27.
32. Jeffrey A. Lefebvre, "Kennedy's Algerian Dilemma: Containment, Alliance Politics, and the 'Rebel Dialogue,'" *Middle Eastern Studies* 35 (April 1999): 61–82.
33. Ball, *Past Has Another Pattern*, 276–82.
34. Noer, "New Frontiers and Old Priorities in Africa," 269–74; Borstelmann, "'Hedging Our Bets and Buying Time,'" 455.
35. Meeting with the president on Portuguese Africa, July 18, 1963, *FRUS, 1961–1963*, vol. 21: *Africa*, 573; meeting with president on Portuguese Africa, July 30, 1960, ibid., 577–78; memorandum of conversation between president and Foreign Minister Franco Nogueira, November 7, 1963, ibid., 581–85.
36. Noer, "New Frontiers and Old Priorities in Africa," 274–78.
37. State Department to Embassy in South Africa, August 25, 1961, *FRUS, 1961–1963*, vol. 21: *Africa*, 598–601; Assistant Secretary Williams to Deputy Secretary of Defense Gilpatric, September 16, 1961, ibid., 601–602.
38. Memorandum of conversation between Rusk and South African ambassador, July 17, 1963, ibid., 639–43; Bowles to Bundy of NSC, September 21, 1961, ibid., 603–605.
39. Larry Grubbs, "'Workshop of a Continent': American Representations of Whiteness and Modernity in 1960s South Africa," *Diplomatic History* 32 (June 2008): 405–39; Massie, *Loosing the Bonds*, 97–156.
40. Wiesner to Bundy, October 18, 1961, *FRUS, 1961–1963*, vol. 21: *Africa*, 607–8.
41. Rusk to Harriman, June 15, 1963, ibid., 633–35.
42. Rabe, *Most Dangerous Area*, 48–54.
43. Memorandum of conversation between Rusk and South African ambassador, July 17, 1963, *FRUS, 1961–1963*, vol. 21: *Africa*, 639–43; Massie, *Loosing the Bonds*, 152.
44. Memorandum from State Department to NSC on Chief Luthuli, November 13, 1961, *FRUS, 1961–1963*, vol. 21: *Africa*, 612.
45. CIA report, May 10, 1963, and Ambassador Satterthwaite's comments in Kenneth Mokoena, ed., *South Africa and the United States: The Declassified History* (New York: New Press, 1993), 188–96.
46. Weiner, *Legacy of Ashes*, 362; David Johnston, "C.I.A. Tie Reported in Mandela Arrest," *New York Times*, June 10, 1990.

Chapter 9: John F. Kennedy: The Future Versus the Past

1. Robert A. Divine, "The Education of John F. Kennedy," in *Makers of American Diplomacy: From Theodore Roosevelt to Henry Kissinger*, ed. Frank J. Merli and

Theodore A. Wilson (New York: Charles Scribner's Sons, 1974), 317–44.

2. Kennedy quoted in Leffler, *For the Soul of Mankind*, 185.
3. Sorensen, *Kennedy*, 822–23; Schlesinger, *A Thousand Days*, 821–23.
4. Commencement Address at American University, June 10, 1963, *PPP: JFK, 1963*, 459–64.
5. Fursenko and Naftali, *Khrushchev's Cold War*, 507–26; Leffler, *For the Soul of Mankind*, 182–89.
6. Divine, "Education of John F. Kennedy," 325.
7. Address before the 18th General Assembly of the United Nations, September 20, 1963, *PPP: JFK, 1963*, 693–98.
8. Address in Salt Lake City at the Mormon Tabernacle, September 26, 1963, ibid., 733–38.
9. Remarks Prepared for Delivery at the Trade Mart in Dallas, November 22, 1963, ibid., 890–94.
10. Leffler, *For the Soul of Mankind*, 190–92.
11. Dallek, *Unfinished Life*, 709.
12. Ibid., 710.
13. Hess, *Vietnam: Explaining America's Lost War*, 57.
14. Giglio, *Presidency of John F. Kennedy*, 305.
15. Dallek, *Unfinished Life*, 574.
16. Nelson, "President Kennedy's National Security Policy," 9.

Recommended Readings

Bass, Warren. *Support Any Friend: Kennedy's Middle East and the Making of the U.S.-Israel Alliance*. New York: Oxford University Press, 2003.

Beschloss, Michael. *The Crisis Years: Kennedy and Khrushchev*. New York: Edward Burlingame Books, 1991.

Bohning, Don. *The Castro Obsession: U.S. Covert Operations against Cuba, 1959–1965*. Washington, DC: Potomac Books, 2006.

Brinkley, Douglas, and Richard T. Griffiths, eds. *John F. Kennedy and Europe*. Baton Rouge: Louisiana State University Press, 1999.

Dallek, Robert. *An Unfinished Life: John F. Kennedy, 1917–1963*. Boston: Little, Brown, 2003.

Donaldson, Gary A. *The First Modern Campaign: Kennedy, Nixon, and the Election of 1960*. Lanham, MD: Rowman & Littlefield, 2007.

Freedman, Lawrence. *Kennedy's Wars: Berlin, Cuba, Laos, and Vietnam*. New York: Oxford University Press, 2000.

Fursenko, Alexsandr, and Timothy Naftali. *Khrushchev's Cold War: The Inside Story of an American Adversary*. New York: W. W. Norton, 2006.

———. *"One Hell of a Gamble": Khrushchev, Castro, and Kennedy, 1958–1964*. New York: W. W. Norton, 1997.

Giglio, James N. *The Presidency of John F. Kennedy*. 2nd edition, revised. Lawrence: University Press of Kansas, 2006.

Herring, George C. *America's Longest War: The United States and Vietnam, 1950–1975*. 4th edition. New York: McGraw-Hill, 2002.

Hersh, Seymour. *The Dark Side of Camelot*. Boston: Little, Brown, 1997.

Hilsman, Roger. *To Move a Nation: The Politics of Foreign Policy in the Kennedy Administration*. Garden City, NY: Doubleday, 1967.

Hoffman, Elizabeth Cobbs. *All You Need Is Love: The Peace Corps and the Spirit of the 1960s*. Cambridge, MA: Harvard University Press, 1998.

Hunt, Michael. *Lyndon Johnson's War: America's Cold War Crusade in Vietnam, 1945–1968*. New York: Hill and Wang, 1996.

Jacobs, Seth. *Cold War Mandarin: Ngo Dinh Diem and the Origins of America's War in Vietnam, 1950–1963*. Lanham, MD: Rowman & Littlefield, 2006.

Jones, Howard. *The Bay of Pigs*. New York: Oxford University Press, 2008.

Kochavi, Noam. *A Conflict Perpetuated: China Policy during the Kennedy Years*. Westport, CT: Praeger, 2002.

Kornbluh, Peter, ed. *Bay of Pigs Declassified: The Secret CIA Report on the Invasion of Cuba*. New York: Free Press, 1998.

Kunz, Diane B., ed. *The Diplomacy of the Crucial Decade: American Foreign Relations during the 1960s*. New York: Columbia University Press, 1994.

Latham, Michael E. *Modernization as Ideology: American Social Science and "Nation Building" in the Kennedy Era*. Chapel Hill: University of North Carolina Press, 2000.

Leffler, Melvyn P. *For the Soul of Mankind: The United States, the Soviet Union, and the Cold War*. New York: Hill and Wang, 2007.

Little, Douglas. *American Orientalism: The United States and the Middle East since 1945*. Chapel Hill: University of North Carolina Press, 2002.

Mahoney, Richard D. *JFK: Ordeal in Africa*. New York: Oxford University Press, 1983.

May, Ernest R., and Philip Zelikow, eds. *The Kennedy Tapes: Inside the White House during the Cuban Missile Crisis*. Cambridge, MA: Belknap Press of Harvard University Press, 1997.

McMahon, Robert J. *The Cold War on the Periphery: The United States, India, and Pakistan*. New York: Columbia University Press, 1994.

Merrill, Dennis. *Bread and Ballot: The United States and India's Economic Development, 1947–1963*. Chapel Hill: University of North Carolina Press, 1990.

Munton, Don, and David Welch. *The Cuban Missile Crisis: A Concise History*. New York: Oxford University Press, 2007.

Noer, Thomas J. *Cold War and Black Liberation: The United States and White Rule in Africa, 1948–1968*. Columbia: University of Missouri Press, 1985.

Paterson, Thomas G., ed. *Kennedy's Quest for Victory: American Foreign Policy, 1961–1963*. New York: Oxford University Press, 1989.

Preble, Christopher A. *John F. Kennedy and the Missile Gap*. Dekalb: University of Northern Illinois Press, 2004.

Rabe, Stephen G. *The Most Dangerous Area in the World: John F. Kennedy Confronts Communist Revolution in Latin America*. Chapel Hill: University of North Carolina Press, 1999.

———. *U.S. Intervention in British Guiana: A Cold War Story*. Chapel Hill: University of North Carolina Press, 2005.

Schlesinger, Arthur M., Jr. *Robert Kennedy and His Times*. Boston: Houghton Mifflin, 1978.

———. *A Thousand Days: John F. Kennedy in the White House*. Boston: Houghton Mifflin, 1965.

Sorensen, Theodore C. *Kennedy*. New York: Harper & Row, 1965.

Taffet, Jeffrey F. *Foreign Aid as Foreign Policy: The Alliance for Progress in Latin America.* New York: Routledge, 2007.

Taubman, William. *Khrushchev: The Man and His Era*. New York: W. W. Norton, 2003.

White, Mark J., ed. *Kennedy: The New Frontier Revisited.* New York: New York University Press, 1998.

Wyden, Peter. *The Bay of Pigs: The Untold Story*. New York: Simon & Schuster, 1979.

Zelikow, Philip D., Timothy Naftali, and Ernest R. May, eds., *The Presidential Recordings: John F. Kennedy*. Vols. 1–3: *The Great Crises*. New York: W. W. Norton, 2001.

Index

Acheson, Dean, 22, 45, 57, 65, 104, 129, 169, 170
Africa: civil rights and, 165–67; Cold War strategy and, 17, 177; colonialism in, 165, 169–71; covert interventions in, 10; discriminatory practices against diplomats from, 18, 167; leaders from, White House visits with, 167, 168; nationalistic aspirations in, sensitivity to, 11, 123, 165–66, 171, 177; Peace Corps volunteers in, 168–69; as priority of JFK administration, 26, 164–65; Soviet assistance in, 143, 181; U.S. interests in, 167–69. *See also specific countries in*
African National Congress (ANC), 176–77, 188
Algeria, 17, 108, 169, 188
Alliance for Progress program: failure of, 2, 82–86, 96–97; goals of, 75, 76–77, 80–81, 89, 187; as measure of foreign policy, 10; origins, 76–82; senatorial support for, 17
American University commencement address, 9, 179, 180–81, 183, 213–15
Angola, 170–71, 189
apartheid, 172–77
Argentina, 78, 79, 86, 92, 96, 188
Asia, 11, 16, 17, 26, 123, 143, 181, 185–86, 187. *See also specific countries in*
Ball, George, 24, 96, 111–12, 123, 170, 207–9
Batista, Fulgencio, 51, 52, 53, 55, 87
Ben-Gurion, David, 154, 160–61, 162, 163
Berlin: Berlin Wall, 46–50, 184; Checkpoint Charlie confrontation, 48; defense of by U.S., 10, 44–46, 121–22, 198–99; division following World War II, 41–42; solidary with people of, 4; speech by JFK in, 9, 49, 50, 184; unification of, 50; Vienna summit, 40–41, 42, 44, 194–96
Betancourt, Rómulo, 78, 82, 88–91
Bissell, Richard, 56–57, 58, 60, 200
Bowles, Chester, 23–24, 57, 132, 135, 144, 145–46, 151, 156, 174, 175
Brazil, 77, 78, 86, 91–97, 122, 185, 188
British Guiana, 80, 86, 97, 122, 147, 185, 188
Bundy, McGeorge, 22, 62, 63, 96, 110, 111, 123, 135, 138, 203–4

Carter, Lillian, 6
Castro, Fidel: assassination plot against, 51, 62, 72, 73, 185, 200–202; Bay of Pigs invasion, 56, 59; Cuban missile crisis, 63, 68; Cuban Revolution, 19, 51–54, 87; domestic policy, 53; ideological doctrine of, 52, 54, 60, 185; Latin America, relationship

with, 86, 91; overthrow of, 20, 55–56; rise to power by, 51–52, 54; surrender of, 72
Castro, Raúl, 52, 54, 59
Central Intelligence Agency (CIA): assassination of foreign leaders, 24, 87, 185; Brazil policy, 94–95; China policy, 137, 138; Cuba and Castro policy, 24, 58, 185, 200–202; destabilization of governments by, 2, 54–55, 94–95; directors of, 24
Chiang Kai-shek. *See* Jiang Jieshi
Chile, 85, 96, 188
China: attack on by U.S., talks about, 139–40; characterization of Chinese people, 131, 141; civil war in, 127–29, 130–31; commando raids on, 137; communism in, 15, 20, 122–23, 127–32, 134; diplomatic relations between U.S. and, 125, 130–31, 133; food aid to, 135, 136, 147; friend and protector role of U.S., 125–28; Great Leap Forward, 135, 136; immigration ban, 127; India, relationship with, 135–36, 147, 150–51; military aid to, 128; nuclear weapons development, 137–40, 185, 211–12; nuclear weapons threat against, 130, 132; Open Door policy, 126, 128; People's Republic of China, 128–32; policy of JFK toward, 132–37, 140–41, 187; Qing Dynasty, 126–27; records from, declassification of, 11; Sino-Soviet relationship, 37, 131–32, 134, 136, 139, 181; two Chinas plan, 130–31, 132, 133; UN seat, 129, 130, 133–35, 147, 187, 210–11; Vietnam, aid to, 105; world domination plan of, 28
civil defense initiatives, 15–16, 33–34, 46, 197–98
civil rights: Africa and, 165–67; discrimination, 9, 18, 127, 167; equal justice, commitment to, 8, 9; influence of Gandhi on, 141; racism, 18, 83, 127, 131, 167; segregation, 6, 9, 18, 166, 167, 215; support for, 8–9
Cold War: demilitarization of, 37, 41; dogmatic anticommunist stand, 11, 13–14, 97, 189; India and, 142, 146–50, 151, 152; initiatives against Soviet Union, 15; loss of, 20; nationalism strategy for, 17; policy failure during, 100; as priority of JFK administration, 26; records from, declassification of, 11; Truman's policy toward, 13, 15; victory in, 13–14, 18, 26
Colombia, 81, 84, 205
colonialism, 11, 16, 17, 102–5, 108, 126, 165, 169–71
commencement address at American University, 9, 179, 180–81, 183, 213–15
communism: in China, 15, 20, 122–23, 127–32, 134; in Cuba, 20, 52, 54, 60, 205–6; dogmatic anticommunist stand, 11, 18, 20, 97, 189; enlightened anticommunist, 24; expansion of, threat from, 35, 63; in Laos, 121; in Latin America, 54–55, 78–80, 86–88, 92, 97, 188, 205–6; in Middle East, 156–58; nationalism and, 75, 123; in South Africa, 176; speech by JFK against, 120, 184, 215–18; struggle between capitalism and, 37, 40; in Vietnam, 103, 105, 108, 122–23, 186
Conein, Lucien, 116–17
Costa Rica, 17–18, 78, 81, 187
Cuba: anti-American movement in, 19; Bay of Pigs invasion, 24, 51, 56–59, 86, 121; Castro and Cuban Revolution, 19, 51–54, 87; communism in, 20, 52, 54, 60, 205–6; containment policies against, 73–74; covert war in, 25, 55–56, 63, 72–74, 122, 185; diplomatic relations between U.S. and, 55, 72; invasion by U.S., 63–64, 70; Latin America, relationship with, 86, 91,

92; military plans against, 10, 61–62; missile crisis, 33, 51, 63–70, 86, 92, 122, 202–3; Mongoose, Operation, 61, 63–64; nonintervention policy, 92; organized crime in, 53, 55; peace offer from, 60; Platt Amendment, 53; policy of U.S. toward, 55–56, 57–58, 60, 62–63, 72–74, 199–200; poverty and economic conditions in, 53; as priority of JFK administration, 59–60; sabotage and terrorism campaign, 51, 70–73, 203–4; Soviet-Cuban cooperation, 54; speculation on JFK's policy toward, 184–85; threat to U.S. national interest by, 60; trade embargo against, 61; U.S. presence and influence in, 52–53

defense budget. *See* military spending and defense budget
Defense Department, 22–23, 61, 159, 168, 173
"A Democrat Looks at Foreign Policy" (Kennedy), 18–19, 21
Diem, Ngo Dinh, 105–7, 108, 109, 113–19, 121, 122, 207–9
Dillon, C. Douglas, 22, 76, 78–79
domestic policy, 8, 9, 10
Dominican Republic, 73, 77, 83, 87–88, 188
Dulles, Allen W., 21, 24, 55
Dulles, John Foster, 22, 130–31, 155, 165, 169, 188

economic development, 8, 9, 17, 25, 26, 125, 143–46, 152
Ecuador, 77, 85, 205
Egypt, 37–38, 154–59, 160, 187
Eisenhower, Dwight D.: Africa policy, 165, 166, 169, 172–73; Berlin, defense of and Khrushchev, 46; China policy, 130–31, 132, 133, 136, 187; Cold War policy, 13; colonialism, opposition to, 104; criticism of administration of, 19–21, 28, 109, 188; Cuba and Castro policy of, 55–56, 57, 199–200; destabilization of governments by, 188; Egypt policy, 154–55; election of, 16, 130; foreign policy team, 21, 22; India policy, 142–43; Israel policy, 160, 164; Laos policy, 121; Latin American policy, 54–55, 78; military-industrial complex danger, 31; military spending and defense budget, 16, 20, 24, 28, 30, 31, 109; national security policies of, 29, 30–31, 102; NSC decision-making process, 19, 21; nuclear weapons test ban, 19, 30–31, 34, 180; Pakistan policy, 142; Vietnam policy, 102, 105, 106, 108; West Berlin, defense of, 44
Eshkol, Levi, 163, 164
Ethiopia, 168–69

fallout shelter program, 15–16, 33–34, 46, 197–98
foreign policy: globalist policy of Truman, 15; interest in, 1–2, 8, 10; priorities of JFK administration, 25–26, 59–60, 75, 80, 91, 108, 109, 164–65; rating of record on, 8, 9, 10–11, 186; team for, 15, 21–26
Formosa. *See* Taiwan (Formosa)
France: Algerian independence, 108, 169, 188; Berlin, defense of by U.S., 44; China policy, 126; denouncement of by JFK, 17; Germany division following World War II, 42; nuclear weapons test ban, 138–39; Vietnam, colonial war in, 102, 103, 104–5; Vietnam, U.S. aid in, 15, 16, 104–5, 108

Galbraith, John Kenneth, 144, 145, 148
Gandhi, Mahandas, 141
Germany: Axis alliance, 128; China policy, 126; division following World War II, 41–42; Dresden, 34; East Germany, 40, 41, 42–44, 45, 46–48; Munich meeting, 14, 15, 20;

recovery following World War II, 42–43; Soviet Union, invasion of, 43; unification of, 43, 46, 50; Vienna summit, 40–41, 42, 44, 194–96; West Germany, 40, 41, 42–44, 45, 46. *See also* Berlin
Giancana, Sam, 55, 62, 200–202
Gilpatric, Roswell, 32–33, 39, 48
Goa, 149
Gordon, Lincoln, 79, 80, 94, 95, 96
Goulart, João, 86, 91, 92, 93–96, 97, 185, 188
Great Britain. *See* United Kingdom
Guantánamo Bay military base, 53, 61, 66
Guatemala, 54, 55, 57–58, 77, 86, 188, 205
Guevara, Ernesto "Ché," 52, 54, 60, 71, 78–79, 93
Guyana, 97, 188

Haiti, 77, 83, 175
Harkins, Paul D., 110, 111, 208–9
Harriman, W. Averell, 39–40, 121, 135, 139, 150, 151, 181, 203–4, 211–12
Helms, Richard, 60, 62
Hilsman, Roger, 4, 140–41
Hitler, Adolph, 14, 15, 43, 159
Ho Chi Minh, 15, 102–5, 107, 122

India: allegiance to the West, 125; British Guiana population, 97, 147; British imperialism in, 141; China, relationship with, 135–36, 147, 150–51; Cold War and, 142, 146–50, 151, 152; economic development assistance, 17, 125, 143–46, 152; Goa, seizure of, 149; government in, 142; nuclear weapons development, 150; Pakistan, relationship with, 141–42, 147, 149–50, 151–52; partitioning of, 141–42; Peace Corps volunteers in, 6, 144; U.S., relationship with, 142–43, 149–50, 151–52
internationalism, 13

Israel, 153, 154, 155, 156, 159–64, 187
Jagan, Cheddi, 86, 97, 147, 185, 188
Japan, 103, 126, 127–28
Jiang Jieshi, 127, 128, 129–31, 132, 133, 134–35, 136, 139–40, 187, 211
Jiang Jingguo (Chiang Ching-kuo), 139–40
Johnson, Lyndon Baines: Cuba and Castro policy, 72–74, 185; destabilization of governments by, 188; Egypt policy, 159; fact-finding tours, 25; India policy, 146; influence on foreign policy, 25; Israel policy, 161–62, 164; Latin American policy, 85–86, 95; legislative success of, 8, 9; Vietnam policy, 99–100, 101–2, 108–9, 111, 119, 120, 122, 123, 187; in West Berlin, 47
Joint Chiefs of Staff, 24, 61, 65, 68, 110, 111, 123, 173, 182, 202–3

Kashmir, 141–42, 147, 149–50, 151
Kennedy, Jacqueline Bouvier, 2, 38, 39–40, 76, 147, 148
Kennedy, John F. (JFK): affection for and popularity of, 2–7, 11; buildings, monuments, and roads named after, 4–5; character and integrity of, 2, 8, 9, 17–18; characteristics of, 40; early career of, 14–19; global outlook of, 13–14; health problems of, 8, 14; idealism of, 6, 7; Khrushchev, relationship with, 39. *See also* presidency of Kennedy
Kennedy, Joseph "Joe," 14, 34
Kennedy, Joseph P., 14
Kennedy, Patricia, 16, 143
Kennedy, Robert: attorney general appointment, 25; Castro assassination plot, 62, 63, 72, 73, 200–202; credentials of, 25; Cuba and Castro policy, 59–60, 65, 69, 185; in India, 143; influence on foreign policy, 25; King, intervention on behalf of, 166; Latin American policy, 94–96; Middle East and Asian tour, 16;

poverty in U.S., 17–18; presidential campaign and platform, 6; Vietnam policy, 120
Khrushchev, Nikita S.: Berlin, correspondence with JFK about, 47–48; Berlin, war plans to defend, 46; Berlin Wall, 46–47; characteristics of, 40; Cuban missile crisis, 33, 63, 64, 65, 67, 68, 69–70; domestic policy, 36–37; foreign assistance from, 143; Germany, attitude toward, 43; international policies of, 37–39, 79, 109, 143, 181; JFK, relationship with, 39; nuclear weapons test ban, 19, 30–31, 139, 180, 181, 182, 187, 211–12; removal from power, 181; rise to power by, 35–36; Sino-Soviet relationship, 131–32; Soviet-American cooperation, 27–28, 35, 38, 50; Stalin, relationship with, 36; United Nations speech, 38; Vienna summit, 11, 38, 39–41, 42, 44, 194–96; war, attitude toward, 36
Khrushchev, Nina Petrovna, 39–40
King, Martin Luther, Jr., 9, 141, 166
Kubitschek, Juscelino, 78, 93, 94, 96

Laos, 121, 147, 187
Latin America: Cold War strategy and, 17, 86; communism in, 54–55, 78–80, 86–88, 92, 97, 188, 205–6; conditions in, 77; Cuba, relationship with, 86, 91, 92; destabilization of governments in, 54–55, 86–88, 94–97, 187–88; interventions in, 10, 17–18, 83, 86–97, 122, 187; legacy of JFK, 187–88; military aid to, 29, 90–91; nationalistic aspirations in, sensitivity to, 11, 123; population growth in, 84; poverty and economic conditions in, 60; as priority of JFK administration, 26, 75, 80, 91; Soviet–Latin American relationships, 54–55, 92. *See also* Alliance for Progress program; *specific countries in*
LeMay, Curtis, 35, 68, 122
Lodge, Henry Cabot, Jr., 16, 116, 118, 208–9
López Mateos, Adolfo, 205–6

Macmillan, Harold, 44, 80, 133–34
Mandela, Nelson Rolihlahla, 176–77
Mao Zedong, 37, 127, 128–29, 130, 132, 134, 138
Marshall Plan, 15, 42–43, 75, 82–84
McCarthy, Joseph, 16, 17, 129–30
McCone, John A., 24, 73, 138, 203–4
McNamara, Robert S.: appointment of, 22; Berlin, war plans to defend, 45; credentials of, 22–23; Cuba and Castro policy, 62, 64, 65, 66, 68, 200, 203–4; missile gap statement, 32; nuclear weapons of U.S., 32, 182; Vietnam policy, 101, 110, 111, 116, 117, 123, 207
Mexico, 81, 85, 205–6
Middle East, 11, 16, 26, 153–54, 155, 156–58, 159, 160, 161, 162–64, 181
military-industrial complex, 31
military spending and defense budget: Eisenhower administration, 16, 20, 24, 28, 30, 31, 109; increase in, 15, 21, 28–30, 33, 46, 198
military troops: arms race and, 16–17, 27; expansion of, 27, 29–30; special forces personnel, 29; Vietnam deployment, 110, 111–12, 121; West Berlin, defense of, 47–48, 198–99
Minh, Duong Van, 118, 119
Mongoose, Operation, 61, 63–64
moon exploration. *See* space program

Nasser, Gamal Abdel, 154–57, 158–59, 161, 162, 164
nationalism: as champion of, 4, 17, 188; communism and, 75, 123; power of, 16, 17; sensitivity to nationalistic aspirations, 11, 123, 153, 155, 165–66, 171, 177
National Security Council (NSC), 19, 21, 22, 64, 68–69, 202–3

National Security Council Memorandum No. 68/2 (NSC 68/2), 15, 18, 20, 24, 29–30, 38
National Security Council Memorandum No. 162/2, 29
Nehru, Jawaharlal, 141, 142–43, 144–45, 146–49, 150–51, 152
Nhu, Ngo Dinh, 107, 115–16, 118, 122, 207–9
Nicaragua, 83, 189
Nitze, Paul, 15, 24, 29–30, 45, 60
Nixon, Richard M., 4, 5, 19–21, 28, 78, 101–2, 165, 166, 188
Norstad, Lauris, 45, 198–99
North Atlantic Treaty Organization (NATO), 15, 29, 43
nuclear war: Berlin, war plans to defend, 45; confrontations with Soviet Union and threat of, 10; fallout shelter program, 15–16, 33–34, 46, 197–98; first-strike capability, 33; limited nuclear war, 34–35, 39; threat of, 1–2; victory in, 39
nuclear weapons: arms control treaties, 182; arms race, 16–17, 27, 32–34, 50, 160, 161, 162–64, 186–87; Chinese development of, 137–40, 185, 211–12; increase in, 28–29, 32–33, 38; in India, 150; as JFK legacy, 182; in Middle East, 160, 161, 162–64; military-industrial complex, 31; in Pakistan, 150; power of, 33; as priority of JFK administration, 25–26; Soviet weapons, 15–17, 19–21, 31–33, 38–39; test ban agreement and treaty, 19, 30–31, 34, 138–39, 179, 180–84, 186–87, 211–15; testing of, 38–39, 48, 180, 182; U.S. strategic advantage and superiority, 31–33, 45, 48, 66

Obama, Barack, 7

Pakistan, 97, 141–42, 147, 149–50, 151–52
Palestinian Arabs, 153, 154, 160, 161, 162
Peace Corps, 2, 6, 10, 144, 168–69, 186
Peru, 77, 78
poor people and poverty, 17, 53, 60, 145, 187. *See also* Peace Corps
Portugal, 149, 169–71
presidency of Kennedy: approval rating of JFK, 4, 180; Berlin, leadership during defense of, 44–46, 50, 121–22; as champion of peace, 184, 187; corruption and scandal, lack of, 9; Cuban crises, leadership during, 44, 51, 56, 58–59, 65–66, 68–70, 121, 122; inaugural address, 4, 7, 191–94; legacy of, 182, 186–89; length of, 1; maturity gained during, 179; rating of record during, 8, 9, 10; scholarly analyses of, 7–11; speculation on JFK's policies, 99–100, 101–2, 119–23, 184–86, 209–10; Vietnam, leadership in, 111, 117–22, 209–10. *See also* foreign policy
presidential election: campaign leading to, 19–21, 160, 164; closeness of, 4, 21, 132; criticism of Eisenhower-Nixon administration, 19–21; debate between Nixon and JFK, 19, 20, 21, 108
prestige survey, 19–20
Profiles in Courage (Kennedy), 18
public service, 6, 7

Quadros, Jânio, 91, 92–93

rate-the-president surveys, 5–6, 8
Reagan, Ronald, 5, 49, 175, 189
Roosevelt, Franklin Delano, 3, 5, 14, 39, 112, 181
Roosevelt, Theodore, 5, 13
Rosselli, John, 62, 200–202
Rostow, Walt Whitman, 24–25, 80, 81, 109–10, 111, 123, 137, 144–45, 185
Rusk, Dean: Africa policy, 173, 175–76; Bay of Pigs invasion, 57; Berlin, war plans to defend, 45; China policy, 132, 134; credentials of, 22; Foreign Service, diversity in, 167; India

policy, 150–51; Israel policy, 161, 162; Latin American policy, 96–97; nuclear weapons capacity, U.S., 32; as Secretary of State, 22, 23; Soviet Latin American policy, 79; Vietnam policy, 110, 123, 206–7

Salazar, António de Oliveira, 170–71
Satterthwaite, Joseph, 173, 174, 175
Saudi Arabia, 154, 157, 158–59
Schlesinger, Arthur M., Jr., 3–4, 24, 57, 62, 80, 81, 87, 97, 169
South Africa, 168, 171–77
South America, 19, 78, 79, 92, 96. *See also specific countries in*
Soviet Union: collapse of, 49; confrontation with, 10, 27; Cuban missile crisis, 33, 63–70; defeat of as priority of JFK administration, 25–26; distrust of, 35; economic growth in, 54; Eisenhower administration policy toward, 30; foreign assistance from, 143, 181; German invasion of, 43; initiatives to contain, 15; international policies of, 37–39, 143, 181; military superiority of, 16–17, 19–21, 27, 181; nuclear weapons of, 15–17, 19–21, 31–33, 38–39; nuclear weapons test ban, 138–39; records from, declassification of, 11; relationship with, risks of general war for, 29; Sino-Soviet relationship, 37, 131–32, 134, 136, 139, 181; Soviet-American cooperation, 27–28, 35, 38, 39, 50, 73, 180–84; Soviet-Cuban cooperation, 54; Soviet–Latin American relationships, 54–55, 92; Vietnam, aid to, 105; world domination plan of, 15, 18, 28, 38. *See also* Khrushchev, Nikita S.
space program, 2, 10, 25, 183, 186
Stalin, Josef, 15, 36, 37, 39, 44, 48–49
State Department, 22, 159, 174
Stevenson, Adlai, 16, 17, 23, 66, 141, 149, 171, 173
Strategy of Peace (Kennedy), 18

Taiwan (Formosa), 128, 131, 133–35, 136–37, 187, 210–11
Taylor, Maxwell, 24, 109–10, 111, 116, 117, 123, 185
Trade Mart speech, 120, 184, 215–18
Trujillo, Rafael, 83, 87, 88
Trujillo, Ramfis, 87
Truman, Harry S.: Africa policy, 169, 172; China policy, 112, 122–23, 129–30, 132; Cold War policy, 13, 15; colonialism, opposition to, 104; globalist foreign policy, 15; Israel policy, 159–60, 164; NSC 68/2 adoption, 15, 29; Soviet policy, 15; Vietnam policy, 102, 104–5; West Berlin, defense of, 44
Turkey, 33, 65, 66

U-2 program and spy planes, 19, 20, 31, 32, 68, 137, 138, 139
Ukraine, 35–36, 38, 43
United Kingdom, 14, 42, 44, 126, 133–34, 138–39, 159, 171–72
United Nations (UN), 23, 38, 47, 129, 130, 133–35, 147, 187, 210–11
United States: duties of in the world, 13; isolationist stand, 14–15; political and moral superiority of, 27; Soviet-American cooperation, 27–28, 35, 38, 39, 50, 73, 180–84
Uruguay, 60, 76, 78, 92, 96, 188
U.S. Congress, 8, 15–19, 30

Venezuela, 71–72, 77, 78, 81, 85, 88–91, 158, 187, 205
Verwoerd, Hendrik, 172, 173, 176
Vienna summit, 11, 38, 39–41, 42, 44, 194–96
Vietnam: civil war in, 107, 112; colonialism, liberation from, 102–5; communism in, 103, 105, 108, 122–23, 186; coup d'etat in, 116–19, 121, 122, 207–9; fact-finding tours, 25; France, U.S. aid to, 15, 16, 104–5, 108; Geneva Accords, 105, 106, 108,

110, 142, 147, 186; limitations on military involvement in, 10; national security and, 102; as priority of JFK administration, 108, 109; records from, declassification of, 11; religious intolerance in, 114–16; strategic hamlet program, 113; U.S.-Vietnam relationship, 101
Vietnam War: Ap Bac battle, 113–14; atrocities during, 100–102, 111; casualties of, 100–101; events leading to, 102–7; expansion of military involvement, 107–13, 119, 185, 206–7; failure of, 2; idealism of JFK and, 6; legacy of JFK, 187; opposition to, 24; speculation on JFK's policy toward, 99–100, 101–2, 119–23, 185–86, 209–10; troops deployed to, 110, 111–12, 121; withdrawal from, 185–86

Why England Slept (Kennedy), 14–15
Williams, G. Mennen, 166–67, 171, 173, 175, 176
Wilson, Woodrow, 8, 13, 14, 102
World War II, 14–15, 34, 43, 128

Yemen, 158, 162

About the Author

Stephen G. Rabe is a professor of history and holds the Arts and Humanities Chair at the University of Texas at Dallas. He has previously written or edited eight books, including *The Most Dangerous Area in the World: John F. Kennedy Confronts Communist Revolution in Latin America* (1999) and *U.S. Intervention in British Guiana: A Cold War Story* (2005). His *Eisenhower and Latin America: The Foreign Policy of Anticommunism* (1988) won the Stuart L. Bernath Book Prize from the Society for Historians of American Foreign Relations. He received the Stuart L. Bernath Lecture Prize in 1989. Rabe has taught or lectured in fifteen countries, conducting seminars on modern U.S. history in Argentina, Brazil, and Ecuador. He has also served as the Mary Ball Washington Professor of American History at University College–Dublin in Ireland and the Fulbright Bicentennial Chair in American Studies at the University of Helsinki in Finland.